PARCELS

Latinidad

Transnational Cultures in the United States

This series publishes books that deepen and expand our understanding of Latina/o populations, especially in the context of their transnational relationships within the Americas. Focusing on borders and boundary-crossings, broadly conceived, the series is committed to publishing scholarship in history, film and media, literary and cultural studies, public policy, economics, sociology, and anthropology. Inspired by interdisciplinary approaches, methods, and theories developed out of the study of transborder lives, cultures, and experiences, titles enrich our understanding of transnational dynamics.

Matt Garcia, Series Editor, Professor of Latin American, Latino, and Caribbean Studies, and History, Dartmouth College

For a list of titles in the series, see the last page of the book.

PARCELS

Memories of Salvadoran Migration

MIKE ANASTARIO

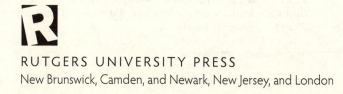

RUTGERS UNIVERSITY PRESS

New Brunswick, Camden, and Newark, New Jersey, and London

Library of Congress Cataloging-in-Publication Data

Names: Anastario, Mike, 1981– author.
Title: Parcels : memories of Salvadoran migration / Mike Anastario.
Description: New Brunswick, New Jersey : Rutgers University Press, [2019] | Series:
Latinidad: transnational cultures in the United States | Includes bibliographical
references and index.
Identifiers: LCCN 2018043724 | ISBN 9780813595221 (pbk.) | ISBN 9780813595238
(cloth)
Subjects: LCSH: Salvadorans—United States. | Collective memory. | Emigrant
remittances—El Salvador. | El Salvador—History—Civil War, 1979–1992—Social
aspects.
Classification: LCC E184.S15 A63 2019 | DDC 973/.04687284-dc23
LC record available at https://lccn.loc.gov/2018043724

A British Cataloging-in-Publication record for this book is available from the British
Library.

All interior photos by the author

♾ The paper used in this publication meets the requirements of the American
National Standard for Information Sciences—Permanence of Paper for Printed
Library Materials, ANSI Z39.48-1992.

www.rutgersuniversitypress.org

Manufactured in the United States of America

To all my teachers, especially the ones who never learned to read or write

CONTENTS

PARCELS

INTRODUCTION

As I write this, some members of the Trump administration doubt whether all Salvadoran migrants deserve to be referred to as human,[1] while some Salvadoran migrants doubt the integrity of what U.S. Americans call food. The study of diasporic remembering is one way to elucidate both of these renderings of the Other, and perhaps memory studies hold promise for unraveling the repetitious harms inherent to both.

In 2018, there is little doubt that Salvadoran migration is an issue of public concern in the United States. Salvadorans in the United States represent approximately one-fifth of the total population of El Salvador.[2] It is well documented that a mass exodus of Salvadorans began during El Salvador's civil war (1979–1992).[3] The United States contributed billions to that war in an effort to defeat an insurgency and implant democracy.[4] Years after that war ended, the U.S. Border Patrol has cumulatively apprehended 175,978 non-Mexicans from the southwestern border of the United States[5] and reported 6,704 southwestern-border deaths for the same time period (from 2000 to 2017).[6] In El Salvador, Amparo Marroquín writes that "mine is a fugitive country, which reinvents itself at every border in a piece-meal way."[7] The mass-migration phenomenon and its diasporas are so advanced that Salvadoran scholars are investigating *memories* of flight and of repatriation.[8] These statistics and ways of approaching human mobility raise serious questions about the impacts of the U.S. nation-state in Central America. Is there a relationship between the non-Mexicans who have been apprehended and previous U.S. investments in counterinsurgency efforts in Central America? Is a democratic U.S. nation-state capable of acknowledging and reconciling the complex effects of its previous interventions abroad? Memory studies is a nascent field that can examine questions such as these and to educate future generations on ways to approach the complex pasts of places that have been deeply affected by U.S. power. Throughout this book, I illustrate how collective forms of diasporic remembering and forgetting can obfuscate and provide ways of answering those questions.

Sociologists clarify that collective memory is not something we have but something we do.[9] Indeed, memories can be categorized, classified, sequenced to tell histories, and epistemically leveraged to speak truth to power. Memories can certainly do those things, but it is also important to recognize that memories do many other things for those who make them. Memories teach strategies, generate pleasures, preserve knowledge, and form the basis of imaginaries that are unimaginable to others. Similar to a color negative in photographic processing, collective memories can inversely map the black holes of *forgetting* for Others who are not doing the remembering. Memory *practices* in the Salvadoran diaspora include particular styles and methods for connecting to and moving nonhuman actors through transnational space. These nonhuman actors include food, medicine, plants, documents, photographs, clothes, hammocks, electronics, school supplies, letters, and remittances that are transmitted at a high throughput across national airspaces, intercepted at national ports of entry, and examined by uniformed agents of the state before being delivered to kin separated by diasporic divides. Memories can fuel diasporic economies. The development and relative size of the Salvadoran diaspora have given rise to a competitive market of Salvadoran couriers who transport nonhuman parcels through transnational space, relying upon and stoking memories in diasporic networks.

Today, the Salvadoran government formally recognizes hundreds of *gestores de encomiendas* (parcel managers). Colloquially, parcel managers are known as *viajeras/os* (travelers), *gestores de encomiendas*, *encomenderas/os*, and couriers, but for consistency, I will refer to them throughout as couriers.[10] Salvadoran couriers transport millions of U.S. dollars in cash and thousands of pounds of merchandise annually between El Salvador and the United States.[11] They collect parcels in El Salvador, travel to the United States, and deliver objects (and sometimes people) within diasporic networks, repeating collection-and-delivery sequences on the way back to El Salvador. In a way, couriers are rapid-cycling migrants, being "here and there" all at once. Salvadoran couriers have made a market out of the movement of parcels that they collect, care for, defend, and deliver. The parcels they move often have deep mnemonic values and memory-triggering potentials. In the everyday practices of their work, couriers link kin separated by diasporic divides, they transfer information, and they manage affects and intimacies across borders. In this study, I focused my work on Salvadoran couriers who provided services to a diaspora emanating from one rural community in northern El Salvador. I focused my work on this memory-rich space to gain context for diasporic memories that I believe have incredible value in understanding the ways in which remembering and forgetting elucidate and obscure mechanisms of power.

CAMPESINX MEMORY

Often represented as the poorest and most illiterate actors in Salvadoran society, Salvadoran *campesinos* (peasants) were disproportionately affected by the

Salvadoran Civil War,[12] and several migrated as a direct result of the violence occurring in their homeland. Depending on who is doing the remembering, Salvadoran campesinos may be remembered by noncampesinos as the actors who were persuaded to participate in the insurgency during the war or as the actors who were rallied to rebel against the oppressive forces of the U.S.-backed Salvadoran state. Historian Erik Ching documents the relative scarcity of campesino voices in the memory communities that have emerged and informed discourse regarding the Salvadoran Civil War.[13] This scarcity reflects the epistemic marginalization of campesinos, which itself can have denigrating effects.[14]

In the Salvadoran countryside, campesinos I interacted with were often illiterate, did not go to school beyond the eighth grade, and had limited access to telephones. Some engaged in subsistence agriculture that did not generate cash income, and some spoke a style of Spanish that took months for me to begin to better understand. Some spoke argot to avoid being understood by others in public. It is no surprise, then, that in El Salvador campesinos are often dismissed, advocated for, denigrated, pitied, subject to state security force harassment, spoken over and spoken for.

Among campesinos with migrant family members, cash remittances from the United States can quickly permit campesinos to access markets and communication technologies that were previously inaccessible to them due to the material restrictions of economic poverty. In the earlier days of the mass-migration phenomenon, rural Salvadoran migrants grew up with limited media images of the United States, where their isolation from urban Salvadoran and global affairs generated ideas of the United States fashioned mostly by word of mouth.[15] Now in the era of smartphone technologies and undocumented migration, there is still a great deal of everyday campesino life that evades virtual networks and remains transmitted through the oral history tradition of the Salvadoran countryside. While epistemic power and privilege may have marginalized Salvadoran campesinos from the written and remembered word, epistemic inferiority should not be mistaken (as it frequently is) for backwardness.

To counter the conceptualization of rural Salvadorans as flat, undynamic, suffering, humble characters who are good at being poor, oppressed, and subjugated, I refer to Salvadoran peasants throughout this work as *campesinxs*. My use of the *x* in campesinx is meant to challenge assumptions of readers who may be tempted to classify or conceptualize Salvadoran campesinxs using such sweeping generalizations.[16] Campesinx memory practices made me conscious of other forms of knowledge and of my own ignorance when I began collecting data. I present those findings in this book using a grounded-theory framework. Grounded-theory methods are flexible yet systematic guidelines that researchers sometimes use to collect and analyze data, typically qualitative, to construct theories grounded in data.[17] I provide a more technical description of my data collection and analytic methods in appendix A. Since grounded theory involves both me (the researcher) and the campesinxs who informed the theoretical work I develop in this book, I owe you a brief explanation of who I am and how I went about collecting data.

I am a U.S. citizen who grew up conditioned to listen to migrant narratives. As a child, my Italian nana told me stories about Napoli during World War II, in which she remembered ancestors who could predict whether deployed soldiers in Africa were dead or alive, homemade liquors, the alternative ways in which gender was expressed on the street, the mafia, fascists, homicides, and bombs, and her memories were couched in reminders that this is where my people came from. My non-Italian grandma remembered the "DPs" (displaced persons) flooding into Plainfield, New Jersey during the Second World War. I grew up listening to my parents infrequently remember the 1967 Plainfield riots, when black Plainfielders clashed with the police and National Guard over multiple injustices, including preexisting tensions with local law enforcement.[18] My parents remembered and I imagined gunshots and National Guard tanks rolling through the streets of my U.S. birthplace.

When I was finally a teenager working my first job as a waiter in a U.S. retirement home, one of the elderly white residents at the establishment flagged down my manager to complain that he didn't want an Italian WOP serving him food. That derogatory term, *WOP*, was once used to refer to Italian Americans (*without papers*, reflecting folk etymology in the United States a few decades prior). This was the first and only time I was the target of xenophobic rhetoric for being Italian American. More interesting to me than this man's antiquated xenophobia were the stories of my black coworkers who jumped in to tell me about their own experiences with, and family stories about, racism. I was just a teenager at the time, but listening to the stories of my black coworkers made me conscious of the ways in which the past weighs heavily upon the present. I heard family memories filled with experiences of hate and alterity that emerged as a result of my brief experience under a xenophobic gaze. In the twenty-first century, Italian migrants are no longer the denigrated migrant class, but blacks continue to be disproportionately brutalized by the police, who also surveil, capture, and facilitate the deportation processes for Salvadoran migrants. The U.S. nation-state is a curiously forgetful actor. When I leave El Salvador and visit my U.S. birthplace, I today see a growing Salvadoran migrant community that is already serviced by couriers delivering parcels from El Salvador. Salvadoran migrants are the newest generation of residents in my personal experience of U.S. history, and their memories are filled with information about the reach of U.S. power, sometimes telling U.S. citizens what we least want to know about what we are.

I collected most of the data for this book in El Salvador from 2015 to 2018. I focused on one localized diaspora emanating from a rural Salvadoran town that

I refer to throughout the rest of this book with the pseudonym "El Norteño."[19] El Norteño is a rural municipality located in the northern Department of Chalatenango, which borders Honduras. When I conducted this study, approximately 37 percent of the Salvadoran population lived in rural areas. Taking this into account, over 99 percent of El Norteño's residents were classified as rural in a census conducted by the Salvadoran government.[20] Frequently unable to access the capital needed to enter the United States with documentation, many (but not all) of El Norteño's migrants to the United States are and remain undocumented. Several are cyclical migrants, returning to El Norteño as deportees, voluntarily, and very few return having obtained some type of status (e.g., residency, citizenship). Some live in El Norteño and engage in cyclical travel on tourist visas, sometimes working short stints in the United States and then returning. El Norteño was heavily impacted by the civil-war violence, but this was not one of the Chalatecx communities that reestablished itself in Honduran refugee camps and then repatriated after the war. During the civil war, El Norteño's residents died, they migrated to the United States and other places, and others managed to survive. The Salvadoran Civil War is the index period that many of El Norteño's residents and ex-residents use to describe family memories of migration. As such, I repeatedly focus on the Salvadoran Civil War as a period of interest throughout this book.

As the migration phenomenon specific to El Norteño developed over time, some networks of El Norteño's residents increasingly made their way to Colorado (including Boulder County and the Metro Denver area) and Long Island, New York (Suffolk and Nassau counties).[21] Split between El Norteño and these U.S. metro and suburban locations, one of the ways in which kin remained connected was by sending parcels to one another through couriers that service El Norteño's diaspora. My two key informants for this study deliver parcels between El Norteño and Colorado and New York—sometimes helping one another do so. They are family members who service entirely different, but closely related, clientele. From 2015 to 2018, I lived in El Salvador and participated in couriers' labor and sometimes travel, increasingly familiarizing myself with seventy members of eleven families that sent parcels between El Salvador and the United States.[22] I spent an intensive four-month period doing work with couriers on a full-time basis, and I spent the remaining 2.7 years intermittently observing and participating in their work and travel. I am a relatively inefficient courier, but I was able to use my privileges and physical labor to assist couriers when they needed extra help here and there. I never received or accepted monetary payment.

My method was to immerse myself in a world of objects that had mnemonic values and potentials, but what exactly does that mean in the context of a twenty-first-century diaspora? How do those parcels, these nonhuman objects, interact with human memory? Here, as a way of crossing over into the book as a whole, I will provide a brief example of how corn seed can do so.

FLIGHT OF THE *MAÍZ BLANCO*

In some parts of the Salvadoran countryside, *maíz blanco* (white corn) seeds are kept and cultivated by families who plant them yearly. The Salvadoran government's national germplasm bank has five versions of white corn seed varieties electronically documented on record,[23] and white corn seed is commercially available throughout El Salvador, but none of these documented and/or marketed varieties represent the heirloom corn seeds that one farmer remembers cultivating and keeping since his childhood. In the second decade of the twenty-first century, he drops maíz blanco seeds into earth that has been partially scorched with a fire-farming method that is reminiscent of, but not quite the same as, what farmers remembered practicing in the 1950s, before synthetic fertilizers and herbicides made their way into El Norteño. The corn will be cultivated as farmers bring portable radios in their *chulas* (bags) to the farm, blasting 1980s "civil-war hits" into the soundscapes of Chalatecx corn rows, saturated with the hum of buzzing insects and Madonna's "Lucky Star."

Sometime during the corn's cultivation this rainy season, a human nearby dies young for reasons that everybody seems to understand but that are foreign from the ways in which law enforcement officers and nongovernmental organizations document it. El Norteño could be classified as a "community at risk" by security programs present in the country, at the same time that several of El Norteño's campesinx youth consider "risk" to be the chance of being physically assaulted by armed members of the Salvadoran state while walking to work—something that is all too familiar for civil-war survivors. Rural family members in the United States will learn about the early death but digest false narratives until the real narratives, backstories, and explication of critical details are provided in person.

In a rural farmhouse, campesinxs compile the harvested maíz blanco seeds into a woven sack that is brought to a Salvadoran courier who apologetically tears it open to see if narcotics have been stashed inside. The seeds are emptied into a clear plastic bag, marked for delivery, and catapulted to high altitudes, destined for U.S. ports of entry. In Texas, a U.S. Customs and Border Protection (CBP) agent will grab the plastic bag full of the maíz blanco seeds and say, "What is this? Is there consommé in this? Is this a poultry product?" Depending on how these interactions go, the bag of maíz blanco may be confiscated or simply tossed back into the courier's luggage.

In El Norteño, two pounds of maíz blanco seeds are typically shared and not sold. But in Colorado, migrants from El Norteño will pay $14 to support the work of the courier, who will, in person, send greetings from the farmer who cultivated the corn and perhaps fill in the backstory of the death that everyone is talking about but in a way that doesn't reflect the state's record of it. In Colorado, the corn seeds will be used to make nixtamalized tortillas. As the tortillas are eaten, the eater may remember and even talk about the person who sent the corn or the distant family of the recently dead or the way in which maíz blanco was grown or the way in which maíz blanco used to be grown in El Norteño. If I turn on a tape recorder and ask the parcel's recipient questions about why she requested the maíz blanco, she will likely tell me that tortillas here in the United States are not the same as they are in El Norteño. She might take cues from me that she is supposed to perform acts of nostalgia for the recording. One can certainly obtain other types of relevant information from tape-recorded interviews, but I immersed myself in the memory-charged agency of parcels to use a different methodological lens for approaching memory in one local diaspora emanating from an area that was affected by U.S. counterinsurgency efforts approximately three decades prior to this analysis.

GROUNDED THEORY

As a participant observer, I rarely conducted cold interviews, learning early on that the presence of a tape recorder radically affected the way in which memories were spoken to me and thus entered into the record. Participant observation and field notes were my primary data-collection method, which I supplemented with focused audio-recorded interviews and the documentation of migration *testimonios* when the moment and topic were appropriate. Over three years, I transported approximately 1,500 pounds of parcels between the United States and El Salvador,[24] and I passed through international state security checkpoints with El Norteño couriers on twelve occasions.[25] While the data in this book focus on the seventy interlocutors and eleven transnational families that I documented, I engaged with and remained connected to dozens more but did not follow through on their diasporic connections. Over three years, I listened to hundreds of unrecorded conversations and memories about migration. Despite these numbers, I try my best to present this work in the spirit of public sociology, focusing on accessible stories about a relatively small number of recognizable actors.[26] This is not an analysis that is powered by numbers but one that is focused on dimensions and depths of memory.

As my networks grew with my time spent in El Salvador, I had numerous unexpected experiences that provided further context for the subject matter I write about here. During fieldwork, I briefly served as a volunteer escort for the U.S. government's Central American Minors program,[27] where I had the privilege to listen to numerous stories spoken by parolee and refugee children as they were destined to be reunited with their parents in the United States. My volunteer service was no longer needed after U.S. president Donald Trump issued an executive order freezing refugee admissions to the United States.[28] My fieldwork occurred during Trump's rise to power in the United States, and his ascension acted as an external intervention that deeply affected conversations and initial perceptions of me in El Salvador. The memories of El Norteño's diaspora, narrated in El Norteño's diasporic communities, are the focus of this work. For readers who might be interested in a more detailed description of the grounded-theory methods I used to collect and analyze data for this book, I have provided a lengthier explanation in appendix A.

The way I practiced grounded theory included, more than anything, everyday conversations with the people I interacted with. Judith Halberstam writes that "conversation rather than mastery indeed seems to offer one very concrete way of being in relation to another form of being and knowing without seeking to measure that life modality by the standards that are external to it."[29] My key informants, the Salvadoran couriers who delivered parcels between the United States and El Salvador, filled in gaps that I could have never understood as an outsider. They accounted for me and ensured my physical safety. They weighed in to help me change names, identities, and identifiers throughout this work. Couriers provided me with a sounding board for my developing ideas and theories. I wrote parts of this book in couriers' homes, discussing nascent ideas with them as we reclined in hammocks at the end of the day. This was the grounded, everyday way in which I as a sociologist attempted to treat those who helped me most during this study "as the agents, instead of the patients, of theory."[30] In this complex era of identity politics, I try the best I can to be cognizant of the shifty experiences of becoming and unbecoming, majoritarian and minoritarian agency, passing and not passing, and humanity and inhumanity that occur during fieldwork for a gringo sociologist who is out of place in rural El Salvador. I repeatedly assert that despite our differences, social remembering and forgetting implicate not one but multiple groups. Navigating our way out of states of collective forgetting will require complex solutions that go far beyond internally reproducing the same power dynamics that redefine the present memory field.

STRUCTURE OF THE BOOK

This book is the outcome of my reliance on a constructivist framework, and I have thus divided it into two sections. The first section orients the reader to memory practices of campesinxs in El Norteño's diaspora. It illustrates memory practices that inform, preserve, emote, please, and project—practices that can also be thought of as *not forgetting*. In the second section of this book, I explore the dynamics of collective forgetting regarding the structuration of violence for campesinxs in El Norteño's diaspora. I develop a working idea of the "U.S. fugue state," which I characterize as a transnational manifestation of collective forgetting that comprises silences, contemporary national strategies, and practices of implementing disarticulated U.S. foreign and immigration policies. In psychiatry, a dissociative fugue is a facet of dissociative amnesia, where the patient is unable to recall autobiographical information.[31] Taking into account the U.S. nation-state's disarticulated approaches to immigration and foreign policy, my use of the word *fugue* builds on the concept of "state amnesia" to include the strategies and disarticulated practices employed by a regional hierarchy that reinforces collective states of forgetting.[32] My use of the word *fugue* is also meant to bring attention to multiplicity in the memory field, where dynamic relationships between narratives, counternarratives, and other narratives coexist with everyday mnemonic practices.[33] In El Salvador, Amparo Marroquín writes that "with the end of the armed struggles, emigration multiplied and has gradually transformed El Salvador into what could be called a fugitive nation, in the double sense of the word. In musical terms, experts consider the fugue the highest form of counterpoint. Its name comes from the Latin *huida* and indicates how voices and melodies respond to each other, overlap, and flee from each other."[34] The U.S. fugue state as I describe it in the second half of this book is about ways that U.S. North Americans and campesinxs collectively forget.

The first four chapters concern campesinx remembering. Chapter 1 orients readers to the social economy of Salvadoran couriers who transport parcels in transnational spaces—it provides context for how nonhuman objects are valued, exchanged, and managed in El Norteño's diaspora. In chapter 2, I draw upon campesinx memories to reconstruct a narrative of undocumented migration through Mexico and examine how remembered elements synchronize with structural pressures that shape and modify harms in the shifty social arena of clandestine migration. In chapter 3, I directly address practices of nostalgia among campesinx migrants, exploring practices of longing that cultivate diasporic intimacy and stoke imaginaries of return to the Salvadoran countryside. In chapter 4, I explore the role of memory in campesinx imaginaries of transnational movement. In particular, I focus on how hybridized expressions of sexuality, language, and movement are linked with subversive liberationist concepts. The first four chapters are relatively independent of one another, but each broadly implicates generative aspects of campesinx remembering.

Chapters 5 through 7 are an analysis of collective forgetting in transnational space. Chapter 5 examines ways in which silences map everyday violence that structures forgetting. Chapter 6 examines "fields of violence" that are repetitiously structured and forgotten amid their ongoing production. Chapter 7 examines the possibility of emigration as an unintended consequence of U.S. counterinsurgency efforts in El Salvador during the Cold War, where disarticulated immigration and foreign policies correspond to renewable strategies of national security.

I hope these chapters can be used to bridge some divides—if minimally, expanding some readers' exposure to Others' memories and stimulating more thinking on the subject of forgetting. I believe there is great potential for memory studies to elucidate the ways in which national forgetting is and has been structured relative to postconflict settings in Central America and U.S. counterinsurgency efforts abroad and for reconciling disarticulated practices of nationstates. As I contend throughout the book, understanding the systematic ways in which nations and people forget and remember can provide new ways of thinking about and imagining different futures.

PART I DIASPORIC REMEMBERING

1 · *ES BARATA Y ES CARA*
Couriers and Parcels in Transnational Space

Forty *pupusas in* El Salvador = $20
Forty *pupusas in* Colorado *from* El Salvador = $112

In El Norteño's diasporic communities, couriers move parcels in ways that organize the emergence of affects and memories. Prices are calculated and discussed with *campesinx* clientele as couriers recall recent conversations with distant family members who are connected to rural temporalities. In this chapter, I provide an overview of the everyday economic and occupational practices of El Norteño's couriers, illustrating how affectively charged transactions are linked with the exchange of memory-interactive parcels in one rural diasporic network. This chapter specifically focuses on socioeconomic aspects of the courier trade in El Norteño's diaspora, providing a basis for understanding the ways in which memory and affect are repetitiously structured through couriers' economic participation in a quasi-documented, transnational profession.

Who are couriers, and what do we, the people who study them, owe them? In short, couriers transport parcels to Salvadorans in transnational diasporic networks who are separated by diasporic divides (space, the ability to cross national boundaries, legal statuses, etc.). At the time this book is being written, approximately twenty-five years after the end of the Salvadoran Civil War,[1] the Salvadoran government has formally recognized *gestores de encomiendas* (parcel managers). Couriers are a formal occupation in El Salvador, where, as of mid-2017, approximately 767 active couriers had registered with the Asociación Nacional de Gestores de Encomiendas y Cultura (National Association of Parcels and Culture Managers in El Salvador; or ANGEC by its initials in Spanish) and where more than two thousand had over the course of recent history been registered as parcel managers by Salvadoran customs.[2] Salvadoran couriers transport hundreds of millions of U.S. dollars in cash and thousands of pounds of merchandise annually between El Salvador and the United States.[3] They collect parcels in El Salvador, travel to the United States, and deliver them within diasporic networks, serving a transnational base of clients. The relative proportion of Salvadorans living in the United States (approximately one-fifth of El Salvador's population[4]) frames the development of such economies, where a transnational client base can sustain the work of Salvadoran couriers enough so that they are able to make it their profession. Sociologist Alisa Garni explains that what sets Salvadoran couriers apart from other transnational traders (such as higglers in Barbados or women shuttle traders in the former Soviet Union) is that Salvadoran couriers tend to engage in long-distance air travel, deliver goods to clients' homes or from their own stores, and leverage resources cultivated in their home country to build their businesses.[5]

For those of us who have studied couriers, the question of what we owe back to them is a local one. My key informant says that we who study couriers owe them a finished research product that engenders "respect, tolerance, and for people to learn that this is professional labor."[6] My key informants have also asked me for help directly related to their work, and I always try to fulfill their requests. In this chapter, I take these requests into account as I reconcile the important role that couriers play in structuring the production of affects and memories in diasporic communities. At the end of the nineteenth century, the American ethnologist Otis Mason wrote about the different devices used by couriers who transport human objects, noting that "there is no doubt that all of these various devices have had their influence in shaping and deforming the human body."[7] That is to say, the immense amount of physical stress that couriers experience is a salient aspect of couriers' livelihoods. The stress is more than physical. In the twenty-first century, Garni writes about a Salvadoran courier sitting down to sew the seams of the duffel bags she drags through the airport.[8] The temporal and affective stressors that couriers experience occur as we observe and interview them and as couriers transfer parcels that stoke and invoke memories in intimate diasporic environments. When couriers implicate me in their stress, I try (in an interactionist way of knowing) to navigate that stress with them.

The willingness of El Norteño's campesinx clientele to pay a 560 percent markup for stuffed tortillas reflects an everyday acknowledgment of couriers' professional labor. Salvadoran couriers regularly talk with their clients about showing up at U.S. ports of entry with hundreds of pounds of Salvadoran food packed at maximum weight restrictions in their luggage. Campesinxs who pay those marked-up prices require little explanation of who couriers are. Couriers, however, seem to repetitiously provoke anger and confusion among U.S. Customs and Border Protection agents, as couriers defend and sometimes lose parcels as part of the everyday risks they experience in their quasi-documented profession. Couriers are known travelers, transporters, defenders, and deliverers of mnemonically valued objects that are wound up in affective diasporic networks.

In El Salvador, ANGEC membership helps couriers facilitate interactions with the Salvadoran government upon entry into El Salvador with parcels from the United States. Membership reduces the paperwork burden, reduces the tariffs that couriers pay on imported parcels,[9] and provides a structured way for couriers to interface with Salvadoran migration agents at the Comalapa Airport when they return from the United States with hundreds of pounds of merchandise. ANGEC members pay monthly fees and attend biannual meetings. ANGEC's defined objectives include establishing and maintaining permanent relationships between Salvadoran families and fostering economic and social development.[10] Historically, ANGEC has lobbied the legislative assembly in El Salvador to influence language surrounding laws governing baggage and courier services.[11] While U.S. CBP officers may perceive the courier profession as informal labor,[12] and while there are indeed unregistered couriers, ANGEC professionalizes and legitimizes the occupation in El Salvador. It is not the Salvadoran government that needs to understand couriers and their labors but rather agents of the U.S. state and the sources of information they draw upon when they confiscate and trash *pupusas*, transferring the cost of the confiscated item to a professional Salvadoran courier who has little room for retaliation or objection.

In the United States, agents of the state such as CBP officers can frequently become confused by, irritated by, or even aggressive with ANGEC and non-ANGEC Salvadoran couriers alike who arrive at U.S. ports of entry on tourist visas (sometimes with business visitor [B-1] visas) with hundreds of pounds of chicken, cheese, beans, and other food items packed into thin duffel bags (reducing the overall weight of the cargo so that more parcels can be packed inside). Before the 2004 negotiations of the Dominican Republic–Central America Free Trade Agreement (CAFTA) in El Salvador, ANGEC had hoped to secure a special class of visas for Salvadoran couriers.[13] Despite being transnational economic producers, Salvadoran couriers are too small a class, often with relatively too little capital, and instead must settle for business visitor B-1 visas, which offer less reliable methods for validating their professional work in transnational space. The B-1, B-1 combination, or simple tourist visas that are typically issued to Salvadoran couriers create uncertainty in courier travels. Inspectors from the U.S. Department of the Interior, U.S. Fish and Wildlife Service and U.S. CBP have asked me, at the time they are reviewing a courier's luggage, to tell them more about the very people standing before them whose luggage they are inspecting (due to my fluency in the English language and the fact that I stated I was a sociologist who was studying couriers). In the spirit of my key informants' request, I also write this chapter for those agents who read to learn. English-speaking inspectors and Spanish-speaking couriers are often unable to engage in the type of dialogue that could promote mutual understanding and decrease anxieties felt at the moment when couriers interface with the fabric of the U.S. nation-state.

I should finally add that as a participant observer who feels he owes something to the couriers he studied, I participated in the work of two ANGEC couriers from El Norteño. As a courier, I was slow and inefficient, but I could be useful when it came to lifting heavy objects, providing vehicular transport in the United States, or providing simultaneous translation for couriers as they negotiated their entry into the United States.[14] My work earned me no direct pay, but it did afford me free flights between the United States and El Salvador for the 250 extra pounds of parcels that my passenger ticket allowed couriers to carry for that particular trip. To learn more about the nonhuman objects that couriers labored to move, I treated couriers as my mentors while conducting this research. This was also how I learned more about the socioeconomics of the courier trade, which in part organizes memory practices. Here I focus on salient aspects of the socioeconomics of El Norteño's couriers that are relevant to understanding how the courier trade structures mnemonic practices in a local diasporic network.

ENCOMIENDANOMICS

Campesinx migrants in Colorado who choose to pay a 560 percent markup for a food product (aware that the cost of the markup exceeds daily wages of their kin in the rural Salvadoran countryside) need little explanation of how couriers make their money and the risks they face to run their businesses. There are indeed business secrets and outstanding mysteries particular to individual couriers that I will not divulge here, but rather, I try to explain to unfamiliar readers how El Norteño's couriers produce and reproduce their market and business operations. Here I do not focus on market demand for a parcel but more so focus on the implementation of couriers' transnational production of delivered parcels, centering on the ways that couriers navigate and negotiate multiple costs to arrive at a price that is generally understood and accepted by networks of diasporic clientele. The marked-up values of food, medicine, documents, photographs, clothes, hammocks, electronics, school supplies, letters, remittances, and sometimes even people in transnational space reflect much more than a nostalgia among clientele for the Salvadoran countryside. Couriers repetitiously invest and structure inputs to drive their business operations, successfully delivering these myriad parcels in conditions that are at minimum adequate and at best pristine.

The business operations I document here are specific to El Norteño's couriers and are likely to be somewhat unique to Chalatenango and somewhat variant from couriers who provide services to diasporic communities linked with other Salvadoran departments, such as La Libertad or San Miguel.[15] To help readers make sense of the business practices of couriers who provide services to clientele in El Norteño's diasporic networks, I detail segments of transnational journeys with couriers to present a "restructured composite" drawn from the nonfictional incidents and details of multiple trips obtained from my field notes. To do this, I

FIGURE 1.1   Cheese being sent as a parcel from El Salvador to the United States.

draw inspiration from Jason De León's restructured composite of migrant journeys and combine "events occurring within one or more ethnographic investigations into a single narrative."[16] I also focus on these composite narratives because
they form the basis of my understanding of socioeconomic factors that structure
couriers' affectively and mnemonically charged interactions with clients. In her
ethnographic work with Chalatecxs, Irina Carlota Silber writes that "traversing
time and place are critical components of my theorizing because this traversing is embodied in the lives of Chalatecos."[17] Traversing time and place are also
important to the theorizing in this chapter, so I begin with a restructured composite of the segment of a courier's travel sequence here.

TRAVERSING RURAL, URBAN, LAND, AND AIR SPACE WITH A COURIER

Forty-eight hours before we leave for Colorado, I am in the Salvadoran countryside at Mateo's house collecting and packaging parcels. Mateo is one of my key

FIGURE 1.2   A tub of coffee after it has been inspected by couriers in El Salvador, who puncture the parcel using wooden skewers in order to evaluate if anything is hidden inside.

informants and works as a courier to transport parcels between Chalatenango and Colorado (including Boulder County and the Metro Denver area). In one day, dozens of parcels that collectively weigh hundreds of pounds will flow toward Mateo's business/home in El Norteño, and he needs additional labor to process the parcels accordingly. His mother, father, sister, nephew, and I are present to assist with the collection, inspection, weighing, and repackaging of each parcel.

As we collect parcels at the table, an older man in a cowboy hat with a machete strapped to his belt approaches us. He is holding a hammock and two bricks of cheese destined for his daughter in Colorado. The courier's father and sister stretch open the hammock to make sure nothing is stashed inside as the courier stabs a wooden skewer through the bricks of cheese to make sure nothing has been hidden in the cheese. The man in the cowboy hat is an old friend, but he is accustomed to having his parcels scrutinized by the family in this manner, and he watches his parcels be subject to inspection without showing visible or verbal signs of personal offense. The old man tells me that his wife finished making the cheese this morning. No contraband is found in the hammock or in the cheese. The hammock and the cheese are tightly repackaged by Mateo's sister and bound with masking tape. She weighs the packages and writes the daughter's name and the parcel weight on each package. The cheese will go directly into one of the large freezers behind the collection table. As this inspection process takes place, other farmworkers arrive, forming a line to deliver parcels of their own that, likewise, the laboring family unit will collect, inspect, weigh, package, and, more often than not, freeze.

Clients converse with Mateo's family and casually comment on each parcel as members of the family inspect and weigh them. One woman in line hands me a plastic bag full of what looks like a dark powder. Mateo's father recognizes it as *maíz negro* (black corn) flour and comments that it is produced from small corn stalks that are unlike the genetically modified corn produced in the United States. He says this particular black corn flour is best for making *Atol Shuco* (a hot, fermented beverage), and the client confirms that this is exactly why she is sending corn flour.

Some clients arrive with items that Mateo rejects. For example, one woman arrives with a box of lidocaine injections and syringes intended to assist with a minor surgery for a client in the United States. Mateo politely tells her that he will not be able to bring these items through U.S. customs. Acetaminophen, antibiotics, and antiparasitic medications also arrive, along with statements such as *fíjate que el cipote está enfermo* (the boy is sick), where clients communicate brief tales of sick campesinx kin who refuse to go to a doctor's office or pharmacy in the United States.

An older woman arrives at the collection table with two tubs of sugarcane honey (similar to molasses). She asks if I know her daughter Cristina in Colorado. I respond that yes, I met Cristina in Boulder, and I remember that her daughter misses the *frijoles de seda* (silk beans) and *quesillo* (a type of cheese similar to mozzarella) used to make pupusas. As I say this, Cristina's mother stares at me with laser-sharp attention for an uncomfortable moment or two after I finish speaking. She then asks me if Cristina missed anything else. Cristina's mother is taking inventory on what Cristina says that she longs for so that she can deliver it to Cristina next time the courier makes a trip. Friendly couriers who engage their clients in small conversations and who are attentive to the details of longing in their clientele networks can facilitate conversations such as this one that will result in more parcels being delivered in the future. I do remember that Cristina joked with me about the frequency with which her mother asked for cash remittances, but I choose not to disclose this information to her mother. I am not simply being friendly with Cristina's mother—I am mimicking conversational tactics I learned by watching Mateo interact with his clients. This is one of the ways that couriers participate in the production of longing, reproducing demand that moves objects through transnational space.

Mateo and his family spend the morning receiving, weighing, and repackaging parcels. When the sun sets, Mateo and his father begin loading parcels into cardboard boxes, which they then transfer into thin duffel bags. The thin bags create a light, makeshift suitcase that will store delicate food items loaded onto an international flight destined for Texas. Mateo and his father continue to puzzle together boxes and bags until each one reaches the seventy-pound limit that Mateo is permitted to board the airplane with given his elite status with his commercial airline of choice. Couriers rapidly accrue such statuses with commercial airlines that compete for their loyalty. Some couriers even make inroads with commercial airlines to reach private agreements to carry additional cargo so that they can guarantee the transport of more weight than is permitted for most passengers.

When Mateo and his father are done packing for the trip, Mateo eyes the backpack in which I carry my field notes, audio recorder, and laptop. He tells me that my bag is thin before instructing me to shove eighteen pastries into it. Then Mateo opens my carry-on luggage and crams coffee, hammocks, and blankets into what I had originally perceived to be a fully packed suitcase. We go to sleep with pieces of luggage packed to the absolute brim. Frozen items will be packed at two in the morning before we leave for the airport.

The next day, I wake up at 2:30 in the morning and Mateo's family is already awake and working to help him pack the frozen items and to load the vehicle. We depart the house at 3 a.m., but we immediately stop at a farmhouse in El Norteño and pick up an elderly woman who will be visiting her son in the United States. The woman has never flown; nor has she been to the United States, but she managed to get a travel visa and her son, who is living in Texas, has paid Mateo to accompany her to the U.S. port that we will enter. The vehicle continues moving out of Chalatenango. As we pass through Apopa, a municipality in the Department of San Salvador, we stop at a gas station where two individuals were shot dead hours earlier. The police tape is still there but the numbered cards used to identify the bodies have been removed. A young woman enters the car. She is carrying a restraining order against a family member in El Salvador who has recently abused her, along with her newly obtained visa. I learn that the courier already has a copy of her restraining order in case *we* are targeted on our way to the airport. As we drive, I learn that the girl's aunt woke her up in the middle of the night, just two hours before we picked her up at the gas station, to tell the young girl to pack a bag because today was the day that she would be heading to live in the United States, presumably forever.

Our caravan arrives at the airport, and Mateo quickly runs to what Celia Rivas describes as "The Pollo Campero in El Salvador's Comalapa Airport, one of numerous locations in the country . . . Travelers often buy boxes of chicken to take with them on the plane."[18] Mateo purchases three large boxes of fried chicken from Pollo Campero that he will gift or sell to his clients in the United States. He distributes the boxes of chicken to the three of us who are traveling with him, and we waddle toward the gate with our overstuffed luggage and chicken boxes as he manages our tickets and passport with each agent. We board

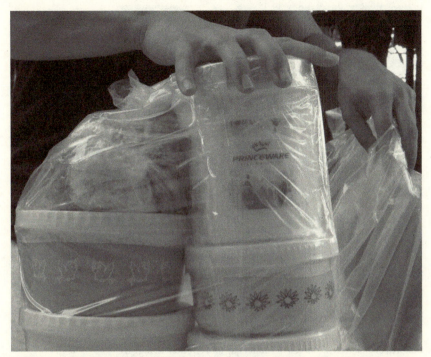

FIGURE 1.3 Various parcels (including beans and cheese) that have been inspected and repackaged by Salvadoran couriers prior to bringing them to the United States.

FIGURE 1.4 Food parcels being packed into a freezer in El Salvador the day before they are brought to the United States.

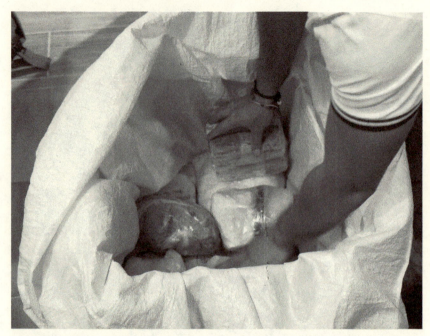

FIGURE 1.5 Parcels in El Salvador being sorted into a polypropylene-lined cardboard box that will be inserted into a canvas duffel bag and checked as luggage.

and I sit with the girl and the woman in the back of the airplane as the courier assumes his customary seat in first class (benefits that come with frequent flights). The grandmother and girl have never flown before, so I manage their carry-on stowage, buckle and unbuckle their seatbelts, explain how the toilet in the bathroom works, and order their beverages for them. Throughout much of the flight, the two women stare wide-eyed out the window. The young woman who was informed hours earlier that she would be forever moving to the United States cries throughout the flight. I purchase a turkey melt sandwich from the flight attendant and split it between the three of us. The women instantly consume their portions of the turkey melt and politely thank me for sharing food. Realizing that this was their first time trying food outside of El Salvador, I ask the women what they thought of the sandwich. They both hesitate. I say that I didn't like the way it tasted, and they both assure me that it was disgusting. The grandmother is shocked that I spent the equivalent of a day's wage in the Salvadoran countryside for one off-putting turkey melt.

We land at the George Bush Intercontinental Airport in Houston, and I break apart from Mateo and the two women as we are processed by the U.S. Department of Homeland Security (DHS). Mateo gestures toward the line for U.S. citizens and says, "Your flag is waiting for you." I am rapidly processed, a CBP agent

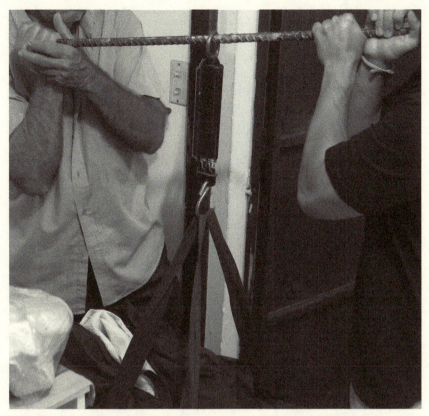

FIGURE 1.6 A courier and a family member in El Salvador weighing a packed duffel bag to evaluate whether it meets the maximum weight restrictions for checked luggage.

stamps my passport and says, "Welcome home," and I go to baggage claim and collect the five large black cloth bags from the luggage carousel. All the luggage and passengers from our flight disappear, and there is still no sign of Mateo and the two women. The smell of cheese rises from the bags, and I take a seat on the abandoned luggage carousel as I wonder what happened to them.

PRODUCTION INPUTS

Salvadoran couriers are transnational producers. They transport parcels and people between family members who are kept apart by national boundaries that do not allow for the fluid movement of undocumented bodies in transnational spaces. The speed of the delivery and condition of the delivered product define a courier's reputation among clientele. While ANGEC does not set price limits, Salvadoran couriers typically charged $5 to $7 per pound at the time I collected data for this book.[19] Within the $5–$7 per pound price spectrum, price per pound may vary with airline ticket costs that are dependent on the U.S. state to which couriers are delivering parcels. Multiple couriers delivering parcels to adjacent or overlapping diasporic networks will compete with one another for clients. The transported parcel is almost always paid for by the U.S.-based family member, mainly due to the elevated incomes in the United States. For a single trip managed by a single courier, hundreds of pounds of parcels can be transported for dozens of transnational families. The 560 percent price markup I presented at the beginning of this chapter is not truly a markup, since the product itself is not ultimately what the client is paying for (the cooked pupusas were a gift from a family member), but rather, clients pay for the cost of *transport*.

The distance and logistics involved in rapidly transporting parcels from points of origin (Chalatenango, El Salvador) to points of destination (Boulder County / Metro Denver area) imply standard capital inputs and repetitive transportation costs. Freezers, telephones, suitcases, backpacks, scales, and travel documents (such as travel visas with the B-1 specification, residencies, or citizenships) are required to ensure the preservation and delivery of parcels. Reputable couriers often freeze perishable food products (like cooked game hen or cream) immediately upon receiving them in El Salvador and transport these products in their frozen state to prevent spoilage. As such, having adequate access to freezers at the points of origin (Chalatenango) and destination (United States) are important for delivering parcels in good condition. After seeing the cover of this book, one of my key informants wanted to clarify that he would never deliver a parcel in such poor condition (although he did appreciate the creative way in which the aged parcel provoked attention to memory). Having mobile and fixed scales can be helpful in estimating the price at the time of parcel delivery and in maximizing the weight per item of luggage prior to arriving at the airport. There are also financial costs associated with internal transport in El Salvador and the United States (duffel bags, vehicles) and international transportation (flights and extra cargo) that affect the price per pound for a courier.

El Norteño's couriers repetitiously leverage kinship and friendship networks to conduct business. While standard physical capital (freezers, scales), transportation costs (gasoline, airline tickets), and labor inputs (time spent collecting, transporting, and distributing parcels) affect a courier's budget, the cultural capital that couriers draw on to leverage profit cannot be underestimated—the existence of the courier profession itself is based on the existence of relationships that span points of origin and destination in transnational Salvadoran-U.S. migrant networks and on affective and mnemonic practices implicated in these relationships.

In the context of courier production, I use the term *cultural capital* to refer to the social assets that couriers use to get ahead in their markets, taking into account the relationships between "economic production and the system producing the producers,"[20] where couriers employ mannerisms, cultivate personal relationships, and engage in affective and mnemonic management to maintain and advance their businesses. For example, couriers encounter basic transportation costs (airline tickets, gasoline) in their occupation, but these costs can be reduced by leveraging favors within familial networks, where a U.S.-based family member may provide free rides to reduce their Salvadoran courier family member's overall costs. Perhaps the courier will repay these favors in the form of small token parcels repetitively delivered to kin who provide cost-reducing favors. Couriers' relationships with private airline agents can also result in special discounts, and some ticketing agents go out of their way to help favored couriers identify better-priced flights and deals. At one private airline agency in San Salvador, where I listened to Mateo engage in small talk for what seemed like an inordinate amount of time, the airline agent gestured toward him and explained to me that Mateo was *buena gente* (good people). Reciprocally, Mateo provides this agent and others with gifts that are reciprocated in discretionary efforts and favors afforded to Mateo when he runs into problems with airline tickets or pricing.

Couriers leverage interpersonal relationships within their diasporic communities to establish and maintain clients. Human affects surround the transfer and delivery of parcels, which are objects that stoke intimate memories of kin who are physically separated by diasporic divides. A campesinx migrant can buy wholesale cheese in the grocery store, but having cheese made and sent by a grandmother whom a campesinx hasn't seen in ten years assigns a mnemonic value to that internationally transported cheese. If parcels arrive in excellent condition with a few friendly words and a backstory, a courier can gain a type of intrafamilial trust that distinguishes this courier from others who may be known for their bad attitudes and/or tendencies to deliver ruined food parcels. In the case of the ruined food product, not only does the parcel lose mnemonic value, but because of the parcel's mnemonic value, the ruination has affectively intense outcomes.

As part of their occupation, couriers physically link family and kin located through the transnational spaces of diasporic networks, and El Norteño's couriers grew into their professions through these links. Some couriers begin their first travels as I did, tagging along with close friends or family members who are already working as couriers but whose work volume requires the additional support. Junior couriers can draw upon senior couriers' relationships that are built in transnational families in order to earn trust, establish a reputation, and form his or her respective client base. Couriers who train their own kin to become couriers benefit, in the end, by the familial pooling of resources in El Salvador. Further, the ability to obtain a visa (typically tourist visas) to conduct the transnational work of a courier is often linked to the socioeconomic status of the

Salvadoran visa applicant inside El Salvador. Obtaining a visa often includes being able to show proof of savings, land, economic productivity, and other factors that tie the individual back to El Salvador.[21]

Finally, couriers attempt to balance hundreds of pounds of parcels sent between dozens of families with the cost of an airline ticket and airline weight restrictions on luggage. Variability in weight restrictions, airline ticket costs, and the final weight of all parcels received for a flight is absorbed by the courier's cultural-capital inputs. At a moment's notice, the ability of a courier to call on highly trusted people with visas, within kinship and friendship networks, affects the consistency with which a courier provides services to clients. Thus it is important for couriers to cultivate these working relationships to maintain consistency with clientele. I was once helping Mateo collect parcels for one of his upcoming trips when he quickly exceeded his weight restriction for his ticketed flight. He turned to me and asked if I could travel to the United States with him for the week, where we would be leaving El Salvador in thirty-six hours. I was personally one of about four individuals he regularly drew upon for last-minute needs such as this.

TRAVELING WITH A COURIER: TRANSPORTING PARCELS INTO THE UNITED STATES

On my trip with Mateo and the two women he was escorting into the United States, I waited at the baggage-claim carousel until all apparent passengers from our flight had collected their luggage. When Mateo and the two women emerged from passport control, Mateo explained that they were held up because the CBP officer who reviewed their passports and visas was a bilingual Mexican American who refused to speak in Spanish to Mateo and his monolingual Spanish-speaking travel companions. This type of intra-Latinx racism is a common source of frustration for Salvadoran couriers, who feel that CBP officers (particularly Mexican Americans or other U.S.-born Latinxs) sometimes go out of their way to make transactions more difficult and denigrating than they actually need to be.

There is no narrative that I can provide to describe what it is like to pass through U.S. customs with a courier, because the experience changes every time and is marked by a feeling of unpredictability. In 2018, Salvadoran couriers entering the United States are reviewed by a CBP agent, who confirms couriers' visas and then flags and escorts couriers through baggage claim and straight to *inspección—el estrés de nuestra experiencia* (inspection—the stress of our experience). Here Mateo is referring to the X-ray machines and inspection tables managed by CBP agents who inspect the items declared by couriers. In 2018, couriers are supposed to be filling out prior-notice forms with the U.S. Food and Drug Administration (FDA), which are presented to the CBP officers who inspect declared items. On instances where I have passed through customs alone, a CBP agent quickly spots my bag from a distance and sends me to the X-ray machines. In line, I recognized a few Salvadoran couriers. Despite the fact that English is my first language, the questions asked by CBP agents have often been quick, semiaudible, and somewhat confusing. As a native English speaker, I have usually had to do a double take to understand CBP agents, who fire these questions at individuals who do not speak English as a first language. For example, as I am instructed to place my luggage on the X-ray belt, I hear "You gahporkufroo?" I ask the agent to please repeat the question, and he frustratedly yells back, "Do you have pork or fruit?" As I try to think about whether I am carrying pupusas that might have pork in them, the agent is already visibly frustrated with my delayed response. The entire experience is somewhat anxiety provoking, which does not lend well to the provision of accurate responses, even though it is my intention to provide accurate responses. This experience is far worse for couriers on travel visas who do not speak English as a first language, particularly when Spanish-speaking CBP agents will not speak to them in Spanish. On other occasions, the U.S. FDA form may provoke different CBP agents to declare that the parcels are merchandise (even if all parcels are technically gifts), resulting in couriers' luggage being confiscated. The lack of consistency in CBP agent understandings of the courier occupation is rivaled by the discretionary interpersonal aggression that is haphazardly applied to couriers at various ports of entry.

Older couriers remember U.S. inspectors regularly destroying parcels during customs inspections back in the 1990s, where officers would cut tamales in half and toss them back toward the suitcase as though they were trash. One older courier remembers it felt like some carnivalesque juggling game, where he would anxiously attempt to catch the airborne food parcels as customs agents tossed them back toward his suitcase. Nearly twenty-five years later, CBP officers may be aware of who couriers are and what they are carrying, but CBP inspection concerns over drugs and contraband remain a priority. Instead of working with couriers to understand what is in their luggage, I have found that CBP officers' dispositions and demeanors confuse and provoke anxiety in couriers, many of whom want to provide honest and direct responses about what they are carrying. After once communicating on behalf of a courier who had his entire suitcase of parcels confiscated by CBP (a significant financial loss for the courier), CBP explained to me that "the CBP officer who speaks with you upon arrival determines the admissibility of goods and visitors."[22] I would add from my personal experience with couriers that CBP agents might actually have an easier time implementing inspections if basic communication issues were addressed in a systematic manner. For example, a Spanish-speaking CBP agent who refuses to speak Spanish to a Spanish-speaking courier reduces the conversational accuracy about what the courier is attempting to bring into the United States, thus making linguistic ability (as opposed to an accurate description of what the courier is carrying) the focal point of the interaction.

When possible, Mateo put me in charge of communicating with the U.S. customs inspectors. Despite the fact that we had examined all the parcels in our luggage, I still felt nervous about whether someone could have slipped something in there. These doubts plague couriers as they pass through customs, particularly those who have been caught with narcotics that have been hidden in tamales, candies, or clothes. I asked Mateo how he feels during these moments, right before the CBP inspectors open his luggage, and he responded that "customs in the U.S. is a little box of surprises. You never know what's going to happen, nor what will be the surprise. Sometimes you are fearful, but what I think in that moment is 'I hope to be free one more time after this inspection is over.' Like I told you, customs is a little box of surprises."

On one occasion, as we approached the CBP X-ray machine and inspection tables, Mateo recognized one of the agents from the Department of the Interior U.S. Fish and Wildlife Service Office of Law Enforcement and explained that he perceived her to be malicious. She had previously confiscated cooked iguana eggs from him that he incorrectly identified as "turtle eggs" in the citation that was provided to him. I greeted the inspector and spoke with her in English, introducing myself as a sociologist who was studying the work of this particular courier. She smiled and said that she remembered confiscating items from Mateo. Then the questions began. They were not, however, about what Mateo had in his luggage. She wanted to know what Mateo did for a living, who he was bringing these items to, and why people wanted them. I translated. We talked with her about El Norteño's diaspora and how couriers like Mateo transmit parcels to family members. During this CBP inspection process, nothing was confiscated, and the customs officers thanked us for the interesting conversation. Afterward, Mateo told me that his previous experience with the same agent was completely different, and he told me that it was my status as an English-speaking gringo that made it so.[23]

After passing through U.S. customs, we leave one of our traveling companions (the elderly mother) in Texas and board our connecting flight to Denver, Colorado. At the airport in Denver, we deliver the girl from Apopa to her mother, and we are then picked up and driven to a friend's home in the greater Denver area. When we arrive, Mateo begins unpacking his bags and placing items in the freezer and refrigerator. Campesinx migrants begin arriving at the door of the house. Their behavior and dress are familiar and foreign to me all at once. Mateo's campesinx migrant clientele are dressed in winter clothes and appear to be somewhat impatient with the pace at which Mateo moves—despite being accustomed to the slower temporality of the Salvadoran countryside, Mateo's clients expect him to move faster here. The kitchen is crowded with Chalatecxs, and Mateo is delivering parcels to each of them, handing out parcels and collecting cash using a system that is so particular that I am unable to step in to help. After being awake for twenty-one hours, I begin to fall asleep on top of my field notes as Mateo continues to distribute parcels. I rouse myself to walk to my room, where I fall asleep as Mateo continues to work.

In the days to come, we will shuttle between campesinx migrant enclaves located on the outskirts of Denver and Boulder. The days will be long and boring, with extensive periods of time spent sitting in trailers, kitchens, and parking lots with nothing to do as we wait for Chalatecxs to arrive to pick up and pay for their parcels. I will be put in charge of transporting Mateo around the greater Denver area. The task used to be nightmarish, as neither of us had functional phones in the United States and both of us were without GPS navigation (technological advances in Google Maps offline downloads have since remedied this issue). As the trip wears on, Mateo becomes more stressed and stops assisting me with directions. I have to stop at gas stations and ask for directions to arrive at apartment complexes and trailer parks as I drive Mateo around, with both of us becoming increasingly tired and agitated with one another. We spend ample time in trailer parks, where we are usually without food. Of all the time I spend working with Mateo, our time in the United States is the most stressful, miserable, and conflict ridden. It is not just the intimacy of the memories attached to parcels that couriers manage—they also manage affective responses directly to their clients and the individuals they leverage in their interpersonal networks to do business.

EMOTIONAL LABOR

I spent the most time in the field observing Mateo, a Chalateco courier who learned the trade from his mother, Mercedes. Mercedes had been working as a courier for nearly twenty years as the matriarch of the household, and her son both benefitted from and generally followed her business model. Alisa Garni has described that Salvadoran couriers can buck the traditional gender-development lens that would emphasize couriers' reliance on social networks to conduct their businesses and has argued that women couriers are not passive but shape variable forms of capitalism by drawing on histories of trading goods produced on household-owned lands to launch their businesses. In line with Garni's observations, Mateo's mother launched herself as a courier as the economic matriarch of her household, shaping a career trajectory for herself, and eventually her son, to generate family income. This emphasis on social ties is what traditionally genders the courier trade, where women are presumed to be more apt at cultivating these relationships.[24] Presuming Garni's critical approach to the courier trade, I want to delve more into ways in which couriers manage affect, as their affective management is simultaneously an enacted mechanism of symbolic violence that campesinx migrants experience in the United States.

While campesinx clientele understand that couriers navigate a complex and risky transnational business, clients' exposure to life in the United States and American styles of client-centered business interactions can discipline the "bodily hexis" of Salvadoran couriers, who are pressured to accommodate the more North American presumption of client-centeredness.[25] Mateo's approach to his customers' attitudes in the United States had an observably positive effect on his profits but taxed his personal emotional capacities.

El Norteño's couriers deliver parcels to campesinx migrants who are often located in the economic margins of U.S. society at large. Clients are often overworked and stressed at the time they come to receive parcels delivered by couriers. Clients may scrutinize the quality of the delivered product given the high prices they pay for them. Paying $112 to receive forty pupusas is unheard of in El Salvador, and if those pupusas are not in pristine condition, the courier will receive a loaded complaint. Strings of clients will remind Mateo that they could consider sending parcels with another courier, maybe one who charges a lower price (but whom Mateo knows to deliver ruined products), and Mateo will respond politely to each client who threatens him with his competition. Couriers constantly interact with parents who are worried about their sick children in the United States or U.S.-based clients who are worried about their economically poor parents back home. Sometimes clients claim they don't have enough cash on hand to pay Mateo, where despite having completed "the job," Mateo is not paid for the parcel he has just delivered. Some couriers navigate interactive experiences with everyday violence as they depend on individual favors to conduct their own work. Mateo regularly listened to stories regarding child abuse, mental health problems, and sexual issues experienced by family and kin split between borders, and Mateo often became implicated in these dynamics as he transmitted particular parcels within families that composed his clientele. Couriers experience secondary trauma from some of these interactions and bear the cumulative stress of all he or she has gone through to arrive with the parcel (not to mention the stress of U.S. customs revisions), including the emotional stress of their clientele.

Couriers engage in ample emotional labor, which involves the management of emotions to generate observable facial expressions and bodily displays in order to create a particular emotional state in another person.[26] I have seen couriers employ a wide range of tactics to manage emotions with their clients, from emotional dissonance (continuing to maintain positive emotions with difficult clients who in fact anger and frustrate the courier) to total emotional concordance (the courier expressing how he or she feels toward a client at that moment in time, such as "snapping back" with biting commentary at a client who is expressing anger). Emotional labor is typically presumed to be gendered. Hillary Clinton recently wrote that emotional labor "describes all the unpaid, uncounted, unseen work that people, overwhelmingly women, perform to keep their workplaces humming along."[27] Numerous studies on the sociology of emotion have illustrated how workers who experience emotional dissonance are more likely to experience emotional exhaustion, and it would go without saying that the traditionally feminized labor of couriers assumes more emotional exhaustion for more women in the courier trade.[28] However, the depth of emotional exhaustion can affect couriers of any gender identity. As a courier who was deeply trusted among his clients and who elicited countless personal stories told within families, Mateo was prone to emotional exhaustion and compassion fatigue. He exhibited emotional dissonance with his clients, where he provided a very positive and apologetic emotional response to clients when in fact he felt frustrated, irritated, and stressed about the other tasks he had to complete in a short timeframe. In turn, this made it very difficult to be around him during parcel distribution in the United States. In the United States, I would document hours of gracious interactions with clients, on the one hand, and irritable, dismissive, and argumentative moments with me, on the other. In front of his clients, Mateo not only had a professional disposition; he also placated their emotions at the expense of his own. I tried my best not to take these moments personally, as I was observing and understood the great deal of emotional stress that Mateo was dealing with.

As I learned while traveling with Mateo in the United States, Salvadoran couriers do not necessarily ponder the larger social forces at play when an overworked and emotionally difficult client arrives to pick up a parcel, and couriers can instead take out their frustrations on the same interpersonal networks of friends and family they rely upon to manage the consistency of their businesses. This lashing out is, in part, a mechanistic transfer central to the expression of symbolic violence—a "product of the 'inert violence' of economic structures and social mechanisms relayed by the active violence of people,"[29] which results in the misrecognition of the larger factors at play. The stressful life experiences of undocumented migrants in North America interfacing with the stressful occupational experiences of the courier (who is often misdocumented by the United States) intensify the emotional labor of couriers. The general socioeconomic marginalization that I observed among campesinx migrants inside the United States resulted in migrants struggling to meet basic needs for their transnational networks of families and kin. Couriers become frustrated with the impatience and anger of their U.S.-based clientele, not the unfair U.S. immigration policies that limit campesinx migrants' documentation accessibility that generates its own set of socioeconomic and corresponding emotional consequences. Consequently, couriers dealing with their emotional dissonance by lashing out within the very networks they cultivate to leverage favors for their business operations is another way in which everyday violence obfuscates latent violence. While couriers generate cultural capital that can be leveraged to get ahead, the symbolic violence that infiltrates these networks (as a result of participating in the courier occupation) diminishes this very capital.

JOURNEY WITH A COURIER: RETURN TO EL SALVADOR

In Colorado, we begin collecting parcels for the return trip "home" to Chalatenango. The parcels we collect in the United States are markedly different from those in the Salvadoran countryside. In the United States, we collect shoes, clothes, electronics, children's toys, school supplies, letters, legal documents, and cash that will be sent from Colorado to Chalatenango. Cash remittances are sent with couriers despite the availability of banking services that might be more efficient, since client trust makes couriers an alternative to the otherwise elite-dominated banking industry.[30] Further, temporal prospection in financial planning among campesinxs with limited access to permanent statuses increase reliance and demand on courier remittance services.[31] As a result, we collect cash that generates labor in the Salvadoran countryside, including construction projects and terrain purchases that would have never been accessible on a campesinx's daily wage in Chalatenango.

As we collect parcels in the United States, Mateo hangs items in plastic bags from a mobile scale he keeps on him at all times. The scale determines the weight, and the client pays at the moment of delivery. There are fixed prices for parcels that do not weigh much (e.g., documents and photographs). In the basement of the house we are staying in, Mateo begins combining parcels into suitcases and asks me to lift each bag until we reach the perfect seventy-pound limit for each suitcase. Mateo will push the weight limit by one or two pounds, and when the airline employees at the ticket counter in Denver refuse to let him check the bags because they are each about two pounds over the weight limit, Mateo asks me to translate multiple Spanish-language curses at them.[32] Seventy-two- and seventy-one-pound bags are opened and shifted around until the bags become seventy pounds each. Mateo opens up my carry-on luggage and crams a computer, two cell phones and their chargers, a Teenage Mutant Ninja Turtle backpack, three pairs of shoes, a pair of high heels, a box of Trojan condoms, T-shirts, and a three-pound packet of random clothes items into my backpack and carry-on bags.

Before we board the plane, Mateo has strapped parcels all over his body, under his armpits and around his waist. My carry-on luggage and backpack look fat. Mateo looks like any other traveler with normal carry-on luggage. His jacket is concealing all the extra cargo, but he has this practice down to a science, and we board the plane without being stopped by the airline's ticketing agents. On the flight back to El Salvador, I sense that Mateo's tension and anxiety are beginning to dissolve. Nothing is going to rot or ruin in our luggage, and when the plane lands, the Salvadoran government has predefined processes for dealing with couriers—a profession that the Salvadoran government recognizes. Navigating xenophobic presumptions of criminality has given way to expectations of validation as our direction of movement is oriented toward El Salvador.

As an ANGEC-registered courier, Mateo has already prepared a Salvadoran declaration form for small packets that is specifically devoted to bringing in new and used items from the United States. He filled out the form in the United States and transmitted it to ANGEC with additional specifications, including the flight information, his passport, his Salvadoran business documents, the amount of weight he is carrying, the number of pieces of luggage he has, the number of parcels he is carrying, and additional documentation indicating whether electronic items are present. The electronic items include apparatuses with Wi-Fi, headphones, and smartphones, which will be taxed an additional 5 percent beyond the 13 percent paid to the Salvadoran government for the items. ANGEC prepares a summary document, and the ANGEC representative delivers the document to Mateo after he passes through a migration checkpoint in El Salvador. The ANGEC documentation facilitates for Mateo and other couriers a smoother revision process at Salvadoran customs, where taxes are paid and couriers present identification cards provided by Salvadoran customs. Mateo trickles through the Salvadoran government's processes before leaving the airport.[33]

A FIELD OF RISKS

Transnationally, couriers work in a quasi-documented profession. While it may be easy to assume that couriers enjoy a degree of privilege operating in partially undocumented spaces, the anxiety and tension produced by being treated as suspect in the United States appeared to be quite the opposite. Mateo's characterization of his expectations that U.S. customs is a little "box of surprises" and his corresponding "hope to be free one more time after this inspection is over" are repetitive occupational experiences he has in a profession that is recognized by his government but made suspect by another. The instability surrounding couriers' interactions with the U.S. DHS reduces assurances of occupational and personal security, and these increased moments of stress and fear are experienced by individuals who often net annual incomes near or below the U.S. poverty threshold.[34] Beyond the occupational risks and stressors that couriers experience, they face myriad risks inside El Salvador.

The first time I sat down to write this chapter, I was housesitting for Mateo after he had just returned from a trip to Colorado. There were thousands of dollars of merchandise from the United States scattered around his dining-room table and living room. As I was working on my laptop computer, a thief jumped over the wall and entered the house I was watching. Luckily, neither of us used a weapon against the other, and neither of us ended up physically harmed. A few weeks after this incident, Mateo's most aggressive guard dog was poisoned and killed. A few days after that, someone attempted to break into Mateo's vehicle. Mateo has been "doubling and tripling" his security since these incidents, adding rows of razor wire to his house. Mateo's risks in El Salvador are only part of the security risks he faces daily in his occupation. Every time Mateo passes through customs in the United States, he risks falling victim to any one of his clients placing contraband into one of the hundreds of parcels he is delivering. For Mateo, the direct risks he experiences from his clientele are all part of the reality of working as a courier. He talks frequently about his desire to switch jobs, but in doing so, he realizes he would take a massive pay cut. Personal security is only one of the numerous risks he and other couriers experience, and being a courier means that he expects those risks to keep on materializing in his field.

Couriers are constantly moving fifty- to seventy-pound bags, which leads to chronic back and neck pain. Couriers often deal with these bodily effects by paying for back and neck massages, chiropractic treatments, or muscle relaxants provided without prescription by pharmacies in El Salvador. Several couriers strap on weightlifting belts as they exit their vehicles at the Comalapa Airport, strapping on and removing the belts throughout multiple phases of their transnational journeys. Mateo and I were once loading fifty- and seventy-pound bags into the car on a snowy morning in Denver when he slipped and hurt his back. Mateo's solution was to stretch a little bit in Denver and to get a massage in El Salvador. I typically carried muscle relaxants and ibuprofen ready at a moment's notice in the backpack that contains my voice recorder and field notes. Carrying large, heavy bags in strange positions while traveling is an occupational reality that impacts couriers' bodies. Courier travel behavior can also result in self-reported eating irregularities; fluid retention in feet, ankles, and legs; and alterations in diurnal and sleep rhythms.

When couriers traveling on tourist visas experience acute illness, they are rarely in situations where they can make time to seek adequate health care, treatment, and rest. For example, I knew one courier contracted Chikungunya (a mosquito-borne illness) in Chalatenango but developed symptoms while distributing parcels in the United States. In this case, her U.S.-based campesinx clientele prepared "raise the dead" soup and took care of her until she got better—she never once entered a hospital in the United States, because she was unaware of where she could receive reasonably priced health care. Other couriers will go directly to the emergency room of a hospital and not pay their bills, which are often far too expensive for them to pay (a full day in a hospital can generate costs that are roughly equivalent to a courier's annual salary) and are forwarded to collection agencies in the United States. Navigating the U.S. health-care system and emergency department is a frightening task, as health insurance in the United States is unreasonably expensive for couriers. When a real health emergency arises in the United States, the stress surrounding the health care emergency filters through networks of Salvadorans who attempt to help the courier solve the problem. Back in El Salvador, I regularly observed couriers paying for private health care to treat health issues generated by or exacerbated by their current occupation.

CONCLUSION

The courier trade depends upon and reproduces the diaspora of Chalatecxs that has grown since the Salvadoran Civil War. Couriers cultivate and utilize cultural capital to turn profits in a quasi-documented transnational profession that helps them get financially ahead in El Salvador while also incurring additional risks. The quasi-documented nature of couriers' work produces ample stress when couriers interface with the U.S. DHS. Despite the continued existence and pro-fessionalization of couriers in El Salvador, U.S. government agents treat couriers who are traveling with food on tourist visas as suspect, as potential drug smug-glers, and as individuals who may not deserve to be spoken to in Spanish by Spanish-speaking CBP agents responsible for their inspection. Within a single day, couriers travel from a place where they work in a recognized occupation to a place where unpredictable things happen to them and the parcels they are carry-ing, enacted by people who do not recognize their profession upon arrival.

Working in a quasi-documented profession and serving a clientele base with mixed documentation statuses in the United States is reflected in the stress and emotional labor of El Norteño's couriers. Couriers' experiences of emotional dis-sonance and emotional stress draw attention away from the inert social factors that marginalize and denigrate both couriers and their clients. This emotional labor synchronizes with the transfer of mnemonically charged objects (parcels) in diasporic networks. Memory is a strong component of campesinxs' demand for parcels, and attentive couriers are able to leverage memories that move par-cels through transnational space.

In the next chapter, I specifically focus on couriers' campesinx clientele who migrated from El Norteño without documentation and who remember different periods of undocumented migration through Mexico that correspond to shifts in transnational structural violence. I sequence these memories to map social factors that affect couriers' campesinx clientele, whose memories continue to interact with parcels in transnational space.

2 · A SEQUENCE OF UNDOCUMENTED MIGRANT MEMORIES

While migrants had always faced danger crossing the border and many died before INS began the Southwest Border Strategy, following the implementation of the strategy, there was an increase in border-crossing deaths resulting from exposure to either extreme heat or cold.

—U.S. Government Accountability Office[1]

This federal enforcement strategy is known as Prevention through Deterrence (PTD). PTD along with ever-evolving technologies of enforcement control have increasingly turned the U.S.–Mexico border into a militarized zone where Border Patrol practice a strategy modeled on the Pentagon's Low-Intensity Conflict Doctrine, a policy first designed to suppress domestic insurgencies in the "Third-World."

—Jason De León, anthropologist[2]

those who were shot with bullets while crossing the border,
those who died of malaria or scorpion stings or pit viper bites
in the hell of the banana plantations,
those who cried drunk for the national anthem
under the Pacific cyclone or northern snow,
the hustlers,
the beggars,
the potheads,
Guanaco sons of bitches,
those who could barely make it back,
those who had a little more luck,
the eternally undocumented . . .

—Roque Dalton, poet, 1974[3]

I was unpacking parcels in a Long Island kitchen with Mercedes, one of El Norteño's couriers. Mercedes was wearing a weightlifting belt around her jeans and blouse. Smoke from cooking *pupusas* emanated from the kitchen, and there was snow on the ground outside.

We sat down to rest and wait for Mercedes's clients to begin arriving at the house to pick up the parcels she had brought from El Norteño. As we chatted, Mercedes gestured toward the youngest girl of a group of children that was playing with toys in the adjacent living room. Mercedes explained that the girl had a mother who left El Salvador with a *coyote* (guide / human smuggler) two years ago, but the family lost track of her when she neared the border in Mexico. Nobody has heard from her since. She is presumably dead or, worse, kidnapped and forced to work as a sex slave. Nobody knows. She is *desaparecida* (disappeared).

I stupidly point at the little girl. *Her?* Mercedes nods. She talks about the girl's disappeared mother with the same solemnity that individuals in my peer network talk about someone falling ill with Alzheimer's—it is extreme and unfortunate, but it happens. There are words like *desaparecida*, words that have existed and that continue to exist, which campesinxs use to explain these types of things. Friends and family disappear in Mexico. Being trafficked into sex work is within the range of possible outcomes for young women who migrate from El Norteño to the United States. Couriers' clients experience feelings of being *targeted and hunted* inside the U.S. nation-state's borders. As Mercedes and I continue talking about the young girl's *desaparecida* mother, another teenager from El Norteño is just now disappearing. As we distribute parcels in New York, this young man leaves El Norteño with a coyote who is a known alcoholic. That was the last time anyone from El Norteño saw him. Nobody will know what happened to him, and for a while, he, too, will be *desaparecido*. We will learn about his death on Facebook a few weeks later.

The undocumented migratory terrain that spans Northern Triangle takeoff points, Mexico, and the southern border of the United States is, as I will argue throughout this book, an expansion of the field of violence that campesinxs today both live in and remember. In this chapter, I draw upon campesinxs' memories of the undocumented journey northward to resequence a narrative that spans multiple storytellers and points of combined reference. The temporally ordered sequence of memories that I construct here corresponds to massive structural movements that took place, give shape to, and inform imaginaries in the undocumented flow of people from El Norteño to the United States. Undocumented migration is a behavior that El Norteño's diasporic communities engage in, and memories of this behavior illustrate ways in which campesinxs have been targeted by and subject to state interventions that repetitiously structure harm.

The harms that are in part attributable to structural violence synchronize with the way in which states have targeted nonhuman (narcotics) and human (migrants) flows that emanate from or traverse the "Northern Triangle" of Central America. Throughout this chapter, I will make reference to the Mexican drug cartels and coyotes that have emerged in my interactions with campesinx memories of undocumented migration. As I review these stories, I ask the reader to suspend judgment of who coyotes may be in their imagination, even though coyotes have been known to cause a great deal of direct harm to their clients.[4] Locating the coyote in a longer temporal narrative helps us understand the pressures coyotes have faced that have changed the way in which they provide services to their undocumented clients today. Indeed, it is from coyotes themselves that we have learned that "it is the authorities that represent the greatest danger because they don't keep their word; they charge a fee and then they turn people in. They say yes, but they do not mean it. That's where the danger comes from, not from the control exercised by organized crime."[5] Coyotes are actors who have also been affected by and are subject to the forces structured by the U.S. and Mexican nation-states as those states attempt to intervene in transnational human flows. As I will argue in this chapter, those shifts affect human and drug-smuggling dynamics, and those changes are reflected in the memories of El Norteño's residents as they have made the undocumented journey northward over time.

Finally, I should mention that I do not set out to provide documentation of violations of the human rights of campesinxs in the transnational space of undocumented migration. I take that as a given.[6] The repetitious proclivity of states to structure harm for migrants is what interests me here. Throughout this work, I contend that the continued structuration of power's deleterious effects on human lives is permitted in part by the complexity and generative capacities of state power in transnational space.[7] That power continues to kill Central American migrants as it feeds xenophobic imaginaries, where migrants are denigrated and labeled criminals and animals. This chapter aims to acknowledge and analyze the capacity of states to produce repetitious harm by sequencing the memories of campesinxs who have survived and continue to survive it.

CHANGES IN THE SOCIAL MEMORY OF LAND MIGRATION THROUGH MEXICO

Across the generations of couriers' clientele who have clandestinely migrated through Mexico to reach the United States, the story of the journey has changed over time. Older clientele remember what it was like to migrate in the "early days" of the Salvadoran exodus, back in the 1980s, when El Norteño's residents were living the civil war. Campesinxs remember traveling northward with a single coyote. Journeys were described as occurring in small groups that did not merge with larger groups, where a single coyote guided the group from their home in El Norteño straight to the U.S. drop location. Back then, coyotes were known members of the community who provided a trusted service. The reliability of a single coyote was reflected in the oral histories of El Norteño's residents who made the journey with that coyote.

As human smuggling is not a legal profession, El Norteño's residents evaluated coyotes given the orally transmitted knowledge that attested to the coyote's reliability. For example, in the testimony of one refugee who left El Salvador during the civil war, she recounts having traveled for *one month and eighteen days* with a coyote who guided her from El Norteño to San Diego. She didn't have enough money to pay the coyote up front, so she cooked for the group along the way. In San Diego, she remained with her coyote until a cousin helped her cover the remainder of her travel fee that she still owed the coyote after arriving, and then she went on to receive asylum and get a job. Years later, she sent her daughter to the United States with the same coyote. I interviewed her daughter, and in her daughter's testimony, she recounts traveling for *one month and twenty days* with the same coyote that her mother recommended to her. The length of the journey was automatically included in their *testimonios* of undocumented land migration. The specificity of this particular detail (one month and eighteen days or one month and twenty days) communicated the reliability of this particular coyote for getting campesinxs from El Norteño to the United States. Between two women traversing the Northern Triangle, Mexico, and the United States, the coyote's delivery timeline varied by no more than two days. Both women crossed the desert on foot, but neither described a shortage of water or problems with the trip.

In the late 1990s, something happened in the coyote market. What used to be a journey with a single coyote transformed into campesinxs being relayed northward through a "chain of guides,"[8] with a corresponding series of pickup and drop-off points that involved an increasing number of individuals (particularly in Mexico). Whereas the civil-war migration route involved being escorted by a single guide from El Norteño and into the United States, rural Salvadorans in the late 1990s began describing human delivery chains, where campesinx bodies were managed by new actors unknown to El Norteño's residents.

I was in a trailer home outside of Boulder, Colorado, as Roberto (a campesino migrant in his midthirties) recounted his 1999 border-crossing experience to me. He explained how back in 1999, there were coyotes in each of the Mexican states that he entered, and he could still recall the names of the coyotes in each state. Roberto remembers that the group would hear about the coyote who was about to pick them up and drop them off, and then the group was reliably passed off to the next coyote who was named and who would guide them through a state. He traveled with a small number of people who were never merged with a larger group of migrants. When he finally made it to Mexico's northern border with the United States, the coyote instructed him to enter the trunk of a vehicle with four other people. Roberto recounts how he was told what was going to happen before it happened. The coyote explained to him that he would feel more and more speed bumps as the car approached the U.S. border, and then the car would come to a stop. He recounts that just like the coyote said, the group felt the speed bumps before the car came to a stop. Then he heard the sound of sniffer dogs that approached the vehicle. As Roberto tells me his story, this otherwise shy man prowls around his living room, sniffing realistically like a dog as he recounts his moment in the trunk of a vehicle at a U.S. border checkpoint. His migration memory included specific names and storytelling gestures such as these. His migration memory, although now dated, is less dramatic than it is informative for campesinxs who are constantly trying to understand the shifty landscape of undocumented migration northward through Mexico.

After Roberto's son was born in the United States, his mother made the decision to leave El Norteño and travel to Colorado to visit her newborn grandson. While she only wanted to visit her grandson, she couldn't get a tourist visa to travel to the United States, and so she instead contracted a coyote to bring her to Colorado. Like Roberto, she had already once traveled to the United States in the late 1990s with a reliable coyote, so in 2006, she didn't expect anything to go wrong with her journey. By 2006, things had changed.

By the time I interviewed Roberto's mother, she had long since returned to El Norteño and had no plans to ever travel northward again. I went to her country home in El Norteño, where she eagerly offered me food and tours of her pineapple and banana crops and the free-range livestock that roamed around her farm. Roberto's mother openly spoke about her memories of the Salvadoran Civil War, but she was hesitant to talk about her latest migration attempt through Mexico. When I asked her about what happened in 2006, there were gaps and silences. She recounted how "the coyotes . . . promise one thing, and they do another. It was really ugly there in Tijuana. Ugly. Ugly. I don't like to think about that trip. Everything was more serious . . . for pretty women, young ones, they are left there, depending on their age. Right now, it's really ugly. . . . After that trip, my ex-sister-in-law went, but Los Zetas got her. . . . Although you pay, they treat you horribly. . . . The first time I went was really easy, but the second time, no, it was really difficult." She wished to change the subject, and we did.

A decade after Roberto's mother's migration experience, it is Roberto who tells me that the newest wave of campesinxs arrives telling nightmarish stories. To make the point, Roberto tells me that his cousin just died of hypothermia in the South Texas desert. I am well familiar with this story—he is talking about the young man who was in the process of becoming *desaparecido* as Mercedes and I delivered parcels in Long Island. This story is the most recent one on everyone's lips because not only is it an affectively charged moment for El Norteño's residents, but the unreliability of that coyote and the likelihood of death are outcomes that residents want to avoid.

The shifts in the coyote market over time have transformed human smuggling from a "boutique" doorstep-to-doorstep service, where single coyotes known to El Norteño's residents would escort migrants from their hometowns in El Norteño, through neighboring Honduras, then Guatemala, through Mexico, and into the United States. By 2018, as I am writing this book, the coyote market has developed and evolved into a high-throughput human-trafficking system that entangles human beings with narcotics as they flow northward.

In 2018, I know a trusted driver in El Norteño. He is just a driver—by no means would he ever refer to himself as a coyote. He has a car and drives it. People call on him when they need favors, and he today is also part of a "subcontracted" lot of drivers working erratic errands for multiple individuals, coyotes included, who manage the smuggling chains that feed rural Salvadoran bodies northward. This particular driver sticks to random favors that may involve coyotes, but he refuses to dip into driving massive quantities of cocaine across Central America—which is an opportunity that remains at his fingertips.

On one occasion, without forewarning, the driver receives a call from a woman in Long Island begging him to cooperate with the coyote she has contracted to bring her teenage daughter to the United States. The driver agrees, and the coyote calls him immediately thereafter. The coyote's location is unknown. The coyote begins naming potential drop-off points. A town in Guatemala. *Too far?* A closer town in Honduras. *Not feasible?* Fine, drop her in San Salvador. In a matter of hours, the coyote has named pickup locations in the three countries that make up the Northern Triangle region of Central America. Everyone involved understands that if the girl gets caught while crossing the border from Guatemala to Mexico, she will be apprehended by Mexican authorities and deported back to El Salvador. If she is deported back to El Salvador, the coyote will arrange for her to leave El Salvador the same day she is repatriated. Everyone also understands that the young girl has probably been told to carry birth control and/or condoms for the journey, but nobody talks about it. The chaos surrounding the drop-off points to initiate this particular trip made the driver start to feel insecure for the girl. He makes the chilling comment that he feels the coyote is talking about the girl as though she were an *object for sale*. The emotions surrounding this situation escalate until the young girl brings the journey to a halt, refusing to be driven to any of the drop-off points. The coyote managing this trip is somewhere in Central America, and he is irritated. The girl's mother is in Long Island, and she is furious. The driver in rural El Salvador is concerned. The young teenager in El Norteño is scared. This is just the beginning of an undocumented land-migration attempt in contemporary Chalatenango. In the end, the erratic scene will repeat itself another day, and this particular girl will luckily make it through Mexico and into the United States with limited incidents during her journey northward.

Over three decades, the coyote market has become a series of high-throughput human-smuggling chains that relay undocumented bodies northward through routes that are managed by multiple people and that overlap with Mexican cartel operations. Migrant groups get pooled into homes managed by Mexican cartels, with dozens of unknown people routed northward. Rural Salvadorans who wish to reunite with family members now understand that some will be kidnapped for ransom, some will be sold into sexual slavery, some will perish in the desert, and others will perish in confined spaces. Some will be apprehended and deported at various points through the journey, after which they will be reinserted into the northward-bound delivery routes. Some will find themselves abandoned and wandering alone in the Sonoran Desert, drinking putrid water from cattle troughs. Chalatecxs do not consider this a favorable environment—rather, it is viewed as risky and uncertain. It is navigated through oral knowledge transfers that help El Norteño's residents evaluate the safest bet for the lowest price.

In 2018, when I talk with campesinxs who are preparing to make their journeys northward, we no longer talk about finding a coyote who operates independently of the cartels. We talk about coyotes who reliably navigate Salvadoran bodies *through* the cartels.[9] We talk about the relative safety of joining the migrant caravans making their way northward, but we also talk about the relative improbability of making it into the United States with a high-profile group of migrants tracked by the international news media. The risks and tragedies that repetitively arise but that do not deter rural Salvadorans from making the journey northward in part reflect larger transnational processes that are shaped by state powers. Understanding how coyotes come into contact with the cartels in Mexico helps illustrate these processes and powers.

CARTELS AND COYOTES IN MEXICO

In the 2015 announcement of his presidential bid, Donald Trump drew on a populist rhetoric in claiming that migrants entering the United States through the southern border with Mexico were bringing problems, drugs, crime, and rape.[10] In contemporary U.S. public discourse concerning undocumented migrants emerging from Mexico, rural Salvadorans are often referred to as "illegal migrants," a term that is increasingly conflated with "criminals." These tropes reflect the wake of the Mexican narco wars, where there has been an overlap in human smuggling and drug-cartel operations. As a result, migrants who become caught up in this overlap face a range of grisly risks.[11] Among those who buy into the populist rhetoric that conflates undocumented migrants with illegality and criminality (and increasingly, nonhuman animality), there is general ignorance about the conditions that have pushed rural migrants from their country and also ignorance of how the U.S. nation-state has played a role in fusing the concepts of criminality and migration. Engaging in strategies to keep the allusive *criminal migrant* from entering the United States in part permits the United States to engage in repetitiously harmful strategies, which I seek to unravel by examining ways in which the U.S. nation has, over time and multiple presidential administrations, conflated criminality with migration.

In 1971, President Richard Nixon initiated the War on Drugs.[12] While the United States could have focused a hefty investment inward to understand and treat the underlying issues driving Americans to consume narcotics, it focused ample resources outward, including strategies to diminish the supply of narcotics emanating from the Andean region of South America. Around this same time, unauthorized entry into Mexico became a criminal act under the 1974 Ley General de la Población (General Law of the Population).[13] Undocumented migrants traveling through Mexico could be classified as criminals for their migratory movements, and the United States was solving its drug problem in the Andes. These two factors would begin to synchronize for the U.S. and Mexican states as Mexican marijuana and poppy yields began to progressively make their way northward.[14]

Clients of El Norteño's couriers tell memories of migration that begin to shift around the middle of the first decade of the 2000s. It was in 2006 that Felipe Calderón became the president of Mexico and began the war against Mexican narcos, which resulted in massive violence, deaths, and the unintended proliferation of the drug cartels.[15] During this time, the Los Zeta cartel began to form from members of other drug cartels. Far advanced into its own unsuccessful War on Drugs elsewhere, the United States (under President George Bush), in collaboration with Mexico, signed the Merida Initiative in 2007, which targeted the cartels and included efforts to curtail "the illicit flow of drugs, people, arms, and cash" and aimed to "modernize border security at northern and southern land crossings, ports, and airports."[16] With the Merida Initiative, the U.S. and Mexican nation-states systematically blurred migrants and drugs—both were being smuggled for quite different reasons, but now they were an amalgamated threat to national securities. The Los Zeta cartel, which had specialized in the shipment of cocaine to Europe,[17] began to take an increasing interest in migrant-smuggling routes. Today, coyotes pay fees to Los Zeta, who provides password-regulated entry and passage through cartel-operated territories in Mexico.[18]

In addition to the Merida Initiative, the U.S. Central American Regional Security Initiative (CARSI) was established and funneled millions of dollars into Central American security forces to combat a dystopian fantasia of illegality, crime, smuggling, and trafficking through funding, supplies, and training. The

Merida and CARSI initiatives together represent what anthropologist Wendy Vogt has referred to as a "transnational turn" in state involvement in the militarization, policing, and discipline of everyday life. As drug and migrant routes become more heavily patrolled and controlled by state forces with U.S. support, migrants have been funneled into routes that overlap with those used by cartels to transport drugs northward.[19] Mexican state forces with U.S. support and Mexican cartels are new actors who participate in the distribution of violence for rural Salvadorans, where the *desaparecidos* are no longer those campesinxs who made too much noise during the civil war, but *desaparecidos* are among those who migrate from El Norteño to the United States.

Drugs and migrants, however, are quite distinct entities. The former is an illicit product demanded by the U.S. populace, and the latter is a significant part of the current U.S. population. The massive demand for drugs emanates from the United States, which has been relatively apprehensive about employing public-health harm-reduction strategies that are employed in parts of Europe and Canada.[20] Despite the differences between flows of drugs and people, treating them similarly allows for preventive solutions to be implemented, appearing at once logical and absurd. The new space of undocumented migration includes being killed in ways that are organized, in part, by the way that the United States protects itself.

THE VIOLENCE OF THE U.S. BORDER

El Norteño's residents tell stories of crossing the U.S. border, which often involves walking through the desert. The types of walks, however, have become increasingly lethal as migrant narratives shift into the second decade of the twenty-first century. I listened to numerous memories of undocumented land-migration attempts through Mexico and into the United States that included malnourishment, dehydration, hyperthermia, hypothermia, sexual assault, physical assault (including being beaten and stabbed with a knife in Mexico), kidnappings, and death. In the most recent stories, I hear about hazardous trips through the Sonoran Desert, which is located on the U.S. southern border with Mexico.

In 1993, a study commissioned by the U.S. Office of National Drug Control Policy determined that the southwestern border of the United States was "being overrun." The U.S. Immigration and Naturalization Service (INS) was then under the U.S. Department of Justice, and the INS began shifting its strategy from arresting migrants within the United States to preventing their entry, fortifying more visible and popular urban entry points and "rerouting the illegal border traffic from traditional urban routes to less populated and geographically harsher areas, providing border agents with a tactical advantage over illegal border crossers and smugglers."[21] Anthropologist Jason De León has extensively documented how this strategy has funneled coyotes and their clients into extremely hazardous environments, where evidence of human death in the Sonoran Desert can be quickly destroyed and scattered by turkey vultures (*Cathartes aura*), which since the late 1990s have been eating "the flesh of dead migrants."[22] The Congressional Research Service (within the Library of Congress) has acknowledged that Prevention Through Deterrence (PTD) has been successful in accomplishing "its goal of rerouting unauthorized migrant traffic from heavily populated areas to more remote areas" while explicitly acknowledging that "an unintended consequence of the USBP's 'Prevention Through Deterrence' strategy has been an increase in the number of accidental migrant deaths along the border."[23] De León highlights that "the great irony is that some of the migrants whose movement these defense experts were working to stop were fleeing violence in Central America that US interventionist policies had sanctioned and supported."

As the United States began to implement PTD, coyotes and migrants were systematically funneled toward more dangerous border-crossing zones, where the weather—as opposed to a legally culpable actor (like a U.S. Border Patrol agent)—could become lethal for those attempting to cross the desert. In my own interviews with campesinxs from El Norteño, I have listened to more-recent stories of migrants dying because of exposure (hypothermia, hyperthermia) in border-crossing zones and more testimonios of migrants crossing the Sonoran Desert with limited water. Funneling migrants toward a place where the weather is a lethal factor separates U.S. Border Patrol strategies from culpability for deaths, while simultaneously making the deaths appear to be the result of poor discretion on behalf of the migrants who took the risk.[24] However, the U.S. Congress has gone one step further to intervene in migratory flows in this region. In 2005, the Tucson Border Patrol Sector was "the only sector that is prohibited from having permanently operating checkpoints," where Congress required CBP to relocate its fixed checkpoints every fourteen days to prevent undocumented migrants from predicting the locations of the checkpoints.[25] Changing routes and weather can quickly kill migrants who are funneled into an environment where unpredictability is partially manufactured. As I have learned from desert-crossing testimonios, anything can happen when crossing the Sonoran Desert. More than anything, the unexpected conditions of the desert can result in dehydration, hyperthermia, and hypothermia.

As a result of these testimonios and the unpredictability of this particular environment, I examined the annual temperature in Tucson, Arizona,[26] and compared it to the number of bodies recovered in the desert by the Pima County Medical Examiner's Office by fiscal year.[27] I found that there was no statistical relationship between the number of deaths and fiscal-year average of daily temperatures, but there was a positive and significant relationship between the number of deaths and the *variation* in the temperature. Every one-unit increase in the standard deviation (variation) of the temperature for a given year was associated with an additional thirty-four deaths (see figure 2.1). That is to say, variation in the temperature is associated with deaths in a location where the United States has made checkpoints particularly unpredictable.

U.S. border-protection strategies include diverting migrants toward zones with unpredictable checkpoints with unpredictable temperatures, where unpredictability is lethal. As opposed to scaling back strategies such as PTD, the strategies are now being exported. In 2014, the Mexican government announced a "Southern Border Program" aimed at increasing apprehensions and deportations of U.S.-bound migrants. While U.S. assistance to help Mexico secure its southern border region has increased, there is limited transparency regarding dollar values, recipient units, equipment, and training.[28]

U.S. support and funding for the Merida and CARSI initiatives funneled coyotes and migrants into routes that overlap with those used by cartels to transport drugs northward. For those who are able to successfully navigate these risks and make it into the United States—and there are many who do—they face a new risk. There is a competitive price on migrant heads in the twenty-first

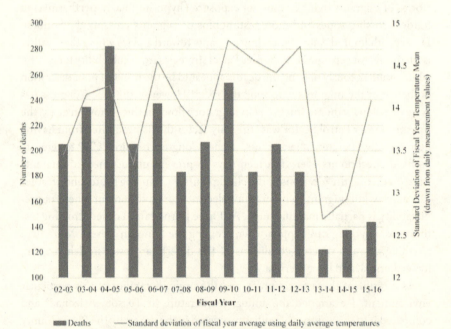

FIGURE 2.1 Deaths and temperature variability in/near Pima County, Arizona by fiscal year.

century—approximately $159 per day in detention.[29] This price is pursued by interested private prison companies through their political involvement with the U.S. Homeland Security Appropriations Subcommittee. The topic of detention (who was in detention, who had just left detention) was salient among members of El Norteño's diasporic communities. I include an attention to detention here as a final step in the sequence of undocumented migration northward for El Norteño's residents.

THE IMMIGRANT DETENTION–INDUSTRIAL COMPLEX

> The Obama administration announced reforms to the immigration detention system, including ways to reduce detention, standardize contracts, and implement more oversight over facilities using a more "civil" model. Advocates championed these goals, which also were supported by an expert consultant hired by the Obama administration to conduct an in-depth evaluation of the detention system. Six years later, the sprawling DHS detention system has only grown farther from those civil detention reform goals. Instead of reducing detention, the administration now incarcerates women and children who flee to the United States seeking protection from persecution.
>
> —National Immigrant Justice Center, 2015[30]

I was seated in the kitchen of a busy Salvadoran household in Long Island as Mercedes delivered parcels to Salvadorans who arrived at the door. As Mercedes worked, two moms living in the house were busy making pupusas with fresh *quesillo* (cheese similar to mozzarella) that Mercedes had just delivered hours ago from El Norteño. Family members and roommates wearing snow hats and parkas walked in and out, always greeting me with handshakes and eye contact. The adults spoke to me in Spanish, and their children spoke to me in gringo-accented English. It was as if Long Island and Chalatenango had been fused together in that busy kitchen. As the mothers made pupusas, they talked about differences in food between the United States and El Salvador, the use of herbal remedies, and the behavior of local racist police officers—the topics flowed faster than I could follow them.

One of the moms, Maria, had an unyielding gaze and a no-bullshit attitude. She began talking about how her husband left El Salvador to work in the United States. After that, a group of men violently assaulted her in El Norteño. Her daughter witnessed the attack. After she was discharged from the hospital, she and her daughter left El Salvador and "traveled with a coyote. I didn't have problems with him. . . . The problem is when one gets to immigration. In Manhattan, they put the shackle on me."

The shackle that Maria is talking about is an ankle monitor—the kind that people on house arrest wear. Maria journeyed through Mexico as an "illegal immigrant" and reported directly to U.S. Immigration and Customs Enforcement (ICE). To her surprise, she was placed in a windowless processing facility for a few days before being tagged with a "shackle":

> When I entered immigration, they told me to take off the shoelaces and that my little girl should take off the rubber bands from her ponytails. They also took off her shoelaces. . . . She was asking, "Mom?" And she was crying and said, "I want to be with my daddy," and I told her, "We're going to get out of here . . ."
>
> There, it is like a . . . like a jail but . . . it's different; it's like being in a cold room . . . no blanket, they just give you aluminum paper. . . . They give that so you can cover yourself. . . . You don't shower there, you don't brush your teeth. . . . From the day that I turned myself in to immigration, I was crying . . . because there are no windows there; one never knows if it's daytime or nighttime. I had to sleep on the bare floor. . . . I held my little girl on my chest because I didn't want her to suffer what I was going through, because it was a really difficult thing.

As Maria told this story, her five-year-old daughter was silently playing with a doll in the corner of the kitchen. I wondered if her daughter should be listening to this story, before remembering that her little girl *lived* this story. This was a family memory:

> When I turned myself in to immigration, a repugnant man said to me, "You think that you are coming to a home, to a nice place?" "No," I answered, "I really don't know, because this is the first time that I've entered this country." So then he said to me, "Many people think that this is a place of luxury." So I told him, "The only thing that interests me is to be with my husband—not in this place, because here one is treated like trash, and one comes to this country to prosper, not to come here."
>
> Every single woman had an ankle monitor put on. . . . The thing that they stick the battery into on that ankle monitor, it's thick and made of pure rubber. . . . It was burning me.

Maria's ankle monitor was an alternative to being placed in a detention facility as she awaited the outcome of the proceedings associated with her asylum claim. The ankle monitor is considered a progressive alternative to placing migrants in detention facilities as they await the outcome of their proceedings, despite the fact that the ankle monitor inflicts a different type of punishment. I asked Maria if she felt stigmatized after she was discharged from the processing facility. She replied, "Nobody gives you work because of the ankle monitor; they think you are a murderer—that's why they don't give anyone work. . . . They put shackles on those who sell drugs, on murders, but we aren't murderers; we don't sell drugs. Like I told you, we are just poor."

After giving her testimony of how she arrived in the United States, Maria said that she wanted to get rid of everything associated with that ankle monitor. She still had the blue charger cable for the ankle monitor she used to wear. She said that she used to spend her days making tortillas with that thing attached to her ankle in the kitchen. After giving her recorded testimony, Maria ran upstairs to her room to grab the cable so that we could discard it at that very moment. When Maria walked upstairs, her five-year-old daughter walked right up to the table where I had recorded her mother's testimony. She was a twig of a human being, with big eyes and black hair. She was grabbing at her fingers in the way little kids do. In a mousy voice, so slight, she told me, "Everything my mommy said is true." I looked down at her and nodded my head.

This tiny girl took a deep breath as if she were about to dive underwater, and with that one breath, she told me that she saw her mom get beat up in El Salvador and that they traveled through Mexico with a coyote and that her father works in New York and that she was stuck in migration prison and that people from migration put an ankle monitor on her mother. She continued to stare up at me, and she repeated herself, "Everything my mommy said is true." I nodded my head. I didn't know how else to respond except by affirming the truth she just spoke—this was one Salvadoran kindergartener's introduction to the United States.

At the time I am writing this book, the U.S. immigration detention system is the largest in the world, with American taxpayers spending more than $2 billion annually to maintain it. Currently, 73 percent of detained migrants are in facilities operated by private prison companies. Two of the major private prison companies reported revenues that have more than doubled since 2008, totaling $765 million in revenues for running immigrant detention facilities in 2015.[31]

Once contracted to run immigrant detention facilities, companies such as the GEO Group, Inc. and the Corrections Corporation of America (CCA) have become concerned with occupancy rates that affect revenue and profitability. As a result, it is a business development strategy of such corporations to seek guaranteed minimums from the U.S. federal government in order to maintain adequate revenues by pressuring members of the U.S. Homeland Security Appropriations Subcommittee to insert migrant detention quotas into their budgets (e.g., the requirement that ICE maintain an average of thirty-four thousand detention beds, regardless of whether or not these beds are being used at a given time). Private prison corporations make direct campaign contributions to members of the U.S. Homeland Security Appropriations Subcommittee, and they include former ICE senior-leadership members on their executive-leadership teams and boards. The prices are competitive, but the market is increasingly dominated by only a handful of companies. One recent report found that the CCA obtained 40 percent of its ICE contracts through a noncompetitive process.[32] The forces driving immigrant detention represent much more than a national security concern—they are structured by elite economic and political decision-makers who have vested interests in detained migrant bodies.

When basic human rights of migrants are violated within ICE detention centers, and when migrants die in these facilities (e.g., the fifty-six migrants who died during the Obama administration), it is difficult for the public to understand why.[33] The obfuscation of details from the public eye is a result of ICE contracting and subcontracting services to private entities, where private entities can invoke redactions regarding funding allocations and avoid direct liability for substandard conditions, shielding large portions of the DHS immigration detention systems from taxpayer scrutiny. ICE does not proactively share information about which of its detention facilities are open or closed, its contracts, or its inspections. To obtain ICE detention-facility contracts and inspection reports, it took the National Immigrant Justice Center four years, one federal lawsuit, two depositions of ICE officers, and a federal court order to obtain the information.[34] The lack of transparency not only raises questions about what is happening inside these facilities but points to the manipulated political and economic markets surrounding the detainment of migrant bodies in the United States.

Campesinxs who disappear into these facilities often remain for an indeterminate amount of time before deportation. The lack of transparency regarding the immigrant detention market, and ultimately, what happens to detained migrants within these facilities, is reinforced by the government's efforts to eliminate evidence of wrongdoing in real time. In 2017, the U.S. National Archives and Records Administration (NARA) stated that ICE was seeking permission to *destroy* "records related to detainees, including incidents of sexual abuse and assault, escapes, deaths while in agency custody, telephone rates charged to detainees, alternatives to detention, logs and reports on status of detainees and detention facilities, and location and segregation of detainees."[35] In the summer of 2018, the American Historical Association sent a letter to NARA opposing the destruction of these records,[36] and the issue is pending.

While experiences of detainment-related abuse and violence will be remembered among the campesinxs who experience these harms, state practices of eliminating records, data, and information will create a void of intelligence such that future generations of U.S. citizens will not be able to evaluate the impacts of these programs. Over time, these are strategies that produce (whether intended or unintended) collective ignorance. After El Norteño's residents make it across the border in 2018, several will continue to live in fear of what this system is capable of doing to them and their family members and will continue to sponsor clandestine journeys of family members that may very well land them in the U.S. immigrant detention–industrial complex. The undocumented migration memories of El Norteño's residents cleave to the present, when the U.S. state illustrated that it was capable of forcibly removing migrant children from their parents.

EMERGENT FRONTIERS IN THE TRANSNATIONAL FIELD OF VIOLENCE

At the time this book is being written, new memories of undocumented migration are in the making, as over two thousand children were recently separated from their parents after crossing the U.S. southern border with Mexico.[37] Despite the public outrage in the United States over this practice, this is not the first time that the U.S. government forcibly removed minority children from their parents. Beginning in the nineteenth century, tens of thousands of indigenous children across North America were forcibly removed from their homes and immersed in federally funded, Christian, English-speaking school environments in order to assimilate them into Euro-American culture.[38] This practice lasted through the twentieth century, and the living terror of it is still recounted in the memories of those who survived, along with their children who remember the memories of their ancestors. The boarding-school era both exposed indigenous youth to systematic violence and reduced indigenous youths' ability to speak their native languages. It was an effective form of epistemicide that indigenous communities in the United States are still recovering from today. The tactic of separating Central American migrant children from their parents is not new, but it is certainly a repetitive imperial practice that can be profoundly destabilizing and terrorizing to those who experience it.

The migrant caravans that have begun making their way northward have attracted ample attention among those with extremely limited economic resources. However, there remains ample suspicion about the likely success of the journey when so much international news media attention has been focused on the movement of these relatively large groups. It is common knowledge that the U.S. president has turned his attention to the caravan(s), and that attention seems to be what is salient among Chalatecxs in everyday conservations about the caravan.

The capacity of U.S. national strategies to harm migrants *en route* to their final destinations is enabled not only by national forgetting but by the factions of individuals who manage the national bureaucracy. In his 2015 presidential bid, Donald Trump stated, "The U.S. has become a dumping ground for everybody else's problems. . . . When Mexico sends its people, they're not sending their best. They're not sending you. They're not sending you. They're sending people that have lots of problems, and they're bringing those problems with us. They're bringing drugs. They're bringing crime. They're rapists. And some, I assume, are good people."[39] Rhetoric such as this circulates through a United States where migrants from El Norteño continue to arrive and exist. The newest waves of everyday botanists, chefs, poets, and artisans are compelled to prove that they are noncriminals. They are increasingly compelled to prove they are human. El Norteño's migrants continue to tell stories to one another that highlight harms experienced along the journey northward, and they continue to send their children to the United States even if they perceive that the U.S. government despises them. The harms experienced today have their own style, but for El Norteño's residents, there has always been harm that is in part navigated through the transfer of oral knowledge in memory.

CONCLUSION

I was back at Mercedes's home in El Norteño, helping her inspect and package parcels for her next trip to Long Island. The house was busy and packed with about two dozen people; Mercedes's grandson and his classmates were using her home to practice a skit for their social studies class. I was standing at a nearby table, revising and repackaging parcels as clients arrived.

A woman walked up to the table with some T-shirts, and she began crying as we unfolded the shirts to inspect them. Printed on the shirts, I recognized the face of a dead seventeen-year-old campesino from El Norteño. He died while trying to make it into the United States just a few months prior. The sender walked somberly over to the place where Mercedes's grandson and his classmates were practicing their skit. I continued to inspect and package parcels. When I was done working, my curiosity got the best of me, and I took a seat next to the young man's family member who had delivered the T-shirts. Just as I did so, the group of teenagers began to rehearse their entire skit from beginning to end. We sat back in our chairs and watched it together.

The skit centered on a group of migrant youth who leave El Norteño to make an undocumented trip northward through Mexico and into the United States. They contract a coyote, who barks orders at them. Shortly thereafter, the protagonist is bitten by a snake in Mexico. He suffers for some time, and then he dies and is gone from the plot. Another character is then stung by a scorpion. She suffers, dies, and disappears from the plot. When the remaining characters make it across the U.S. border, they are caught by U.S. Border Patrol agents. The skit ends.

The U.S. and Mexican states, the Mexican cartels, and the coyotes who move migrants have given shape to experiences of migration that are remembered and relayed to the newest generation of El Norteño's migrants. Those transmitted memories inform youths' imaginaries. Adolescents who performed the skit in El Norteño projected themselves into a future that includes "accidental migrant deaths," and by the time this book goes to press, several of them will have already migrated away from El Norteño. They will migrate with a knowledge of hazards that was transferred to them in spoken memories of undocumented migration.

3 · DIASPORIC INTIMACY AND *NOSTOS* IMAGINARIES

Nostalgia inevitably reappears as a defense mechanism in a time of acceler-
ated rhythms of life and historical upheavals.

—Svetlana Boym[1]

Salvadorans transmit their nostalgia to me when I speak with them.

—Salvadoran courier

Cumbia CDs sent from family members in El Salvador blast the
voices of Los Hermanos Flores from the dry, heated living rooms of hermetically
sealed houses in Colorado. Vulgar utterances (*a la gran puta, me vale verga, que
comas mierda cerote*) in Colorado kitchens with linoleum floors and dishwash-
ing machines produce laughter far out of place. Artisanal *semita* (a type of sweet
pastry) made forty-eight hours ago in El Norteño is unwrapped from its corn
husks and dipped into instant coffee in a trailer park outside of Boulder, Colorado. These mnemonic practices in North American spaces preserve, drive, and
are responsive to the movement of parcels from El Norteño. The ways in which
that past is longed for, conjured, and the intentions surrounding nostalgic gazes
tell us something about the rhythms of life, the transnational chasms, the disparities in privilege, and the transmittable properties of nostalgia that arise in
El Norteño's diasporic networks.

In the previous chapter, I sequenced memories of El Norteño's campesinxs
regarding their undocumented journeys northward, synchronizing those
memories with a narrative of structural harms. While it is important to show
the ways in which people suffer to better understand the structure of repetitious
harms, I am hesitant to ignore the immense capacity for resilience in campesinx
networks. Campesinxs certainly described feeling traumatized in the United

States (much more so as a result of feeling targeted and hunted by the state), but El Norteño's campesinxs also rebound, adapt, create, observe, dream, theorize, care, and long for. At structured sites of transnational disconnects (such as not being able to reliably travel between the United States and El Salvador),[2] campesinxs find and cultivate pleasures. Nostalgia is an emotional memory state that can simultaneously evoke pain and pleasure. Cecilia Rivas writes that Salvadorans are stereotyped as "invariably nostalgic for their home country,"[3] and I will admit that nostalgia was perhaps the most salient memory experience that I documented as I focused on parcels, particularly as El Norteño's campesinxs began to transmit their stories to me. That transmission for a long time provoked me to project my own idealizations onto El Norteño—a practice that I had to first recognize and then be cognizant of when moving forward in collecting data regarding nostalgia. Svetlana Boym wrote that "studying the sociology, politics, and ethnography of nostalgia, its micropractices and meganarratives, remains as urgent as ever. It is always important to ask the question: Who is speaking in the name of nostalgia? Who is its ventriloquist?"[4] I tried to recognize, but at the same time not be enchanted by, nostalgia as it emerged as a salient human factor in the courier economy. Missing the type of cheese that is widely available in El Norteño could provoke a request for a family member to send two pounds of cheese with a courier to Colorado, and eating the cheese once it is received as a parcel could provoke potent memories of El Norteño. The memory practices of nostalgia often led to more nostalgia. When I asked El Norteño's residents about their nostalgia, I found their characterizations of it to be critical of quotidian life in the United States. Boym reminds us that "nostalgia, like globalization, exists in the plural."[5] Indeed, the multiple nostalgic gazes in El Norteño's diasporic networks suggest that collective nostalgia can be at once mending, escapist, prospective, and interpersonally connective. Nostalgia preserves a promise of departure for some, and it is a way forward to becoming a U.S. citizen for others. Nostalgia interacts with intentions to depart as well as intentions to build local intimacy moving forward.

In this chapter, I try not to classify nostalgic types or types of nostalgia. There are numerous ways to gaze nostalgically; they overwhelm, and they can trap a ventriloquist like me in romanticizing times, people, and moments that can also be quite far from romantic for others. Rather, I try to unpack the objects of nostalgic gazing, focusing on both the remembered past and what the associated affect says to the nostalgic gazer. "Stay here," and "go back" are some affectively laden prospections that emerge alongside nostalgic gazing, and I focus on those polar conclusions with the caveat that nostalgia does not cleanly predict a binary outcome for campesinx movement or parcel transfer. I contend that the sense of pleasure and loss wound up in nostalgic gazing both reveals and provides a remedy at critical sites of diasporic discontinuities that campesinx migrants both criticize and affectively manage. Nostalgia, in a way, provides a map for understanding transnational discontinuities, permitting nostalgic gazers to "be homesick and sick of home—occasionally at the same time."[6]

REFLECTIVE AND RESTORATIVE NOSTALGIA

I find Svetlana Boym's work useful in navigating salient components of "nostalgia (from *nostos*—return home, and *algia*—longing)" that emerged in my findings.[7] Boym distinguishes reflective nostalgia (which emphasizes the Greek *algia*, "longing," attention to another time) from restorative nostalgia (which emphasizes the Greek *nostos*, the "return home," the intention to restore the past in the present).[8] Reflective nostalgia necessarily fails at reconstructing the past—it is a way to create diasporic intimacy for migrant communities. Reflective nostalgia is something that is cultivated and shared in the new homeland. After I delivered *semitas* wrapped in corn husks to a campesina mom in Colorado, she shared the dessert with me over a cup of coffee. We took our time eating the *semita*, and we talked about how these *semitas* were made, and we wondered if they could ever be made like this in the United States. She remembered people who made them and talked about campesinxs living in Colorado who knew how to make them, if only the right tools and ingredients were locally available. The weight of her gesture was what mattered—she gave me a gift that we could both appreciate, based on where we had been in the past and what we shared in the present. Her request and payment for the parcel, the act of sharing food, and our conversing about El Norteño were mnemonic practices that build brief moments of intimacy and bind individuals together in the new homeland (the United States).

In contrast to reflective nostalgia, restorative nostalgia aims to conjure the past in the present. Restorative nostalgia can be dangerous, as it is sometimes used to justify racism, xenophobia, and policies of exclusion that harm and marginalize others.[9] That said, I found restorative nostalgia to be salient among campesinxs who construct *nostos* imaginaries, envisioning a return to El Norteño once their time in the United States has come to an end (e.g., be it through a voluntary departure or deportation). Practices such as working to purchase terrain, reviewing corn growth and harvests in El Norteño on social media so as to not lose touch with cultivation practices, and purchasing terrain in El Norteño that one intends to return to are examples of practices associated with restorative nostalgia. What is unique about the restorative nostalgia among my campesinx friends is that none of them ever implied that their agrarian pasts be re-created at the expense of others in a U.S. North American space, whereas the right-wing protesters shouting "blood and soil" at the 2017 protests in Charlottesville, South Carolina, were.[10] Restorative nostalgia can illustrate incredible disparities in presumptions of privilege, highlighting who demands what past be brought into the present. El Norteño's farmers preserve actual agricultural knowledge, including intimately obtained knowledge about soil, and alternative conceptualizations of plants as they work in U.S. day-labor markets for cut-rate wages. In El Norteño's diasporic communities, restorative nostalgia offers a space for the preservation of traditional farming knowledge as it also informs imaginaries of return to El Norteño.

An analysis of reflective and restorative nostalgic gazing reveals fissures in transnational space that permit affective expressions such as pain, loss, pleasure, and comfort in El Norteño's diasporic networks. Various forms of nostalgia arise in rural clientele and provide continuity where nation-states have otherwise structured discontinuity in the movement of Chalatecx bodies. Here I focus on a few objects of collective nostalgic gazing to illustrate these affectively intense mnemonic practices as well as the state-sponsored divides they suture.

FOOD FROM A RURAL PAST IN THE WHOLESALE PRESENT

ME: What are your observations regarding nostalgia among the Salvadorans living there [in the United States]?

COURIER: I think that what flourishes most, or what is above all else, is that feeling, those desires to want to eat and feel Salvadoran flavor, Salvadoran food.

It is notable that food emerged as an object of reflective nostalgic gazing among campesinxs from El Norteño who transmit parcels. Eating is one of the most frequent and earliest human behaviors, with basic food habits presumably formed in infancy and early childhood.[11] Perceptions such as smell that call upon odor neurons in the nasal mucosa are separated by very few neuronal synapses from the hippocampus, an area of the brain implicated in memory functions and affective processes.[12] The experience of food evokes recollection.[13] Campesinxs described food from El Norteño as an extension of local agricultural practices employed to locally produce food, which became inaccessible to El Norteño's residents once they migrated to the United States (other than through the intermittent receipt of parcels). Food was an object connected to known soils, crops, animals, and cultivators in El Norteño, but socioeconomic stressors in the United States contribute to the consumption of wholesale foods in diasporic networks. The food system inside the United States was feeding campesinx migrants, many of whom perceived the food to be of poor quality, and nostalgia for Salvadoran food was one of the factors that moved parcels between the rural past and the diasporic present.

On one Friday night in Boulder, Colorado, I was hanging out with a group of Chalateco men. We were drinking beer, and they were remembering. It was not an interview, just a discussion that felt like a memorial service for Salvadoran food. One of the men would say the name of a traditional food or tropical fruit in El Salvador, and then we would talk about it and compare experiences, sometimes tolerating long silences as someone tried to remember another detail or another food item. The collective conversation involved meditations on the past that were conjured into future collective actions, such as the following: Alguashte *on* mango. *Did you know* alguashte *was ground from* ayote *seeds? Have you seen* ayote *growing in* Chalate? *I remember Don Fernando used to have a small* cultivo *where he grew* ayote. *Have you tried* alguashte *on* mango? *We had a* mango *tree in our yard in* Chalate. *Let's get some mangoes and put* alguashte *on them tomorrow.* The conversation and the future actions emanating from it were examples of restorative nostalgic practices.

Among the men I was speaking with whose nostalgia would soon summon food items to a Colorado kitchen table, Eduardo was my generational peer, who had migrated to the United States over a decade ago. He was captured in Mexico and deported back to El Salvador numerous times during his journey. He remembers being repatriated in El Salvador and his *coyote* (guide) telling him that they were getting a meal at Pollo Campero and then heading straight back to the border of El Salvador. More than ten years after leaving El Salvador, fried chicken from Pollo Campero was the one parcel that Eduardo repeatedly asked for from a Salvadoran courier who delivers parcels in Colorado. It took Eduardo three months to make it to the United States, and he finally made it across the border near Matamoros on his fourth attempt. He remembered crossing a river, being completely naked and unable to swim, and falling off his raft and freaking out as he doggy paddled to shore and trudged into the muddy United States. Similar to other migrants who make the undocumented journey, he arrived in Colorado emaciated from the trip. Speaking with me more than a decade after he crossed the border, Eduardo had already saved money, purchased land in El Norteño, and then lent it to friends and family to cultivate while he remained in Colorado. Eduardo had been in the United States for over a decade, but he constantly compared Colorado to El Norteño when we talked, and despite his time away from El Norteño, his comparisons were unexaggerated. He saw differences in the way that children were raised, differences in relative isolation, and differences in attitudes and the ways in which people restricted their behaviors (in the United States) and felt liberated (in El Salvador). He reviewed pictures and videos of crops cultivated in the Salvadoran countryside. Eduardo was also aware that a full day of work in the sweltering heat of El Norteño might pay nothing more than the food he would eat if he worked his own terrain—and perhaps $8 per day if it were someone else's terrain. This economic reality is what kept Eduardo from hopping on a return flight to El Salvador. As a result of his time in the United States, Eduardo was able to save and purchase his own terrain in

El Norteño. Throughout my fieldwork, Eduardo talked about getting deported as though it were definitively in his future. Eduardo's nostalgia was restorative; he aimed to unite his past with his future, and in doing so, he developed a nostos imaginary of leaving Colorado to cultivate land in El Norteño. Purchasing Chalatecx farmland and talking about return are examples of how Eduardo practiced restorative nostalgia.

Among those in Eduardo's kinship networks who also talked about and shared rural Salvadoran food in the space and time of the Colorado winter, talking about *escabeche* and *pupusas* made from *quesillo* and *frijoles de seda* was not wound up in imaginaries of permanent return. Colorado was the present and future home, and the food was a rare albeit accessible and expensive pleasure. Food was the most frequent parcel that I documented as being sent by family members from El Norteño to the United States. Among El Norteño's couriers, cheese was the number-one food product most commonly transmitted. Couriers would sometimes fill empty space in their luggage with additional cheese purchased in El Norteño because campesinx migrants in the United States would readily purchase the surplus. Other food products that were commonly sent with couriers included *pupusas* (stuffed tortillas), cooked *gallina india* (game hen), *maíz blanco* (white corn), *frijoles de seda* (silk beans), *atado de dulce* (sugarcane paste), and *miel de caña* (sugarcane honey, similar to molasses). Farm-fresh versions of these ingredients were generally inaccessible at local grocery stores in the United States, even at those that catered to Central American migrants in the area. One of these grocery stores was recommended to me when I asked a group of nostalgic food gazers where I could get a Salvadoran breakfast in Colorado.

I entered the grocery store to see that it was familiar and foreign at once, simultaneously appealing to pan–Central American and Mexican clientele. The grocery store included a familiar food station with *comida a la vista* (food in sight), prepared food served from behind a small glass window. The description of the "Salvadoran breakfast" included the same food items I would eat every day for breakfast in the Salvadoran countryside: eggs, cheese, refried beans, plantains, and tortilla. The cashier, to my surprise, was from Chalatenango. I ordered the Salvadoran breakfast, which was four times the price of a breakfast in El Salvador. It included hefty portions of flavorless cheese, watery canned beans, and thin Mexican tortillas (as opposed to the nixtamalized tortillas that were available throughout El Salvador). It was a seemingly inferior, disappointing, and relatively expensive simulation of a breakfast in El Salvador. The ingredients were all there in great quantity, but the flavor was gone. As I ate the only Salvadoran option on the menu in a specialty grocery store, my great disappointment in the quality of the food helped me understand the proclivity of campesinxs to long for the "real" flavor that they (and now I) remembered and longed for from El Norteño.

The everyday differences in food systems, particularly concerning the freshness of local food in El Norteño and the perceived manipulation of wholesale
food in the United States repeatedly arose in response to my questions about
why campesinx migrants longed for food and paid high prices for it to be delivered (in parcels) by a courier. Campesinxs I spoke with in the United States regularly criticized the freshness of wholesale food that was most accessible to them
on their incomes and given their heavy work schedules. One Salvadoran migrant
woman who longed for Chalatecx food described how cheese in the United
States is "old" and that "here there are many factories" that make and distribute
U.S. cheese that is loaded with "chemicals." When I visited this woman's mother
in El Norteño, her mom highlighted the farm-to-table temporality of her food
preferences in the Salvadoran countryside: "In the moment it's really delicious.
But if it's two or three days old, the flavor changes. It's like coffee. The moment
you make coffee and drink it, it's just delicious. But after one hour . . . it doesn't
have the same flavor." El Norteño's migrants moved from situated eating practices in the Salvadoran countryside, where they often consumed fresher food
on relatively low incomes, to lower socioeconomic strata in the United States,
where they consumed wholesale food (also older and preserved) on relatively
higher incomes. These differences also reflect the rural standing of campesinxs
inside El Salvador, where I regularly heard campesinxs scoff at the *old and expensive* food for sale in the supermarkets of San Salvador (the urban capital). The
general availability of fresh ingredients grown in the rural countryside was something that was perceived to affect the flavor of daily food. The strange flavors of
wholesale food in the United States, particularly the perceived absence of flavor,
caused some campesinxs to call into question the conditions of food production and the preservatives used in wholesale food in the United States. Among
campesinxs living in El Norteño, basic ingredients such as cheese, beans, corn-
meal, fruit, game hen, and vegetables are derived locally and rapidly consumed
after being harvested, killed, or processed. Once inside North America, rural
Chalatecx migrants were obtaining prepackaged and preserved versions of similar food items from local grocery stores. They were now engaged with their food
not by drawing it from their kin and local networks but by buying it as consumers divorced from the conditions of cultivation. Reliance on wholesale U.S. food
is a stark gustatory contrast to the farm-to-table eating practices more readily
accessible in the Salvadoran countryside and transmitted as parcels to campesinx
migrants in the United States.

Animal products in the United States were another topic of ample discussion. There was the perception that farm animals in the United States have been
raised differently, resulting in poorer quality meat or animal products (e.g., milk)
than what is available in the Salvadoran countryside. In these circumstances,
campesinx migrants were generally referring to wholesale meat products derived

from factory farming practices that are more accessible to them given time and income restrictions. Campesinxs in the United States regularly asked for animal meat or animal products such as game hen, iguana, and cheese from their family members in El Norteño, noting that the quality of animal meat such as chicken is spongy and flavorless in the United States. In El Norteño, it is common to see game hens foraging at farmhouses, sometimes walking freely around living spaces, kitchens, and yards. Making chicken soup typically implies personally capturing and killing the chicken that will be consumed. This stands in contrast to factory farming practices in the United States, where an increasing number of animals are raised for slaughter in decreasing physical spaces.[14]

Factory farming practices in the United States have historically been characterized by animal overcrowding, the restricted movement of animals, unnatural diets including nontherapeutic doses of antibiotics in animal feed, and unanesthetized surgical procedures.[15] In the United States, factory farming practices also reflect the general reduction in the U.S. farming population to 2 percent of the general population.[16] In El Norteño, over 99 percent of the municipality is considered "rural"[17] and is relatively unaffected by factory farming. Despite the agricultural industry in the United States being more "developed," rural Salvadoran migrants do not necessarily equate more developed with "better." One campesina migrant who regularly paid money for food parcels from El Norteño to be delivered to her in Colorado and who aimed to return back to El Salvador stated that in El Norteño, "There were many people who had livestock, and that's where they made their business. Some sold milk, or they sold it to people who make cheese. There, everything is natural, and here, the truth is things are not so natural." Another Chalateca migrant to Colorado explained how "the cheese here is not the same as in El Salvador. The flavor is different because here, everything here has . . . at its base . . . they put some type of chemical in it so that it lasts . . . but there [in El Salvador], no. Everything is natural." Purchasing locally made, farm-fresh cheese produced from free-grazing cows in El Norteño is markedly different from purchasing a plastic-wrapped block of wholesale cheese in the United States, which may include milk obtained from a cow that has been administered a bovine growth hormone, with the cheese product including additives such as Yellow 5, which is approved by the U.S. Food and Drug Administration.[18] The large quantity of food parcels evident in couriers' luggage was a materialization of nostalgia among rural migrants who were often critical of the way the United States produces its food and many of whom longed for an everyday flavor that was now a rare and thus treasured occurrence.

The emergence of food among nostalgic gazers in diasporic networks points to non-U.S. food systems and modes of agricultural production that are not as accessible in the United States for campesinx migrants, whose time and incomes are restricted. Everyday interactions with nonhuman actors (plants, soil, fire, rain) and natural temporalities (lunar cycles, rainy seasons) in the lifeway of Chalatecx subsistence agriculture are also remembered, recalled, and in some, longed for after arrival in the United States. While the experience of subsistence farming in El Salvador can be physically taxing and difficult, it is also a distinct lifeway that contrasts with the paved roads, fast cars, hermetically sealed homes, and pressured temporalities of North American life.

REMEMBERING THE FORGOTTEN LAND

While food was a more salient focus in reflective nostalgia, subsistence agriculture was more pronounced in restorative nostalgia. Within restorative nostalgia, I encountered alternative ways of existing with the environment—where knowing was part of an interactive process with actants, including plants, the moon, fire, cloud formations, birds, other farmers, and the rain—in El Norteño.[19] Campesinx restorative nostalgia included memories of a subsistence agricultural lifeway that was comparatively more tied to nonhuman temporalities (the lunar cycle, avian migration patterns) and sustained by oral knowledge transfer. In light of restorative nostalgia, some campesinxs ultimately intended to exit the United States and imagined returning to a longed-for place and time where this alternative lifeway was being realized.

For campesinxs who previously cultivated their own *milpas* (plots of land where corn, beans, and squash are typically grown) in Chalatenango, cultivation techniques are often learned through oral knowledge transfer and direct observation—perhaps tweaked every now and then by an extension agent from the Centro Nacional de Tecnología Agropecuaria y Forestal (CENTA, or the "National Center for Agricultural and Forestry Technology"). This type of knowledge acquisition and transfer was particularly important in Chalatenango, where subsistence farmers were often making more decisions about what to do on land that they were in charge of (be it through ownership or rent). Historian Molly Todd has shown how economically poor campesinos in El Salvador's rural north have historically had more control over their land and more freedom to develop their own paths than their counterparts in the larger coffee-export zones of El Salvador that were dominated by a few members of the elite class.[20] El Norteño's campesinxs who engage in subsistence agriculture cultivate crops such as corn, beans, squash, coffee, loroco, sorghum, pineapples, bananas, mangoes, and cucumbers, among others. Heirloom varieties of seeds (such as *maíz capulín*) are maintained and transferred separately from the market economy. The proximity of crops and gardens to the home allows for an easier integration of crop cultivation into everyday behavior and conversations. Due to the intensity of the sun in the countryside, diurnal patterns may include leaving for work at 4 a.m. to avoid working in the midday sun and going to bed shortly after dark. Everyday attention to lunar temporalities, astronomical patterns, the landscape, and the weather governs conversations and dictates work decisions that are made in El Norteño. This quotidian way of being is radically different from the daily experiences of campesinx migrants working day-labor jobs in the United States. It is a lifeway that is longed for among some who intend to return to El Norteño and work in subsistence agriculture. In El Norteño, migrants who save their money in the United States and purchase land in El Salvador are often referred to as migrants "with vision" among El Norteño's current farmers. Indeed, migrants with restorative nostalgia who develop nostos imaginaries often invest their U.S. earnings into housing and land in El Salvador in expectation for their return home.

The distance between subsistence farming in Chalatenango and migrant life in Colorado includes far more than variations in economic development and physical space. Understanding the object of the restorative nostalgic gaze implies an alternative lifeway that is not accessible to Chalatecx migrants, who are pressured to engage in alternative work practices once inside the United States. In writing about biodiversity preservation among Peruvian potato farmers, Virginia Nazarea writes that "whether we see farmers pining for old varieties or realistically relinquishing them, and whether we call what we're doing applied anthropology, development anthropology, engaged anthropology, or public anthropology, anthropologists have a role to play and need to know when to get on with it. Beyond mediating or brokering, anthropologists can try to penetrate and articulate the sand in, as well as the rubber on, other people's shoes—or non-shoes—because we are presented with multiple opportunities for getting as close as possible to walking in them."[21] As a resident in El Salvador, I had a unique opportunity to more closely examine the object of restorative nostalgic gazing for this alternative lifeway. In the latter stages of my fieldwork, I began more closely examining and eventually participating in everyday subsistence-farming activities in El Norteño. It is an endeavor that goes far beyond the scope of this book, but aspects of that experience helped me better understand transnational chasms where restorative nostalgic impulses emerge.

Participating in milpa farming with El Norteño's farmers introduced me to the drastically different temporalities of campesinx life, as well as the informal, orally transmitted knowledge that circulated and was used to cultivate the milpa. The most knowledgeable campesinxs in El Norteño, a disappearing variety, are those who can predict that it will rain. They observe cloud movement and the wind, and some are said to reference astrological patterns, but I never met someone who could do so (I only heard about campesinos *from before* who knew how to use astrological patterns to predict rain). One campesino farmer now in his sixties remembers a time during the dry season: "We were just kids, and [Dad] told us to 'prepare the spades, because tomorrow, we are going to sow.' And my brother, who is now living in Colorado, says 'Fuck, Dad is crazy.' My brother said to him, 'But how are we going to sow if the ground is so hard and it hasn't rained?' Dad told him, 'Prepare the spades, because tomorrow, we are going to sow.' We went along with my father, and we sowed corn in total disbelief. And that afternoon, the storm fell, and the rainy season began. . . . I don't know, they had that—as one would say—that wisdom." Chalatecos admired those farmers who had the ability to predict rain, and they often talked about how that particular type of knowledge was fading with the passage of the generations and the emigration of campesinx youth. My on- and off-the-farm conversations with farmers in El Norteño included constant attention to not only the weather but the moon, and the convergence of these two factors could dictate work schedules (as opposed to a manager or organization determining when an individual works). It was usually the individual farmer who determined what to do on her or his farm, depending on meteorological and lunar temporalities.

As I ate pupusas one day in rural El Salvador, a campesino who was deported from the United States explained to me that in contrast to life in the United States, "the moon determines everything here." In El Norteño, there is still ample conversational and decision-making attention given to the moon—its size and timing in the lunar cycle are frequently talked about among farmers in everyday conversations and in agricultural planning. Farmers will sow particular varieties on predefined segments of the moon cycle, as the moon is understood to affect plant growth. Using the moon to understand plant growth is something that has been somewhat "validated" in the natural sciences, where research on lunar cycles and biological rhythms suggests that plant "roots perceive the tidal acceleration generated by the orbital motions of the Moon and the Earth."[22] Both rural migrants in the United States and farmers in El Salvador would always point me to *los ancianos* (elders) as my questions about the moon became more specific. Older campesinxs were perceived as the best sources for transmitting this type of everyday, occupationally informative knowledge.

When I spoke with El Norteño's elders about the moon, they would regularly talk about and remember the people *de antes* (from before). Much of this knowledge was likely a syncretic outcome of modern agricultural knowledge with traditional knowledge from indigenous communities (e.g., Pipil, Chortí) that have since been subject to genocides and experiences of historical loss. When using astrological or lunar knowledge to cultivate, some farmers described that a key component of the cultivation practice was *belief*. One couldn't experiment with the lunar cycle to see if it might work, one had to *believe* that planting on the lunar cycle worked in order for the plant to grow as intended. Campesinxs talked about what *plants wanted* and whether God would allow the earth to give. Spiritual approaches to milpa farming in El Norteño may again be syncretic expressions of modern-day Christianity with polytheistic devotion to gods that were associated with the sun, moon, and rain.[23] Indeed, the word *milpa* is derived from the word for "field" in Nahuatl, referring to a field cleared by fire before sowing corn (a practice that is also referred to as "swidden" agriculture,[24] better known through the derogatory "slash and burn" attribution).[25] The genocides that have subsequently diminished the indigenous identity in El Salvador and the historical loss of traditional indigenous knowledge and practices in contemporary rural El Salvador subjects what remains in the mestizo oral record that I documented in El Norteño to mere conjecture. However, the remnants of what may be a cosmopraxis implicated in subsistence agricultural practices in El Norteño are a salient component of what is remembered and preserved in subsistence farming practices in Chalatenango. This lifeway contrasts substantially with everyday life in North America, and this difference (perhaps ontological in nature for some) is a component of restorative nostalgia.

PLANT MEDICINE AND CARETAKING

Common to both reflective and restorative nostalgia was the medicinal role of plants in caretaking and traditional medicine. Interactions with plants in El Norteño go beyond subsistence agricultural practices, and memories of interactions with plants provoke the movement of medicinal parcels to diasporic communities in places such as Colorado and Long Island. In those places, it is relatively common that campesinx migrants live in hermetically sealed homes that reinforce discontinuities in physical contact with the natural environment. One can sit inside a house in the United States, for example, and be relatively unaware of a gentle wind. While gardening is certainly evident and practiced among campesinxs in the United States, it is difficult for campesinx migrants to access the same plant-based remedies that were once cultivated and used in El Norteño. Inside the United States, some campesinxs experience illnesses including forms of anxiety, seasonal depression, and a variety of respiratory illnesses that have traditional remedies in El Norteño. While some campesinx migrants quickly adapt to and use the U.S. health care system, others remain fearful and avoidant of U.S. health care due to language barriers and fears of "getting caught" when entering pharmacies, hospitals, or clinics. Some long for their rural caretakers and their remedies when ill. As I learned through following couriers, campesinxs in the United States regularly reach out into transnational space to communicate symptoms to mothers, sisters, grandmothers, and aunts (this was often a gendered practice) still living in El Norteño. While treatment options may be available at arm's length in the United States, campesinxs in El Norteño will attempt to send mixed treatments with couriers, who deliver the rural remedy to the United States. The efficacy of these treatments is not well understood, but I can attest to the perceived efficacy of the remedies through ways in which I directly observed and experienced caretaking from campesinxs in El Norteño.

During the period of time that I lived with El Norteño's couriers, one day, I became ill with the flu. I woke up in a hammock with a wet washcloth on my forehead. Mercedes, one of the Chalateca couriers I had been following, offered me a strange tea. I refused it. I was particularly self-conscious about being an immobile white male who had become an additional caretaking burden for a woman with multiple jobs. I was so sick that I stopped taking field notes. I lost track of what day it was. I only began to take the remedies offered to me when Mercedes started crying because I refused her caretaking attempts. She explained that she brought herbs in from the field and that she made "raise the dead" soup. I told Mercedes not to worry about me, but I eventually ate the soup and fell back asleep. When I woke up, my fever had broken, and I was able to start working again.

As I recovered, Mercedes collected herbs and made soups and teas from berry leaves, orange-tree leaves, lemon-tree leaves, avocado-tree leaves, ginger, allspice, and lemongrass. Pots of water boiled with eucalyptus and chamomile were dumped into buckets that I used for bathing. I never once requested these remedies—they were locally harvested, prepared, and administered by Mercedes, her sister, or her daughter. I regularly observed Salvadoran women from the countryside trying to send extracts or variants of these treatments to the United States, several of which couriers refuse to carry because they are unsure of whether the extracts will pass inspection. Regardless, campesinxs still request and transmit herbal medicinal remedies to resolve illnesses that arise in diasporic networks.

In El Norteño, plant-based remedies are regularly cultivated and utilized. A report by the Salvadoran secretary of culture on El Norteño specifically highlighted the ancestral use of animals and plants to calm pain and cure maladies, recognizing that a supernatural power was associated with medicinal plants.[26] Medicinal-plant cultivation and remedy use were integrated into everyday caretaking behaviors that were generally managed by women to tend to the sick in El Norteño and its diaspora.

I regularly observed illness being addressed through hybrid treatments involving plant-based medicines, modern medicine, and supernatural remedies. Berry leaves, antibiotics, and witchcraft may be administered together for a number of ailments. In El Norteño, residents still talked of treating illnesses according to humoral pathology (e.g., having too much heat, cold, and air). Several of these conceptualizations of health in Chalatenango have been considered to be rooted in medicine brought by the Spanish during the conquests, including variants of outdated Greek medicine that persist in the region, where sickness is explained according to "the humors."[27] But there is also evidence that remedies from the preexisting indigenous (non-Mestizo) communities continue to be

FIGURE 3.1 A courier and a family friend inspect a dropper from a bottle containing a medicinal tincture that will be sent as a parcel from El Salvador to the United States.

widely used and have been incorporated into the humoral framework.[28] Regardless of where health beliefs came from and whether they are "valid," campesinxs continue to reference conditions implicating humoral frameworks in the United States, which are often dealt with through traditional remedies delivered as parcels by El Norteño's couriers.

I regularly overheard couriers reject herbal remedies that were brought to them on the grounds that the herbs would not pass through U.S. customs, and I came to recognize illnesses by the parcels that indicated someone was sick in the United States (combinations of herbal remedies and modern pharmaceuticals). For example, sending berry leaves and antibiotics typically indicated that a family member in the United States had the flu (I later tried to communicate information about self-prescribing antibiotics for the flu in this manner).[29] A Chalateca mother sending orange leaves to her daughter in Long Island during the month of February probably meant that her daughter had nerve problems during the darker months up north, perhaps the result of seasonal depression. In Denver or Long Island, campesinxs from El Salvador often found themselves living in urban houses or trailers, where farmland was inaccessible and where one would have to otherwise go to a pharmacy or a doctor's office to treat an illness. In the United States, I heard of campesinxs complaining about symptoms to their Salvadoran family members back home—seeking a transnational solution to a malady instead of a local one available in the United States.

Ultimately, that some campesinxs in the United States do not utilize the U.S. health care system reflects a multifactorial outcome of health care accessibility, felt xenophobia, and the preservation of traditional knowledge that is in part made possible through the transfer of parcels by El Norteño's couriers. The integration of farmland, family, and treatments that were previously implicated in processes of bodily recovery, regardless of how gendered those practices may be, was a familiar combination that was longed for when illness arose, despite the logistical complications and restrictions of transnational delivery.

CONCLUSION

Collective nostalgia in El Norteño's diasporic networks harbors emotional experiences of pain, pleasure, loss, and comfort. It can fix gazes upon the past, structure intimacy, and inform imaginaries of return. Nostalgia develops at sites of transnational discontinuity and provokes materializations of the rural past in the present as parcels delivered by couriers. The growth of nostalgia at sites where campesinxs' movements are restricted highlights that power, as Foucault reminds us, "doesn't only weigh on us as a force that says no, but that it traverses and produces things, it induces pleasure, forms knowledge, produces discourse."[30] The production of nostalgia harbored criticism of the United States' wholesale food system, while the memory practices associated with nostalgia (reaching out into diasporic networks and moving parcels across transnational space) preserved aspects of an alternative lifeway in the diasporic present. Nostalgia illustrates disparities in privilege, including who is allowed to imagine what past be brought into which present, and highlights disparities in health care accessibility. Diasporic nostalgia did not form the basis of collective actions that would otherwise challenge the policies of the same U.S. nation-state that maintains physical divides for undocumented Salvadorans, but diasporic nostalgia did harbor a critique of U.S. wholesale food. Wholesale food in the United States is being rendered as something disgusting to campesinx migrants who know of, and some of whom long for, alternative ways to cultivate it.

The contradictory senses of pleasure and loss wound up in nostalgic gazing both reveal and remedy critical sites of diasporic discontinuities. What is longed for in El Norteño's diaspora raises questions about the assumed superiority of development paradigms, where wholesale solutions in the United States reduce consumers' connectivity to the circumstances of food and medicine production. Collective practices of nostalgia raise questions about uncertain futures in the United States—and alternatives to those futures. In the next chapter, I examine ways in which campesinx imaginaries draw upon memories that further bridge multidirectional divides in transnational space.

4 · WE DO NOT HAVE TO LEARN TO BE WHAT WE ARE NOT

Memory and Imagination in the Rural Diaspora

No one considers it a secret. Northward migration is a life project for many Salvadorians: young people, girls, the elderly, men and women, sons, mothers, neighbors, friends, students, professionals, peasants, and the unemployed.

—Amparo Marroquín[1]

Like virtual particles in a quantum field, multiple futures pop in and out of possibility.

—Anna Tsing[2]

I was in the Salvadoran countryside eating *pupusas* and drinking Regia beer, listening to a queer Chalatecx friend imagine his drag-queen persona. Who knew if that persona would ever become realized at the annual drag pageant in Chalatenango? What mattered more was the amount of time we repeatedly spent in his imagination, exploring her futuristic visions.

His drag persona, "Elba Lazo," is a peasant girl from a small town in Chalatenango. Elba collects *loroco* (an edible vine flower used to flavor food), which goes for only $1 per pound when it's in season, and sells it at the market. She had been to the United States as a migrant, but she got deported because she was caught "working on the street" in Houston. Elba raises her finger in the air and waves it back and forth as she says, "You might think I was selling sex, but I was actually just selling bubblegum. You know, in El Salvador, you can sell anything on the street, but in the U.S., they put you in jail for that shit." We both laugh sardonically after this joke because it is too real—my friend has actually been deported from the United States. She is using critical humor to call out racial policing practices in the United States, where a banal misdemeanor could very well trigger a deportation.

Elba Lazo explains that she needs to be prepared to *tirar imperio* (take empire) at any time (the English analog of taking empire might best be described as "throwing shade," a practice of casting insults drawn from black culture and employed in drag-ball culture, later popularized by the film *Paris is Burning* and the U.S. television series *RuPaul's Drag Race*).³ Elba Lazo explains that she is prepared to *tirar imperio* the moment that a *machista campesinx* makes cat-calls from the audience, ranging from *mamacita* (little mama) to *te voy a pisar* (I'm going to fuck you). Her prepared responses include comparing machista campesinxs to livestock while undermining their masculinities, which is a logical solution for a drag queen with a subsistence-farming audience. Her fastest line is "Y vos, que sos? Sos perra o sos vaca? Porque a mí me pareces más vaca que perra" (And you, what are you? Are you a bitch or a cow? Because to me you look more like a cow than a bitch).

I ask Elba Lazo if she has a real chance at winning the annual drag pageant in Chalatenango, and she explains that the key to her imagined success is in her backstory. She clarifies that when queens are asked what they will do if they win the crown, they give "bullshit" responses, such as they are going to achieve equality for LGBT people in the municipal offices. She rolls her eyes and says that is not going to happen anytime soon in El Salvador. Elba looks into the distance and tells me, as though she is speaking to the judges, that if she wins the crown, she will use her fame to start a multinational export trade where she sends loroco to diasporic strongholds in the United States, using a number of known couriers who shuttle parcels between Chalatenango, Maryland, Texas, and California. Elba Lazo feels the need to further explain the ingenuity of her winning drag vision: "Do you know how much a pound of loroco costs in Texas? Between $15 to $20. In Chalatenango it's $1 per pound." This fact alone leads us to stop talking about Elba Lazo. Our conversation turns into a defeated comparison of loroco in the Salvadoran countryside and loroco in Latino grocery stores located throughout the United States. My conversation with Elba Lazo was not a structured interview; it was simply one of the myriad ways in which Chalatecxs spend time in their imaginations, meditating on surreal prospections that could, should, and perhaps would happen.

One of the notable qualities of Elba Lazo is that she emerges from the imagination of a gay, communist, churchgoing Catholic who has been deported from the United States. She is crafted by someone who has traversed the Salvadoran diaspora. She emerges from the "diasporic imaginary,"⁴ shifting our focus to the temporal and corporeal, where places such as Chalatenango and the United States are transformed into affective and temporal processes. Elba Lazo's sardonic humor allows for us to openly acknowledge how states surveil, police, restrict, and enforce movement, where the imagined audience can take *as a given* that U.S. law-enforcement officers engage in racialized policing practices that criminalize and lead to the deportation of brown people. Elba is constructed from diasporic memories and campesinx ingenuity. The sexual freedom that Elba's imaginer brings from the United States to El Salvador is both a reflection of his exposure to U.S. North American progressivism as well as the imaginer's conceptualization of liberation theology. It is not one (exposure to life in the United States) or the other (popular liberation theology) that makes space for envisioned queens like Elba Lazo in the contemporary Salvadoran countryside. She is indeed a syncretic outcome of distinctly different places, but she is also an outcome of space-variant memories that coproduce innovative and irreverent visions of nation-states.

During fieldwork, I often found myself in the humorous, surreal, conditional tense of campesinx interlocutors as they were imagining. These moments of imagination were not marked by explicit intentions to *do something particular* in the immediate future, although sometimes they were. Moments of imagination were salient, particularly in places like El Norteño, where poor internet connectivity and questionable telephone service afforded more time away from technology-based communications. These aspects of economic development, however, do not imply that El Norteño is simply a more backward, less developed place that contrasts linearly to more "developed" or "educated" social environments in the urban capital or U.S. diasporic strongholds.[5] El Norteño changes as campesinx migrants cycle in and out of it, as emergent cultural hybrids and novel conceptualizations of what is possible move with minds and bodies as they traverse transnational space, simultaneously orienting the next generation of El Norteño's youth to systems of possibilities. Deported Catholic communists develop transnational drag imaginaries that are now being showcased to campesinxs at annual drag pageants in rural El Salvador. While I showcased Elba Lazo to make this point, I do not in this chapter focus on the myriad diasporic imaginaries that are taking shape in and shaping El Norteño's diaspora. Rather, I focus on the mechanisms by which diasporic memory informs prospection and imagination—ways in which the past is called upon to develop imaginative projections and surreal forecasts that do not predict but shape possibilities for collective practices in transnational space.

Drawing upon Bourdieu's analysis of cultural production, El Norteño's *state of the system of possibilities* changes with time, orienting new generations toward *more innovative possibilities*[6] that include cyclical migration, no matter how dangerous it may be. Following the U.S. federal strategies of "Prevention Through

Deterrence" and the recent dehumanizing forced removal of migrant children from their parents, there grows a contradictory adage that if the United States is that hard to get into, *it's probably worth it*. Diasporic imaginaries modify the value of transnational movement, and those imaginaries are informed by memories of the imaginers.

Understanding these changes in the system of possibilities in the rural countryside, and why they take hold and stick, entails first understanding the hybridity that develops in diasporic communities.[7] This hybridity is more than a simple combination of two fixed locations (rural El Salvador and the United States); it also sutures memories from both spaces that coalesce in prospections, taking on multiple meanings for campesinxs who imagine in the process of orienting themselves to multiple possibilities and envisaged alternatives. To illustrate the ways in which transnational spaces foster the growth of memories that inform diasporic imaginaries, I first use simple demographic and jurisdictional particularities of space in Colorado to describe how some hybrid cultural elements emerge. Then I illustrate how renderings of the past interact with transnational space to inform the system of possibilities that is imagined, acted upon, and that acts as a counterpoint to state-based strategies of prevention and deterrence.

HYBRIDIZED EMERGENCES

Demographic and jurisdictional settings are environmental factors that stimulate the emergence of hybrid cultural elements in El Norteño's diaspora. Demographically, there are apparent age disparities by location in the network of clientele who send and receive parcels. Every time I followed Mateo (one of El Norteño's couriers) from the rural Salvadoran countryside and into Colorado, I was struck by the perceivably larger portion of rural Salvadorans in the United States who appeared to be in my age group (midthirties at the time I was collecting data) compared to their relative scarcity in the Salvadoran countryside, where I was also conducting field research. Age represents a simple demographic difference between the two places that carries consequences for the way in which new cultural elements emerge. In rural Chalatenango, the relative distribution of thirty- to thirty-nine-year-old Salvadorans is proportionately *smaller*[8] than the relative distribution of thirty- to thirty-nine-year-old foreign-born Salvadorans in the United States.[9] The vast majority of Salvadoran migrants to the United States (81 percent) are estimated to be of working age.[10] This disproportionate distribution in age difference reflects the fact that campesinxs are often working in Colorado—making money, saving it, and often sending it "home." Experiences and exposure to coworkers affect language and consumer practices (described later). Campesinxs receive encouragement from kin in El Norteño who recognize their economic mobility and often benefit from remittances. Migrant campesinxs are talked about in El Norteño as contributing to the economic well-being of El Norteño. Nearly all the Salvadorans I met in Colorado were remitting home in some manner or another (this might reflect the fact that I operated in the networks of couriers' clientele). Migrant family members regularly sent material goods and cash to kin in the Salvadoran countryside.

The relative economic mobility produced by the migration of campesinxs to Colorado has complex socioeconomic implications. After migrating to the United States, economically poor campesinxs can make exponentially more money in the United States than they could in El Norteño. *Campesina* migrants may experience even more economic mobility than men, where in one hour of U.S. labor, campesinas can make more than a man's day-labor wage in rural El Salvador. Despite this economic mobility, many enter the United States in the ranks of the working poor, classifiably inhabiting the lower strata of the U.S. socioeconomic spectrum. Thus there is immense transnational class mobility for campesinxs entering the United States, even if they are economically classified as the working poor or working class once inside the United States.[11] This transnational economic gain, as I will argue later, also has imaginative implications for migrants who experience economic "liberation" from the economic poverty of subsistence agricultural lifeways in El Salvador. With a U.S. job and income, campesinxs are increasingly exposed to a consumer culture that can alter purchasing patterns and modes of saving, spending, style, and taste. For example, El Norteño's couriers observed that rural migrants change their financial management strategies once in the United States, opening personal bank accounts and managing transactions with debit cards instead of cash, spending more money than they used to for an increasing number of evolving "needs" once inside the United States. In contrast to the collective pooling of cash among family members in El Norteño, money is digitized and more frequently personalized in the United States.

The individualization and accrual of savings occur relative to a range of kinship dynamics among campesinxs working in the United States. The cost-saving strategies of living within kinship networks in the United States and marriage and the expectation of children do not appear to be as commonplace an expectation in late adolescence and early adulthood once inside the United States as it is in the Salvadoran countryside. In El Norteño, a single individual in their late twenties or thirties is somewhat of an anomaly and can be viewed suspiciously or be subject to immense pressure to marry. Queer Chalatecxs sometimes feel pressured to enter heterosexual marriages and have children, even for those who acknowledge that this is not reflective of their sexual desires. In contrast, being single or unmarried in the United States at an older age can seem like the norm. The average age at first marriage for men and women in the United States is estimated to be 3.2 and 5.0 years greater than the age at first marriage for men and women in El Salvador.[12]

Kinship networks can comprise campesinx migrants with numerous legal statuses inside the United States. For example, a mother with Temporary Protected Status (TPS) could have a daughter who was brought to the United States with a parolee status under the Central American Minors program (before such admission into the United States was eliminated in 2017 under Donald Trump's presidency), and she could also have an undocumented son who entered the United States with a coyote following the reduction of parolee admissions with the Central American Minors program in 2017. As a result, Salvadoran kinship networks in North America involve multiple legal statuses, and family dynamics can be affected in turn by the activity of local and immigration law enforcement.

In 2012, U.S. Immigration and Customs Enforcement (ICE) issued a memorandum[13] that provided guidance on detainers, which are requests from ICE to a jail to continue holding a prisoner for forty-eight hours (excluding weekends and holidays) after their release from custody, such that the custody of the person can be transferred to ICE.[14] The memorandum included guidance to detain individuals where officers "have reason to believe the individual is an alien subject to removal from the United States" and a relatively ubiquitous set of criteria that can be subject to interpretation.[15] I have known Chalatecxs who were apprehended in Colorado and deported back to El Salvador for something as simple as drinking a single beer on the way home from work (consider Elba Lazo's joke that "I was actually just selling bubblegum. You know, in El Salvador, you can sell anything on the street, but in the U.S., they put you in jail for that shit"). In the United States, misdemeanor offenses such as these can trigger deportation proceedings. While I have heard stories about police in Colorado who look for brown people engaging in petty crimes like drinking beer on their way home from work, I have directly observed economically rich white people smoking marijuana on ski lifts in the Rocky Mountains, openly violating the open-container laws that initiate migrants' deportations. This is one example of how policing in Colorado is racialized despite Denver being an alleged sanctuary city, where the Denver Sheriff Department does not claim to hold individuals on a detainer past their normal release time for ICE.[16]

These varying legal statuses have numerous implications for everyday family dynamics. For example, one adult child in Colorado who had DACA (deferred action from deportation) status told me about how she ended fistfights between her parents and siblings, shouting that everyone will surely be deported if the police arrive to the house. The threat of law enforcement and the implications it carries (the potential to trigger deportation) can be enough to bring an end to drunken brawls between campesinx kin living in the same household.

While some campesinx families perceive separation as the price to pay for an economically beneficial strategy, it has profound emotional consequences.[17] Transnational families split between borders (e.g., parents living in the United States with children and grandparents remaining in El Salvador) may include kinship dynamics where communication takes place using an increasing number of social media modalities, including Skype, WhatsApp, Facebook, and Instagram. Younger generations can visualize what life in the United States looks like for their relatives who transmit photographic updates to El Norteño's youth as they grow to imagine their potential futures.

Salvadoran family dynamics have a way of becoming more fluid in the United States, where new definitions of kinship emerge. During the course of my research, the U.S. Supreme Court ruled that state-level bans on same-sex marriage were unconstitutional,[18] and gay marriage could actually become one way in which immigrants could obtain documentation. These new realizations of family disrupt, but do not always counter, the ever-shifting kinship dynamics in transnational family networks. Beyond heteronormative family units, there are also campesinx migrants who enter into romantic partnerships with noncampesinxs in the United States, and there are also queer campesinxs who re-create heteronormative kinship dynamics with single-gender living arrangements in the United States. While the kinship arrangements of queer campesinxs are recognizable and familiar in Colorado (sometimes with an identifiable "mother" figure and "father" figure governing the "household"), these queer manifestations of Salvadoran family dynamics were not yet apparent to me in El Norteño.

Jurisdictional idiosyncrasies between spaces not only shape emergent family dynamics, but they also shape conceptualizations surrounding the consumption and use of substances. Amendment 64 to Colorado's general election ballot in 2012[19] resulted in Colorado State declaring that "the use of marijuana should be legal for persons twenty-one years of age or older and taxed in a manner similar to alcohol."[20] As recreational marijuana began to be sold in 2014, marijuana smoke emanating from one's Colorado residence would not produce a law-enforcement action, whereas in El Salvador, it could. The effects of recreational cannabis legalization in locations such as Colorado, where I spent most of my time following Mateo, are worth noting.

In El Salvador, there is both a stigma and irreverence for the social transgression of marijuana use. In El Salvador, the possession of cannabis can result in a multiyear prison sentence.[21] However, I observed cannabis used for both medical and recreational purposes in El Norteño. This included elderly Salvadoran women making cannabis-based tinctures to treat pain, individuals with Parkinson's disease consuming marijuana to reduce tremors, and also individuals such as gang members who preferred to smoke marijuana (often as an alternative to consuming alcohol). In Chalatenango, I actually encountered one law-enforcement agency that distributed confiscated cannabis to women with instructions never to smoke it but to turn it into "medicine." It seemed that marijuana was perceived as being medicinal when THC (tetrahydrocannabinol), the principal psychoactive constituent of cannabis, was extracted into butters, oils, or tinctures, but it was considered criminal when smoked. Despite evidence of marijuana use in El Norteño, it was not as accepted as it was among campesinxs in Colorado.

The legalization of recreational cannabis in Colorado radically altered the use and perceptions of it among campesinxs now living there. After seeing legal marijuana consumed, these new attitudes are filtering back into the Salvadoran countryside. In several instances, Salvadorans living in Colorado have attempted to send marijuana-based products (such as tinctures and sublingual drops) back to family members in El Salvador for medical issues. However, El Norteño's couriers refuse to carry these parcels due to the risk it puts on them in entering El Salvador.

Among campesinxs in Colorado, there was the perception that the construction or renovation of physical spaces for recreational dispensaries was generating employment and that the taxes associated with recreational marijuana were helping the state. On this same note, migrants complained about urban rent prices skyrocketing following the implementation of recreational sales in 2014, narrated as an internal migration factor that pushed Salvadoran migrants to cheaper housing options located on the outskirts of Boulder and Denver. Several migrants reported originally living in apartments in locations such as Boulder but subsequently moving into trailer homes in towns on the outskirts of the city as a direct result of the legalization of recreational cannabis. Here, a micromigration of Salvadorans was narrated as the by-product of a state government's decision, which was simultaneously narrated as having positive (job-creating) and negative (rent-raising) effects that implicated rural Salvadorans. The role that cannabis legalization has had on the continued migration of Salvadorans is an area that deserves further research.

MOMENTS OF TRANSNATIONAL SYNCRETISM

Understanding that there are basic demographic and jurisdictional differences between spaces implicated in El Norteño's diaspora, it should be little surprise that hybrid cultural elements emerge. In its most basic form, this hybridity that I am writing about has been referred to as *syncretism*—the blending of elements from two different cultures to generate something new.[22] After migrating from El Norteño to the United States, some migrants undergo rapid and unprecedented changes in their everyday lives that give rise to new ways of being in and thinking about the world. Mateo, a Salvadoran courier who delivers parcels to Colorado, used food to explain how his clients who have just migrated to the United States start to say things like: "'I want a hamburger. I could go for a pizza.' It's something that they normally wouldn't do here [in El Norteño]. I say this thinking about the fact that the majority of people come from rural zones. Yes, there are people in the capital who in some form or another have had this life-style, and when they are there [in the United States]—it's not a 'boom' for them. However, everything else changes. Their wardrobe, the way they behave—I love that some of them get into school and try to gradually develop, like learning English." The changes in taste preferences and language acquisition that Mateo describes in his clientele could be framed as moments of acculturation (a change in beliefs, values, identities, or behaviors that occur in "minorities" as a result of prolonged contact with the "majority" culture) and assimilation (an acquisition of the host culture alongside the loss of the heritage culture).[23] While acculturation and assimilation are helpful in terms of thinking about power dynamics inside the United States, this type of representation in diasporic communities risks overemphasizing dualisms that make opaque the multiple emergences of cultural and memorial hybridity, particularly as they are drawn upon in futur-istic prospections that may have little to do with acculturation or assimilation. Diasporic imaginaries can be both syncretic outcomes and comprise syncretic cultural elements all at once. Here I first break down examples of stylistic and linguistic syncretism prior to showing how the imaginary is a spatially moder-ated syncretism that draws from memory.

Style

During my fieldwork with El Norteño's couriers, I observed the shipment of par-cels from the United States to El Norteño that included Tommy Hilfiger wallets, Michael Kors purses, Nike shoes, Nixon watches, Hollister skirts, Paris Hilton perfume bottles, and The Green Solution (marijuana-print) socks. These parcels were in some form or another displayed such that others in El Norteño could readily see or smell the North American product on a campesinx body. I also observed the transfer of parcels that remained hidden inside campesinx homes, including Xboxes, DVD players, Samsung tablets, and iPhones. Despite being carefully concealed so as to not be robbed, these items will be gossiped about in El Norteño. In El Norteño, these artifacts of the U.S. empire define and redefine a constantly emerging *sense of style* among campesinxs that implies an interna-tional taste and transnational connectivity.

In her ethnographic work in rural Chalatenango, anthropologist Irina Carlota Silber describes the development of Flor, a young girl who, in the time after the Salvadoran Civil War, grew to perform a specific set of transnational practices: "During fieldwork, I watched Flor change from an eleven-year-old in flip-flops into a young teenager fully displaying her sexuality. Flor wears makeup and perfume, goes to community festivals and dances with boys, and wears tight, short skirts and tops, as marketed on TV. She skillfully performs these new transnational practices of fashion-conscious teens available through the media and local market reproductions of 'trendy' pop gear."[24] Silber's finding that this trend occurs in youth points to the permeation of fashion into the countryside through various media outlets and to the fact that fashion practices themselves are part of the emerging field in postwar Chalatenango.[25]

While I might see transnational gear that was well cared for and perhaps worn during special occasions in El Norteño, I was dumbfounded by the everyday fashion sensibility of rural campesinxs in the United States. I usually felt like a slob when I was in the presence of campesinxs near Denver, suddenly aware of what I looked like, whether I had shaved, the relative age and condition of my clothes and sneakers (which had become quite worn in El Salvador), and my complete lack of accessories. Whereas in El Norteño my colorful New Balance shoes were *chivo* (cool), they were seen as comparatively "old" among campesinx migrants in the United States. I realized the type of pressure that some campesinxs might feel as I was ordering coffee from a trendy coffee shop in downtown Denver when I heard two white people with North American–accented English making fun of *my* clothing (which was generally the same type of clothing I wore during the fieldwork in El Norteño). I imagined how new campesinx migrants felt when they sensed similar venomous microaggressions in the United States— cosmopolitan acts of shaming that are nonetheless sensed and adapted to with time. The demand for U.S. fashion in El Norteño comes not only from the material presence of U.S. fashion in the space of the Salvadoran countryside but also through viewing the altered fashion and styles of migrant kin who transmit visual representations, particularly selfies, over social media accounts (e.g., Facebook, Instagram, Snapchat, WhatsApp) shared by friends and family members living in El Norteño.

This narrative of syncretic fashion that I've developed here, however, is partial and flawed. It presents a version of cultural hybridity where the passive campesinx subject in El Norteño submits to trends that dominate what is considered desirable on Salvadoran bodies in North America. It presents a somewhat assimilationist narrative that ignores the campesinx behind the drive to purchase, but it nonetheless shows ways in which the diaspora affects taste in El Norteño. There are certainly campesinxs who do not care about U.S. fashion but who nonetheless take on new styles with the passage of time in the United States (particularly the immediate need to purchase clothes for the winter in Colorado). But there are other factors at play, including spiritual beliefs that are wound up with the past, which also underlie the emergent transnational class mobility and syncretic fashion statements being paraded around the Salvadoran countryside.

Anthropologists have begun to examine syncretic cultural elements as sites that exhibit disparate expressions of power.[26] In the discussion of linguistic hybridity that follows, I examine cultural hybrids as sites of diasporic contention. As I have tried to show earlier, the environmental foundations for syncretic emergence can be affected by extremely local dynamics that implicate power. A discussion of linguistic syncretism is one way to show how conflicts emerge in the sensorium of cultural hybridities.

Language

After beginning research for this book in El Norteño, I began to adjust the way I spoke Spanish. I started to regularly use the curse words and *caliche* (slang) that I regularly heard in the countryside as I became more comfortable with that way of speaking Spanish. Cecilia Rivas writes that "the language spoken by Salvadorans is unfixed, shifting, and innovative, and it is intertwined with social, political, and historical practice."[27] The Spanish I heard in El Norteño was markedly different from the Spanish I heard in San Salvador, which appeared to have class-dependent sociolects. I continued speaking my version of Chalatecx Spanish with Mateo the courier as we traveled around Colorado. This was one of the ways in which I came to better understand how syncretic cultural outcomes could also be loaded with contention.

In Colorado, I noticed differences in how men in my age range (thirtysomethings) referred to one another and used explicative adjectives. In El Norteño, I was accustomed to referring to men (and men referring to me) using terms such as *maje, cerote, pendejo, cabrón* (fool, piece of shit, dumbass, asshole), or the transnationalized but less offensive *men* (appropriated from the English *man*) that one might hear among those friends who are *en confianza* (trusted). I could not understand why Salvadoran campesinos in the same age range were calling each other *güey* in Colorado. A Mexican American friend of mine in Colorado explained that *güey* was commonly used in Mexican slang. Linguist Kimberly Adilia Helmer succinctly writes, "Güey is derived from büey, meaning ox. In some contexts güey is 'ass' or 'asshole,' but generally speaking it translates to man, dude, 'homie,' sometimes idiot. Some consider it profane."[28] Further, in the United States, I heard Salvadoran men use an adjective, *pinche*, to make emphatic statements. The clearest English translation would be the use of *damn* or *fucking* as adjectives, such as "the *fucking* car broke down." In the Salvadoran countryside, the analog adjective used would be *puta* (which literally means *whore* but when used as an adjective would translate to *fucking*, with those same gendered overtones). The words *güey* and *pinche* had been adapted from the Mexican vocabulary, and I didn't understand why rural Salvadoran men were using Mexican words in Colorado. Further, I sometimes heard Chalateco men in the United States chiding other Chalateco men for speaking "like Mexicans." The phenomenon was occurring among men, so I asked women why they thought this was happening.

Women explained how language was a contested site with variant forms in the same diasporic network. A household matriarch listened to the examples I just stated, and she began her interpretation by explaining her experience of intra-Latinx racism in her workplace. She described how in Colorado, Mexicans were the dominant group and often looked down upon and discriminated against Salvadorans. While undocumented campesinxs were being classified into the umbrella of *illegal Hispanic migrants* in the xenophobic imaginary, Mexicans indeed outnumbered Chalatecxs. In Colorado, where I was hearing Mexicanized Spanish among Salvadoran campesinxs, it is estimated that there are three thousand undocumented Salvadorans and 128,000 undocumented Mexicans, with Mexicans representing 79 percent of the estimated undocumented population and Salvadorans representing 2 percent.[29] The tendency toward Mexicanized Spanish, she conjectured, was a result of the social pressure that Salvadoran men felt in the presence of the more socially dominant and occupationally established Mexican class of migrants. Other men held onto their Chalateco identity and chided those who *Mexicanized* their utterances, which was a coded way of scolding them for "giving in" to the pressures exerted by the more dominant Mexicans in the workplace. I never once heard women use the word *güey* to refer to one another, but I did hear them use *pinche* (instead of *puta*).[30] Within perceived hierarchies of masculinity and race, Chalateco men in particular were in some ways experiencing pressure to change their everyday utterances. Some did, and some did not.

Discussions about manifestations of linguistic syncretism often emerged when Chalatecxs were exposed to non-Salvadorans in occupational environments. On numerous occasions, Salvadoran migrant men asked me if black men using the word *nigga* with other black men *en confianza* was best translated as *maje, pendejo, cerote,* or *cabrón*. I explained that the term couldn't exactly be translated into any of those terms because there were historical and highly racialized implications behind the use of that word in the United States, particularly based on who is saying it to whom. One Salvadoran man asked if he should start using the word *nigga* to show the *confianza* he felt with his black coworkers. As I tried to provide the man with a brief explanation of structural and historical racism, he couldn't help but see the similarities with his own experiences in North America. Discussions like these with my network of Chalatecx friends often produced discussions of where all these linguistic issues came from, and on numerous occasions, it was Chalatecxs who began talking about the conquest of the Americas and the fact that the U.S. nation-state was overwhelmingly composed of migrant (as opposed to indigenous) groups. That is to say, discussions of linguistic syncretism gave rise to Chalatecx migrants generating everyday theories of power and the American empire.

In both cases—the Mexicanization of Spanish and the curiosity over how to show *confianza* with black coworkers—the discussions about language that I illustrate here emerged among men who were curious, marginalized, and often wished to exhibit friendship or camaraderie, mainly within their occupational environments. This type of comradery is common among rural workers who perform labor in the Salvadoran countryside, where incantations of *cerote* (piece of shit), *culero* (faggot), and *pendejo* (dumbass) are yelled between close friends *en confianza* as they perform grueling agricultural tasks in the expansive mountain fields used to cultivate corn and sorghum. The proclivity of rural Salvadoran migrants to change their idiolects, to inquire about others' idiolects, to use derogatory words as phrases of endearment, and to chide one another for changing their vocabulary are examples of how linguistic syncretism can reflect imbalances of power that are sensed in diasporic communities in the United States. Language, as a cultural element, is subject to hybridization and constantly reproduces meanings and flights of thought through everyday utterances.[31]

When I thought I had finally reached all the conclusions I could possibly come to about this example of linguistic hybridity, I talked with Mercedes (one of El Norteño's couriers) about her thoughts on my findings. Mercedes had been working as a courier for two decades, and she had spent time observing El Norteño's campesinxs migrate and develop hybrid cultural expressions. When I asked Mercedes about what she thought about Salvadoran campesinxs who began picking up a Mexican vocabulary, she nodded and responded emphatically, "Exactly that is what I want you to understand. Vocabulary. Because vocabulary is where we identify ourselves, right? I always criticize, and perhaps I'm always going to criticize: We have to be what we are; we do not have to learn to be what we are not." Mercedes was talking about migrants in the United States, her clients, experiencing pressures to change parts of who they are and how they present themselves *after* migrating to U.S. environments. My observations about language captured some of her frustrations with the responses to vulnerability that she had observed in El Norteño's diasporic communities. As we continued talking about language, I told Mercedes a story about how I was using curse words in casual conversation with a campesina grandmother in Colorado. After a few minutes of conversation, the grandmother began laughing and asked that I never leave because I reminded her so much of El Norteño. I asked Mercedes why she thought that a rural Salvadoran matriarch would feel so nostalgic and emotional when hearing Salvadoran curse words from a gringo who is clearly not from El Norteño. Mercedes had something to add to my findings. Mercedes smiled and nodded, clarifying that "it's because here [in El Norteño], with our vocabulary, we feel free. . . . I have a word, 'shit,' but for me, I feel that *I liberate myself* because that word doesn't make me feel like a bigger person. Instead, using that word *liberates me* from so much shit!" We laughed as she explained this, but Mercedes's observations on language alluded to something much greater than felt social pressures and the need to change one's identity to fit in. She explained cursing, using inappropriate words that are often crude and offensive, as a way to *liberate* oneself. She pitted liberation against felt social pressures to "pass" as something else, which she conceptualized as being partially materialized through language.

The imaginary is a syncretic site where new cultural elements are produced with input from individual renderings of the past. In the context of diasporas, inconvenient and contradictory renderings of the past place can give rise to unexpected imaginaries that underlie behavior. The diaspora gives rise to imaginaries that combine places like El Norteño and the United States. These imaginaries are rendered through narratives that diasporic youth digest, changing the state of the system of possibilities perceived and imagined by the newest generations in El Norteño. Mercedes's use of the concept of liberation in the context of my emergent theorizing on linguistic syncretism pointed my attention back toward a piece of the local and recent history of El Norteño that I had been aware of, but ignoring, for several years. She was using a word that had metaphysical underpinnings, and as I reexamined data, I repeatedly encountered the concept of liberation in campesinxs' descriptions of transnational movements that defy classificatory schemes such as economic migration, security, or family reunification to which campesinx migrants have been epistemically subject by researchers like me.

MIGRATION AS LIBERATION

I was in Colorado preparing for a return trip back to El Norteño with Mateo. We had already packed up nearly two hundred pounds of parcels that included a bottle of creatine, a professional camera, MMA fighting shorts, lip gloss, a microphone, a liter of sexual lubricant, a computer case, a five-gallon tub of protein powder, and dozens of pounds of clothing and shoes. Clients continued arriving at the door to deliver parcels, and a small group of backlogged clients began to congeal at one of the tables in the house as Mateo continued processing requests. The matriarch at the table hollered that I should go grab my tape recorder. I had become accustomed to moments such as these, and I did as I was told. One of the Chalateca women at the table was telling a *historia*, which was also a type of *testimonio*, and she courteously restarted her *historia* from the beginning for my recorder.

This testimony was told in front of an audience of children, women, and men. In the first part of her testimony, she describes living in El Salvador during the civil war in the 1980s and then attempting to deliver food to her injured brother, who is inside a house in an active combat zone. Her testimony included a meticulously detailed account of her movement through rural Chalatenango and toward San Salvador. She described where she got on and off of buses, where she hitched rides, the names of the roads, the approximate travel times, and the names of towns at each stop. These details are an important part of campesinx storytelling not only because they speak to the authenticity of the story, but they also instruct listeners *on how to move through the route* should listeners choose to do so themselves. After hitching a series of rides to get to San Salvador, she describes encountering a Salvadoran Army officer standing at the front line of the urban combat zone where her brother is located. She describes her confrontation with the officer, who has just told her that she cannot pass the line where he is standing.

"Yes," I said, "I'm going to pass."

He told me "Well, pass, but if something happens to you from here to there, it's not our problem."

"No," I said to him. "It's not your problem." I went running.

The lakes of blood. The lakes of blood.

The storyteller slowed down and looked around the table as she repeated, "The lakes of blood. The lakes of blood." She was getting us, the listeners, to focus on how terrible things used to be in another place, where we were not. Her *historia* then transitioned into the key lesson of the narrative: "Because in all reality, who has always been with us is God. And I feel that he is the only one who has guided us. He brought us to this country, and I give him thanks because he has given me this country—to have a better life for me, my children, and even my mother." As a former Catholic and current atheist, listening to metanarratives of migration that included God guiding migrants into El Salvador was not what I necessarily wanted to hear, and I will admit that I was originally drawn to the gory and traumatizing aspects of her testimony (that I could use to paint Salvadorans as refugees fleeing violence) as opposed to the metaphysical component of her testimony. But in practicing a grounded-theory approach, where I repeatedly had to code and recode and conduct more interviews on the themes I detected, I couldn't ignore metaphysical renderings of migration. For some campesinxs, migration was an embryonic act of liberation.

In El Norteño's diasporic networks, memories of liberative movement eschewed epistemically privileged characterizations of the unilaterally poor campesinx. Liberation theologians Leonardo Boff and Clodovis Boff write that "the situation of the oppressed is defined not only by their oppressors but also by the way in which they react to oppression, resist it, and fight to set themselves free from it. The poor cannot be understood without including their dimension as social subjects or co-agents—though submerged ones—of the historical process. This means that any analysis of the world of the poor has to take account not only of their oppressors but also of their own history and efforts at liberation, however embryonic these may be."[32] A rural woman describing how she migrated away from experiences of terror and was *brought by God* to the United States could be framed as an embryonic act of liberation among the rural poor. A rural woman using a curse word that *"liberates me* from so much shit!" is another embryonic utterance of liberation. Similar to Deleuze and Guattari's rhizomes,[33] it seemed that old concepts of liberation had splintered and developed beyond my scholarly understanding of what popular liberation theology was and what it meant to campesinxs who were both affected by and interpretive of it.

During the Salvadoran Civil War, liberation theology was a spiritually charged, socially critical framework that advocated for the liberation of the oppressed and asked practitioners to confront topics such as socioeconomic inequality through analytic approaches such as Marxist analysis. Irina Carlota Silber writes that in the practices associated with liberation theology, including "the social organization, practices, and consciousness-raising of CEBs (Christian Ecclesiastical Base Communities), many people had their first democratic experiences and critiques of social injustice."[34] Liberation theology was often associated with the insurgency during the civil war, and even priests who were perceived as mobilizing communities into action could be subject to extrajudicial killings. Several intellectuals who wrote on liberation theology were executed by U.S.-trained special forces in 1989 at La Universidad Centroamericana (the Central American University, or UCA) in El Salvador. To the United States during the Cold War, liberation theology in El Salvador presented a similar perceived threat as jihad in the Middle East. Popular liberation theology (as opposed to professional or pastoral liberation theology) is the type of theology that emerges among the people,[35] which in El Salvador implied the rural poor (campesinxs).

When I began conducting research with couriers in 2015, I encountered rural Salvadorans spread out across the United States who attended Catholic mass and who talked about the deaths of Rutilio Grande and Archbishop Romero. The repetition of these topics in my data obliged me to better investigate and understand what liberation theology was in order to understand its popular interpretations among campesinxs who referenced it in telling me stories about their personal experiences with liberation. For El Norteño's campesinxs, the act of migration itself was not just a *fleeing* of civil-war violence but an intentional movement with spiritual underpinnings. Historian Molly Todd, writing on the agency of Chalateco refugees during the Salvadoran Civil War, suggests that "at the core of the campesino challenge was the issue of sovereignty. As the Salvadoran state strove for control—often 'performing' its power through military violence—campesinos transformed their individual and political bodies into weapons. They retained as much control as possible over these bodies. They moved them (or didn't move them) to make political statements, and they maintained physical and political attachments to and engagement with their patria."[36] Todd frames the mass exodus of Salvadorans during the civil war not as a passive experience of victimization but rather as a radical form of organized movement that could be compared and reconciled with stories like Exodus from the Christian bible.[37] This reconciliation of action with scripture and the organized movement of rural bodies speaks to hermeneutical and practical mediations of liberation theology and arose repeatedly during data collection, implying that migration is itself an embryonic form of popular liberation.

Liberation theology has historically overemphasized the economic aspects of poverty and underemphasized other types of oppression.[38] The motivations and experiences of poor Salvadoran campesinxs have been undertheorized and absolutized in mainstream academic discourse, boiling inequality and domination down to nothing more than equating the suffering of the rural poor with class oppression. Theologian Marcella Althaus-Reid writes that "not every poor woman is heterosexual, nor do heterosexual women have homogenous behavior either. Sexuality and poverty combine themselves in different ways and reality is constituted with variations. Oppression ramifies itself and is less contained than liberationists used to think."[39] Whether it is campesinxs using metaphysical renderings to describe narratives of movement or queer communist Catholics "throwing empire" in drag imaginaries, the popular and embryonic forms of liberation theology undermine epistemically privileged conceptualizations of campesinxs in classical liberation theology as the unilateral "rural poor."

During my second round of data collection, I interviewed a Chalateco gay man living in Denver. I met him through a courier he uses to sends clothes, shoes, and shirts back home to his family in rural Chalatenango. In return, his family sends him cheese and bread. They were typical parcels sent by an atypical interview subject. He was atypical because he had openly admitted his sexuality to me in the interview. He remembered how things used to be back when he left El Norteño: "There they rape the gays. . . . The guys, those who are men, *supposedly men*, say, 'Well, he's a faggot, so he has to be raped,' and, well, they rape him. . . . They don't consider that if they fuck a man, they are gay. . . . For them, they are 'men.' But they commit the evil of raping another man." He had found a new space for himself in Colorado, one where he did not feel fearful of, nor defined by, his sexuality. For him, in this new place, his sexuality was simply a *part* of him. This particular man had not been back to El Norteño since he left, but our interview was still shrouded in secrecy—he wanted to make sure I would not share his identity with anyone in or from El Norteño. On that note, I asked him that if he could say one thing to people from El Norteño, what would it be? He said, "That they accept us as we are. That we are all humans. We all deserve respect . . . the thing is that *before the eyes of God*, we are human beings, and one has to give respect and love because we are from the same place. We are Salvadorans." Again, I heard a spiritual interpretation of collective experience spoken by a campesino migrant that was directed to other Salvadorans. But in this context, the oppressors that he was referencing were the same that have been historically recognized as victims under the framework of classical liberation theology. That is to say, poor campesinos who experienced class oppression in popular liberation theology were also this man's rapists and oppressors. When I asked him how he would like to address Salvadorans, he spoke of God. In the contradictions of campesinx life, where gay men are raped with impunity but where there are also emerging drag events with queens who imagine transnational enterprises, a gay campesino could hold onto his religious convictions without being overcome by the queer hating that permeates particular factions of Salvadoran society.[40]

Intra-campesinx forms of oppression have given rise to the ways in which micronetworks have formed within El Norteño's diaspora. Oppression carries the capacity to induce fear, and in the face of great oppression, it is not surprising that individuals may choose exit routes that unshackle them from that fear. Marcella Althaus-Reid claims that "the fear of homosexuality in Latin America surpasses any other fear, and it is an active fear which silences and suppress[es] sexualities."[41] When I asked one gay Chalateco migrant to Denver about his first gay experience in El Salvador, he responded, "The first friend I had, I looked at him walking, but I never spoke to him, he was just herding animals—cows, that type of thing. Well, I saw him one morning, and I asked him, 'Are you gay?' And he said, 'Yes, but shut up; don't make any noise about it.' And he asked me, 'And you?' 'Yes, shut up; don't make any noise about it.' That's how I began to get to know him. He lives with me now." While some queer campesinxs lived with family, others lived with each other. Further, some re-created heteronormative family dynamics within same-sex groups of individuals living together, where traditional family roles of a mother, father, and children emerged among friends living in same-sex and same-sexual-orientation households.

The liberation afforded by the act of migration to the United States is slowly shifting perceptions of sexuality in El Norteño's diaspora, which includes the development of rural imaginaries about what is possible both here and there. At the time I was collecting data for this book, expressions of queerness, homosexuality, and bisexuality had already emerged, rarely but also publicly, in parts of the Salvadoran countryside. Adolescent queers in particular increasingly felt that there is less of a stigma in the expression of gender or sexual nonconformance, in part because of social media exposure and in part because of the transnational role models they have available to them in the twenty-first century. Among migrants who have lived for some time in the United States and whose open expression has made headway with transnational family networks, there is also an emergent rural sexual liberation occurring in the countryside.[42] Sexuality illustrates shifts in the Salvadoran countryside that dissolve epistemically privileged renderings of the poor, backward, oppressed, criminalized, passive, and reactive Salvadoran campesino. The Salvadoran countryside is also a social space with hybridized cultural elements that sometimes put factions of "educated," cosmopolitan, yet homophobic Salvadorans in San Salvador to absolute shame.

IMAGINARIES AND THE SYSTEM OF POSSIBILITIES IN EL NORTEÑO

In rural Chalatenango, potential migrants perceive the United States at once as a viable space for liberation and as a nation-state that seeks to evict Salvadorans. It is openly assumed that the United States is a place of economic mobility and individualism but also xenophobia and relative socioeconomic difficulties. In Colorado, pot smokers and queer campesinxs will find relatively "better" access to services, rights, and freedoms of expression. Movement away from El Salvador was and continuously is an act of liberation that transects class, gender, and sexual forms of oppression and that reshapes the Salvadoran countryside. This reshaping is an exportation of not simply North American values but the way in which cultural hybrids are rendered by campesinxs who move through transnational space. The reliance and doubling back on Civil War–era liberation theology to conceptualize sexuality and curse words in the present is not the result of assimilated Salvadorans exporting North American values back to El Norteño, but rather this possibility is potentiated by campesinxs' exposure to North American social environments. Regardless of how difficult the experience of migration might be, migration and all that it promises is within the state of the system of possibilities for campesinxs from El Norteño. Cyclical migrants, deportees, and constant communications within transnational kinship networks shape imaginaries in El Norteño. The imaginary is a productive site where new possibilities are constantly emerging.

In her work on the Salvadoran imaginary, Cecilia Rivas details how imaginaries develop around migration—the generation of connections to one's home country—and around deep local changes that occur relative to globalization. Rivas writes that "the opportunity to connect to the outside world exists through the Salvadorans who already reside outside El Salvador. They can provide the way out of poverty and underdevelopment—not solely through their remittances, but because of their 'unequaled human experience.'"[43] Tight transnational connections within El Norteño's diaspora, mechanized through mainstream media outlets as well as social media, provide some of the foundations through which syncretic imaginaries emerge. Through Instagram and Facebook feeds, youth visualize possible futures in the United States, replete with expectations of what to wear, where they could be living, and how they might be able to grow into their imagined selves. Even the harsh experiences of migration through Mexico and tales of time in detention can be conceptualized as a price to pay for the elusive but collective promise of liberations afforded by migration.

From the vantage point of rural El Salvador in the twenty-first century, I listened to imaginaries that ranged from the practical to totally absurd. The practical included the campesinx migrant "with vision." Some youth, those with "vision," might already form *nostos* imaginaries before leaving El Norteño. They wouldn't be tempted to spend all their money after making it to the United States, and they imagined strategies they would employ after arriving in the United States, including going only once to a clothing store in order to buy weather-appropriate clothes and avoiding malls and other recreational outlets where peer pressure could lead to spending money. Living isolated lifestyles in the United States to scrimp and save could provide a better life in El Salvador, but the felt shame and stigma of nonconsumerist orientations in the United States (consider the venomous microaggressions I experienced in a hipster coffee shop in Denver) may eventually unravel some of these strategies. Totally absurd renderings of the American dream included queer Chalatecxs joking about finding a same-sex gringx partner to marry in order to legally migrate to the United States. In writing about queer diasporas, Gayatri Gopinath reminds us that "'demanding the impossible' points to the failure of the nation to live up to its promises of democratic egalitarianism, and dares to envision other possibilities of existence exterior to dominant systems of logic."[44] As I conducted research for this book, the absurd machinations of some queer campesinxs became an accessible reality when the U.S. Supreme Court ruled that state-level bans on same-sex marriage were unconstitutional. It turns out that campesinxs' imaginaries, no matter how queer or marginalized they may be, could be quite perceptive of one nation-state's behavior.[45]

CONCLUSION

In El Norteño's diasporic communities, the emergence of hybrid cultural forms reflects both disparate expressions of power and productive impulses that implicate memory. I tried to show how some social factors particular to Colorado and El Norteño shape and inform what is real, remembered, and perceived to be within the realm of the possible for campesinxs in diasporic networks. As El Norteño's migrants draw upon the past to understand points of conflict in the present, they also use their own conceptualizations of the past to remember acts of transnational migration. Diasporic imaginaries offer alternatives to and simultaneously undermine the formulaic "push factors" that are studied, known, and treated as points of intervention by states to influence human mobility.

This final chapter concludes part 1 of this book, which aimed to orient read-ers to some dimensions of collective memory and memory practices among campesinxs in El Norteño's diaspora. I concluded with an analysis of campesinx imaginaries that illustrates how campesinx diasporic remembering is implicated in future prospections of transnational experience. Part 2 of this book explores an inversion of campesinx remembering by focusing on a collective system of forgetting. I try to ground that analysis in the active memories of El Norteño's campesinxs, who continue to transmit knowledge, produce pleasures, and develop prospections despite weighted collective states of oblivion. I refer to this particular system of forgetting as the U.S. fugue state, and the next three chapters are focused on its powerful tendency to strategize, intervene, and forget.

PART II THE U.S. FUGUE STATE

5 · SILENCE AND SYSTEMATIC FORGETTING

As this Commission submits its report, El Salvador is embarked on a positive and irreversible process of consolidation of internal peace and modification of conduct for the maintenance of a genuine, lasting climate of national coexistence. The process of reconciliation is restoring the nation's faith in itself and in its leaders and institutions.

—The Commission on the Truth for El Salvador, 1993[1]

The Truth Commission? The truth? I've known so many cases of white-collar crime. People in power can basically do what they want in this country. *The Truth Commission*—that was just another political thing.

—Salvadoran courier, 2017

In the memories of El Norteño's diasporic networks, campesinx remembering preserved and transmitted knowledge, it moved parcels that provoked more memories, and it was invoked to imagine. Amid the forms of remembering I encountered, I also heard alternative memories of how my parental generation's U.S. tax dollars were spent, approximately three decades ago, in places like El Norteño. I listened to memories that narrated the impact of U.S. counterinsurgency efforts abroad. The memories made sense, but much of the information I received was new to me. Listening to campesinxs' memories encouraged me to first acknowledge and then examine the silences implicated in my own forgetting.

One evening, in El Salvador, I was typing up my field notes and filling in gaps that were scattered across them. I was reviewing what seemed like an overbearingly meticulous record of the mundane, checking for missingness and asking various friends to help me fill in the blanks. Mateo, one of El Norteño's couriers, was reclined in a hammock. I fired off questions about parcel weight restrictions and pricing, and he dutifully responded to each one. When I was done, Mateo asked me if there was anything else I was missing. The thought of *data I could be missing* haunted me. I thought for a while before answering him. I asked Mateo to tell me about his first memory in life. He replied quickly, "It's when I was under the bed, and there was a grenade explosion. It was during the war. . . . It was one of the windows in my house where the grenade landed and exploded. . . . We couldn't be sure who threw it. . . . We got underneath the bed . . . the crib, for protection every time there was a confrontation—because I was still using a crib back then." He wasn't quite sure who was to blame, but civil-war violence was Mateo's first memory in life. I also asked Mateo to jump ahead and articulate his dreams of the future. He stood up and put his hand in the air to ensure I gave total attention to the statement he was about to make. "The objective is to leave," he said.

Sometimes, when scholars study topics such as migration, it is easy to forget that migrants themselves have also done quite a bit of thinking and even theorizing about the places they have traversed. Mateo has spent considerably more time than me cycling between the United States and El Salvador. He traverses an appreciable portion of space in El Norteño's diaspora regularly, and he has direct experience with agents who protect the borders of both countries. I asked Mateo to tell me his opinion regarding *the relationship* between two nation-states: El Salvador and the United States. Again, he replied quickly, "Countries like this one—the U.S. *dominates* them. Countries like ours need money, and the U.S. does what they want with us. We live in the shadow of the U.S. You already know this, Mike. Gringos are like that. They treat us like shit."

Mateo and I continued talking, but I was nagged by what I initially perceived to be an aberration in his thinking. I found it contradictory that Mateo desired to migrate to the same place he characterized as abusive toward Salvadorans. This was an often-repeated conversation between me and Mateo, and I have listened to Mateo draw out his arguments about how the United States dominates El Salvador and then describe why he would like to live in the United States. While seemingly contradictory, his stories make a great deal of sense. I hear a narrative of subjugation in transnational space, and I hear a friend express a desire to transcend.

What at first appeared to be logical deviations between spoken memories and expressed affects regarding the United States I later found to be characteristic of the discursive silences that emerge in the absence of reconciliation and the continued structuration of violence in El Norteño's fields.[2] Silence frustrates mainstream notions of justice that dominate tribunals, courts, and truth commissions, and silence inculcates actors in the memory field. Edna Lomsky-Feder conceptualizes the "memory field" as an internally ordered field governed by social power relations that entrench distribution criteria, regulating what memories are available and monitoring the degree of criticism that can be voiced of the past.[3] In the memory field of El Norteño's diaspora, intergenerational silences that do not illuminate components of the past can be both reparative to those who have suffered and corrosive to the capacity of abusers (be they individuals, organizations, or even departments of a government) to acknowledge, reflect, and reconcile. Silence provides benefits, however problematic they may be, to both perpetrators and survivors. Silence is often self-imposed through cognitive processes. Anthropologist Tine Gammeltoft writes that "like the violence of extreme events, everyday violence is often silenced. Not, it seems, because words falter, but because people do not want to speak them, fearing stigmatization, condemnation, and exclusion. The structures of dominance in which violence is exercised often operate in such a way that the victim is held responsible, being assumed by himself or herself and others to have provoked and deserved the violence."[4] In the context of campesinxs who are conscious of the abuses of power but who express desires to migrate toward its epicenter, silence permits reparative forgetting, it corrodes traces of state culpability, and it allows new generations to move forward as it inculcates them with evolving silences.

Campesinxs in El Norteño have experienced ample exposure to violence during both the Salvadoran Civil War and the present-day conflict between Salvadoran gangs and the state systems that target, incarcerate, and execute them. In this context, silence is distributed through the memory field of campesinxs who compose El Norteño's diaspora. The silences surrounding the experiences of violence and its consequences in El Norteño both point to and obfuscate distributive powers in the fields of memory and violence. Silence simultaneously allows for resilience, impunity, peace, and systematic forgetting. Through its repetition in the field, silence can act as both a cause and a component of intergenerational forgetting.

INTERGENERATIONAL FORGETTING

The inculcation of silence is one way in which collective forgetting is produced among memory makers. I will describe this phenomenon as I perceived it in some of my friends before realizing that I was also personally subject to the same type of forgetting as a U.S. citizen.

Within one family representing three generations of campesinxs from El Norteño, most of whom have migrated inside of El Salvador and cyclically between El Norteño and the United States, I tracked the memory of *La Matanza*—or "The Killing." La Matanza occurred in 1932, when thousands of indigenous and Ladino peasants were executed following a military-led coup.[5] Some adults heard stories about La Matanza only from other farmworkers.

Others retained the memories of family members who survived the violence. I have listened to corn farmers in Sonsonate tell transmitted family memories about a time when blood flowed in the fields, and people slept in trees to avoid the slaughter. That slaughter is a horrific memory of genocide that has been transmitted within some campesinx families still living today, and it is a quickly eroding memory.

In one diasporic family, a mestizo grandfather who survived La Matanza in 1932 (he was a campesino, but he was not part of the insurgency, and he is dead at the time I am writing this book) told his adult daughter about his memory of the event. His daughter was fifty-five at the time I conducted my interview with her in El Norteño, and she remembers her father's description of La Matanza in 1932: "My dad . . . said that . . . he was one of the innocent ones. . . . What he said is that he had a little bed . . . so he said that in order to avoid the bullets, he slept underneath the bed and that he felt fear. That—yes, I remember my father telling me about that. And it was really sad. To think of them under the bed like that, under there because of fear." The daughter of a campesino who survived, remembered, and transmitted his memory of La Matanza of 1932 grew up to survive the Salvadoran Civil War. During the civil war, she gave birth to her daughter in El Norteño. Her daughter has since migrated to the United States. The granddaughter of the survivor of La Matanza, who is now in her thirties and living in Long Island, is a friend of mine. As I was interviewing her one day about her memories of migration, I brought up La Matanza. At thirty-one years of age in 2015, she replied that she was *born* during La Matanza. I said this was impossible because La Matanza happened approximately fifty-two years before she was born. She countered that she both was born during and survived La Matanza—the concept of a mass killing so resonated with her experience of the Salvadoran Civil War that she was missing my reference to the 1932 historical event that is also referred to as La Matanza. She did not realize that her grandfather survived that massacre as a child. Over three generations, intrafamilial transmission of the memory of a genocide terminated with the third generation.[6] The upcoming fourth generation, all of whom are now U.S. citizens, are unlikely to be told any stories about their great-grandfather's survival of La Matanza. Silence inculcates, and over time, it structures forgetting.

At the time I interviewed my friend, I was just as ignorant that North American warships were rushed to the coast of El Salvador to prepare for an intervention in the 1932 indigenous uprising,[7] and I imagine that some of my fellow U.S. citizens have grandparents and great-grandparents with memories, perhaps unspoken, of that event. My friend and I both experienced types of forgetting that involved violence in and around the nation-states we were born into. What haunts me most about my friend telling me she was born during La Matanza is that in the Salvadoran countryside today, one still hears about *matanzas* (killings). That word, *matanza,* is sometimes used to refer to phases that rural communities go through when particular actors are taken out. I describe an incident from one such contemporary matanza at the beginning of the next chapter.

SYSTEMATIC FORGETTING AND TRAUMA

Intergenerational forgetting reflects an inculcation of silence, and everyday silence permits survivors of violence to remake their everyday lives, particularly when justice is inaccessible. Silence permits elderly civil-war survivors the ability to smile and to participate in collective expressions of warmth, kindness, and belonging. Silence also permits impunity. I am not arguing for silence, but I have grown suspicious of justice practices that abhor it at the expense of individuals who are asked to break their silences in the name of "justice for all," particularly when liberal notions of justice remain inaccessible to a large portion of the world's population. Kimberly Theidon writes that our historical époque is characterized by a "faith in memory—not its infallibility but rather the work it is alleged to do in deterring future atrocities."[8] Silence is sometimes what helps individuals deter their own future atrocities. The dynamics of silence can also be used to generate power maps of the memory field, where past experiences of violence come into contact with emotional and cognitive states as they are rendered in collective memory.

There is a difference between *not wanting* to recall past events and *not being able* to recall past events, but trauma stemming from violence has a temporal effect in social memory that can accomplish both, sometimes simultaneously in the same person. Trauma is also a biologically mediated phenomenon, implicating neuroendocrine responses that affect the body. Psychiatric disorders with symptoms that directly affect individual memory include post-traumatic stress disorder, which has symptoms including the inability to recall key features of the trauma.[9] In a less biomedical rendering of trauma, Judith Halberstam writes that forgetting is "a gate-keeping mechanism, a way of protecting the self from unbearable memories. And so shock and trauma, as so many scholars have noted, engender a form of forgetting, a cocooning of the self in order to allow the self to grow separate from the knowledge that might destroy it."[10] As a survival mechanism and/or symptom, avoiding triggers of the trauma and not recalling it engenders a silence that allows both survivors and aggressors to remake their everyday lives, even when those everyday lives reflect unjust conditions. Looking backward at similar personal past experiences may generate a range of memories that are narrated and structured in different ways. Traces of power are embedded in the collective memories and forgetting of those who survive violence, and those traces are corroded by silences that can be simultaneously ameliorative for those who remain silent. In survivors of gender-based violence, Gammeltoft writes that survivors "may be aware of their own fragile social position—and yet try to forget about it, to expel it from consciousness."[11] While campesinxs I interviewed had embedded perceptions that the United States was to blame for much of the violence that occurred in their homelands, what would remembering and delineating those details do to rectify that situation in the absence of adequate transitional justice?[12] People move on given the circumstances, with silence and forgetting helping them do so.

As I collected and delivered parcels for campesinxs split by national divides in El Norteño's diaspora, I became familiar with narratives that flowed through communities and collectives, but I also noticed that key memories in those narratives were subject to erosion. They were memories that were integral to understanding the human-rights abuses that some of my friends had suffered and were still suffering today, and they were also memories that spoke of the way my parents' generation and I paid taxes that funded the structuration of such abuses. Intergenerational silences in transnational space both masked an understanding of those abuses and allowed current generations of campesinxs to move forward with their lives. These silences also allow many U.S. taxpayers to continue engaging in the structuration of harm without consciousness of the harms that are being structured with U.S. tax dollars. I use the vignette that follows to illustrate how the emergent silence surrounding the death of a mayor in El Norteño both structures forgetting and inherently muddies an understanding of the hierarchy producing the harm associated with past U.S. counterinsurgency efforts in El Salvador.

A LEGACY OF U.S. COUNTERINSURGENCY EFFORTS IN EL SALVADOR DURING THE COLD WAR

As a result of the individuals I was connected to in El Norteño's diasporic networks, I repeatedly heard about a mayor who was executed during the Salvadoran Civil War (approximately three decades prior to conducting my field research) and whose memory I began to make the explicit focus of my inquiries for well over the course of a year. To avoid revealing the identities of his survivors, I have changed particular details, including his name, and I thus refer to him here as Antonio Rivas.

To reconstruct the events of Antonio's death, I begin with the memory of a daughter of a man (now dead) in El Norteño who had the gift of revelation during the Salvadoran Civil War. Her father could foretell certain events through his dreams. She told me how her father dreamed of Antonio's death a few months before Antonio was executed. In the weeks leading up to his death, surviving friends and family all seem to remember how Antonio would say, "Soon, they are going to kill me." And soon *they* did.

Every time I heard memories of Antonio Rivas, memory makers would focus on details about how he liked to drink *chaparro* (corn whiskey) and how he liberally used curse words. In the United States, when I asked one of Antonio's surviving friends about Antonio, she looked up into the sky and said *hijueputa* (son of a bitch) before breaking into a fit of laughter. *Hijueputa* was one of Antonio's favorite expressions, and this was how she remembered him thousands of days and miles from the time and site of his death. Those memories often brought smiles to faces and injected laughter into the soundscape of memories surrounding Antonio.

I have grown accustomed to these kinds of details about Antonio—warm and relatable memories about how he used to talk and what he liked to drink. For most of the time I asked people about Antonio, these were the salient memories that emerged. These are relatively mundane details when compared with those that are most difficult to excavate—the particulars surrounding who killed Antonio and the reason they killed him. Through a number of Antonio's surviving family members and friends who are split between the United States and El Salvador, I began to iron out the executed mayor's wartime political affiliation. This was a surprisingly difficult thing to do, given that the political affiliation of a mayor assassinated during a civil war should be a relatively straightforward detail to ascertain. One of Antonio's surviving children told me Antonio was affiliated with the political left, and another child told me he was on the political right. One child said Antonio was too close to the insurgents—or maybe the opposing army. She could not remember. At first, it was unclear to me where Antonio was on the political spectrum, thereby making it confusing to infer who his allies and enemies were.

When I asked who killed Antonio, one of Antonio's surviving family members told me about the bombings in the mountains of El Norteño during his time in office. This person remembers that this was one of Antonio's central concerns that got him killed. Campesinx memory makers are aware that the U.S.-backed Salvadoran Army had airplanes and were bombing guerrilla strongholds in the mountains, but these identifying details are left out of the narration of memories that are all too tied up in the present. As I dug for more information, some community members told me that men in a pickup truck killed Antonio. One might infer that a mayor who was remembered for having a problem with the bombing situation in the mountains would certainly be a mayor who had a problem with the Salvadoran Army during the Salvadoran Civil War—a frightening position to occupy in Chalatenango during the war. It is still a frightening thing to talk about in towns where killers continue to roam free as neighbors. "Men in a pickup truck" are the culprits of killing Antonio for his concern about his constituents being killed in the mountains. Antonio's political affiliations, his agenda, and the larger forces he came into conflict with are all but gone from the general utterances of those who narrate his memory and death.

In one of my interviews with one of Antonio's children, I asked her who killed her father. She remembers a word used to describe the people who were responsible for killing him. The word meant "only for us." I pushed harder on this detail. What was that word? She responded that it was "the oligarchy or something like that." Social-science terms used to describe a small group of people having a large amount of power in class-stratified El Salvador were words that were silenced in El Salvador during the 1980s and remained difficult to recall in 2017.

I spent a year trying to find out what happened to Antonio Rivas, and I always wound up spiraling into conflicting details about Antonio's political affiliations and who actually killed him. As I tried to buckle down on the simple, solid details of who killed Antonio and why, the memories of those who survived him became transient and vague. I went to a small museum in Chalatenango where the curator had a photographic record of all the mayors in Antonio's municipality dating back to before the Salvadoran Civil War. Antonio's predecessor and replacement were pictured, but his was the only picture missing from the museum record. It is as though he never existed. Was I being led down a false path? Was Antonio even really a mayor? I pointed this out to the museum curator, and he confirmed that I was correct—yes, Antonio was actually a mayor who was executed, and he thought it was curious that Antonio's was the only picture missing from the record. He promised that he would try to remedy the problem by hunting down a photo for the picture frame.

I almost abandoned my effort to find out what happened to Antonio. It was Antonio's secretary who, after knowing her for about a year and interviewing her numerous times, finally explained who killed him. It is not lost on me that she filled in the gaps from the vantage point of the United States, decades after his death and thousands of miles away from postwar Chalatenango. We sat in her manicured backyard as she explained that Antonio was a member of the Christian Democratic Party (PDC), the party represented by "the little fish. That was it. . . . He won the mayor's office with that party . . . but he never finished his term because they killed him before it was over. . . . For *them,* the little fish was revolutionary."[13] She cryptically referred to *them* when she remembered those who killed Antonio. I pushed on this detail too. She leaned in and, in a near whisper, provided precise names. She clarified that *they* (the killers) were *patrulleros* (patrolmen or patrollers) from ORDEN (La Organización Democrática Nacionalista). As soon as she mentioned that ORDEN was involved, I, too, became silent. I stopped asking questions about Antonio Rivas.

ORDEN

During the Vietnam War (1955–1975), the U.S. Central Intelligence Agency (CIA) and U.S. Department of Defense (DoD) helped develop the Phoenix

Program as a counterinsurgency effort to destroy the Việt Cộng. Despite the publicly recognized disastrous consequences of the Vietnam War, U.S. counterinsurgency tactics that germinated in Vietnam did not remain contained there. The U.S. government took part in developing and relying upon a counterinsurgency program for El Salvador based on the Phoenix Program and aimed at identifying and eliminating rebel leaders and sympathizers.[14] It was called ORDEN, and it was founded in El Salvador in the early 1960s.[15] ORDEN also means "order" in Spanish.

ORDEN was a right-wing vigilante and paramilitary branch of the Sistema Nacional de Inteligencia (National System of Intelligence), which later became ANESAL (Agencia Nacional de Servicios Especiales de El Salvador, or the National Agency of Special Services of El Salvador). ANESAL was an intelligence unit tied to the Salvadoran National Police, Treasury Police, National Guard, and Border Police. Both ORDEN and ANESAL were under the direction of the National Guard's General José Alberto Medrano.[16]

General Medrano was on the U.S. CIA payroll and was sent on a three-month tour of Vietnam to observe U.S. counterinsurgency techniques.[17] Upon his return to El Salvador, Medrano worked with the CIA to build an intelligence apparatus that became a clearinghouse for information gathered from various intelligence units (the Immigration Service, National Police, and the National Guard), and ORDEN allowed intelligence to be gathered in rural towns and villages.[18] Beyond being involved in the development of ORDEN, the CIA provided lists of individuals deemed subversive to ANESAL.[19] Ideas of counterinsurgency grounded in Vietnam War–era strategies were impressed upon the Salvadoran state through government-coordinated efforts, including reports from Public Safety Program advisers, the U.S. military mission, and the Army Mobile Training Teams that reinforced messages about the external threat of communism and the need for civilian-based counterinsurgency efforts in El Salvador.[20] By the time of the Salvadoran Civil War (1979), ORDEN was officially decommissioned but remained active as a functional security network of approximately sixty-five thousand to one hundred thousand grassroots members that posed a direct threat to campesinx worker organizations (deemed insurgents) across the Salvadoran countryside.[21] ORDEN affiliates received work benefits and were provided arms to persecute campesinx opponents, and they contributed to a culture of violence, disappearances, and terror throughout rural El Salvador.[22]

ORDEN was active both before and during the Salvadoran Civil War in towns such as El Norteño. One campesina who regularly sent parcels to her daughter in New York described how she remembers ORDEN first appearing in town: "There were some people who were pastors . . . who came to preach, and after, they would carry out half of their plan to preach, but really, that is where they were given training. I remember that is how it started. They said they were evangelizing and all of that, and they called the youth, and there they gave them training. It wasn't a prayer, but it was a 'restructuring' that they were given. I remember that." Campesinxs I interviewed described how El Norteño's evangelical Christians carried identity cards to prove their ORDEN affiliation so as to avoid harassment from army personnel. On any occasion during the civil war when the army pulled its forces out of El Norteño, residents remained vigilant about who they were seen talking to or what was said because they knew ORDEN informants could generate lethal rumors. Everyday paranoia and suspicion of fellow community members was one of ORDEN's legacies.

In targeting subversives, ORDEN affiliates also targeted *thinking* that could be associated with insurgency. This occurred at a time when, as Matthew Levin describes in *Cold War University*, foreign revolutions "that posed even a potential threat to American interests were labeled as communist no matter the real underlying conditions."[23] During the civil-war years, using "communist" terminology (the same words used that are also used in classical sociology to analyze class stratification) could generate ORDEN informant attention that might result in an extrajudicial killing. In Colorado, I interviewed a civil-war survivor who remembered that simply using words such as *bourgeoisie* to characterize class inequality could generate unwanted and lethal attention from ORDEN informants. He recalled how in the 1970s, just before the civil war really got going in El Norteño, "there was a killing of professors. . . . I remember it well; they captured some of them . . . and they never came back. So I went . . . to the town police, and at the town police, someone showed me—there were some rooms, and there . . . were bloody palm prints where they bludgeoned them to death. They killed those people, and they carried them out in a red car. . . . They say that they brought them to the sea, attached them to stones, and the sea consumed them, and they never came back." The story seemed outlandish, but when I spoke with fishermen in El Salvador's coastal zones about their childhood memories of the civil war in La Libertad (an area often assumed to have been unaffected by the civil-war violence), those fishermen remembered truckloads of bodies that used to be dumped from the cliffs into the Pacific Ocean.

After telling me that ORDEN patrulleros killed Antonio, his secretary added that "they did a lot of bad things. . . . They went around with their guns—that's why they felt strong. . . . The soldiers armed them." She remembered that those same ORDEN patrulleros were the ones who entered people's homes, tied up the fathers, and raped girls in front of the families. After a year of searching for information on who killed Antonio, answers were provided to me among Salvadoran migrants living in the United States. Knowing that these men were still alive, I chose to stop asking questions about Antonio Rivas (both for his survivors' safety and for my own).

A few months after I learned that ORDEN patrolmen killed Antonio, I was helping a courier load parcels into suitcases when a farm worker arrived at the house. He was going to travel with the courier on his next trip to the United States to visit his children who had migrated there. He had an endless smile and curiously chatted with us as we worked. We meandered through conversations, and the old man eventually began to talk about Antonio, a mayor he once knew, whom we all had heard of, and he recalled how Antonio used to drink and liked to curse. He laughed, and so did several of us in the room. When the old man finished speaking, I mindlessly interjected a question, clarifying that "Antonio was killed by ORDEN patrulleros, right?" The man's face went blank; he bowed his head and said nothing. As I write this now, I feel guilty for having been so obtuse. Without looking up, the old man muttered that the same ORDEN patrulleros who killed Antonio also killed his eighteen-year-old son during the war.

DISILLUSIONMENT

In 1993, the year after the Salvadoran Civil War ended, the report issued by the Truth Commission for El Salvador attributed 85 percent of the acts of violence to Salvadoran state agents, generally in rural areas, and only 5 percent to the guerrilla resistance.[24] These statistics are often cited to claim that both sides committed acts of violence during the war, but the quantitative disparity points to imbalances of power during the conflict. The Truth Commission's report was followed by the Salvadoran Legislative Assembly's approval of an amnesty law in 1993 (which was recently overturned in 2016)[25] to prevent any prosecutions for human-rights abuses committed during the war. The amnesty law was widely considered to be an achievement of the peace process. The logic behind the amnesty law was that human-rights abuses need not be investigated in order to move forward with the processes of forgiving and forgetting.[26] Annette Georgina Hernández Rivas writes that "the transition period was the propitious moment for the State to assume a policy of memory, which would guarantee that acts of violence not be repeated. In its place, forgetting was institutionalized."[27] This form of institutionalized forgetting is a component of what makes it difficult to reconcile memories of the dead with the fact that rural patrolmen who worked for a counterinsurgency group generated with U.S. support still roam free today. Silence is one of several mechanisms that permit survivors to move forward, and despite campesinxs' willingness to talk about the civil war, silence is salient in the memory field regarding the particulars of the most powerful actors who participated in the civil-war violence.

I found that the silence that coats details of disproportionately imbalanced war crimes was more porous when it involved memories of those who were supposed to be fighting for social justice in the name of the poor but who failed.

In postwar Chalatenango, where there was an appreciable perception among groups of survivors that insurgents failed to accomplish their mission, the vast majority of campesinxs I interviewed showed little to no alliance with insurgents and the political party they subsequently formed that is active today (El Frente Farabundo Martí para la Liberación Nacional, or the FMLN). I should add that I did not study one of the repopulated communities that spent time in Honduran refugee camps and repatriated following the war. However, even in those communities, Irina Carlota Silber observed that "like the deception in Chalatenango, targets of blame are elusive, unclear. The contours of accountability are not discrete. Uncovering who lies is the central entanglement of contemporary El Salvador."[28] I found that in the memory field of El Norteño's diaspora, campesinxs were ready to show me *who lies* by remembering particular harms committed by FMLN commanders, despite general silences distributed to the memories of the quantitatively disproportionate war crimes committed by the Salvadoran state.

This is well illustrated by an interview I had with a Chalateca friend from El Norteño who was living in Long Island and who talked with me at length about the civil war and her personal migration experiences. During the interview, she chose to restructure our interaction and said that she wanted to provide a testimony of something that she experienced. I agreed. She began by saying, "I'm going to say something that is very personal. I don't talk about it, but you're going to finally understand." She recounted,

> I was thirteen years old when . . . the Left [the guerrillas] kidnapped me; I was thirteen years old, just a schoolgirl. In my village, they kidnapped many young people. They brought me to their zone in the mountains. . . . They never put me in combat; they never made me fight; they had me in a place where there were people preparing propaganda.
>
> We made pamphlets to distribute in the village . . . things like that. . . . There were only six of us there, but they never gave me a pistol; I never carried one. Yes, I was with them, but I never shot at anyone. . . . It was really frustrating because they snatched me out of my parents' arms at that age, and terrible things happened to me during that time.
>
> It was only three months, three months of captivity, but yes, I was abused at that age. At thirteen years of age, one of the bosses of the Left [the guerrillas]—he, I remember perfectly, in the place where there were six houses . . . they had killed a deer, and a woman from one of the houses helped to prepare everything, and I was helping the woman. When everyone went to sleep . . . he was waiting for me.
>
> I didn't know what it was to have contact with a man—a kiss or anything like that—that part of me had yet to be awakened. . . . He was waiting, he put his gun against me . . . took my clothes off, and he raped me.

My friend's testimony depicts child sexual assault committed by a commander of the guerrilla forces against a rural, poor, civilian minor held in captivity by insurgents during the Salvadoran Civil War. It points to abhorrent acts committed by insurgents, forces that were supposed to be protecting the poor and fighting for their liberation as opposed to raping their children.[29]

More often than not, I came upon memories spoken by campesinxs who had something to say about the inconsistencies of the wartime insurgents. In contrast to the lengthy effort it took for me to find out who killed Antonio Rivas (living perpetrators who also raped women but who were supported by the state's counterinsurgency effort), stories about war crimes committed by insurgents seemed to flow into consciousnesses with greater ease. One narrative of culpability is buried, confused, and corroded, while the other is more accessible. Both are traumatic memories, but the power of silence doesn't hold as strong in the face of disillusionment. The larger forces that the wartime insurgents set out to resist are no longer the focus of critical memories. In postwar El Norteño, couriers and their clients continue to have the perception that "the U.S. does what they want with us," and memories are not urgently needed (nor readily available) to flesh out that argument. Among wartime survivors, I encountered what Irina Carlota Silber describes as a "battle against deception (engaño)."[30] This legacy of the war raises important and problematic issues that still have yet to be adequately addressed (e.g., FMLN commanders raping children), all the while obfuscating the culpability of the agents who were backed by a disproportionately larger amount of power (ORDEN patrolmen). Compared to the FMLN leader who raped a child, the ORDEN patrulleros who raped women were more "protected" by collective silences. Traces of culpability in the memory field appear to deteriorate relative to the hierarchy of the rapists in transnational distributions of power.

If the United States is situated toward the upper echelons of power in the hierarchy of El Norteño's diasporic memory field, it is worth examining how the United States remembers its Cold War self. Unlike the personal, family, and community narratives of the past that I became familiar with while working with Salvadoran couriers, state memories emanate from disparate agents, institutions, and branches of government, with shifting controls of political power over time. There are multiple ways that the state structures remembering, both for the public and for itself. In the following section, I examine one of the numerous ways that U.S. national remembering is structured.

SUSPECT MEMORIALIZATION

Here, I examine one dominant memory framework that the U.S. nation-state has invested in to produce a Cold War memory that fills the memory field's soundscapes with a narrative. While there is not a single state-sponsored memory framework in the United States, there are dominant frameworks that marginalize disruptive or conflicting narratives. Historian Yael Zerubavel describes "collective amnesia" as periods or events "that remain unmarked in the master commemorative narrative. Such periods or events that collective memory suppresses become subjects of collective amnesia. Thus, the construction of the master commemorative narrative exposes the dynamics of remembering and forgetting that underlie the construction of any commemorative narrative: by focusing attention on certain aspects of the past, it necessarily covers up others that are deemed irrelevant or disruptive to the flow of the narrative and ideological message."[31] In the following section, I will examine, through a federally funded memory site, how the United States has invested in one dominant memory framework that provides a "familiar" way of remembering its Cold War nation-state-self. To describe that familiarity, I begin with presidential statements made to the U.S. public that provide context for the messages reinforced by a state-sponsored national historic site that emerged decades later.

Archival footage of Ronald Reagan's public statements made while serving as the president of the United States (and whose years in office spanned the broadest amount of time for any single U.S. president relative to the Salvadoran Civil War) provides context for understanding U.S. national interpretations of itself abroad, particularly in El Salvador, during the Cold War period. In a 1983 address, Ronald Reagan addressed the nation, saying, "Now there was a time when our national security was based on a standing army here within our own borders and shore batteries of artillery along our coast, and of course a navy to keep the sea lanes open for the shipping of things necessary to our well being. The world has changed. Today our national security can be threatened in faraway places. It's up to all of us to be aware of the strategic importance of such places and to be able to identify them."[32]

Although the United States had been engaged in Central American affairs for quite some time prior to 1983,[33] the idea that U.S. national security could be protected by engaging in faraway conflicts renewed for an American public, segments of which were already disillusioned by the war in Vietnam, strategies that resulted in foreign interventions involving military violence abroad. The narrative calls for a level of national consciousness that inhibits critical reflection on how U.S. national security will be achieved by participating in and generating conflicts elsewhere. The narrative focuses on self-protection. It is in line with Anna Tsing's observation that "in popular American fantasies, survival is all about saving oneself by fighting off others."[34] Following the logic of the United States protecting its security by engaging in faraway conflicts, Reagan justified to the U.S. public in 1981 that "what we're actually doing is, at the request of a government in one of our neighboring countries, offering some help against the import or the export into the Western Hemisphere of terrorism, of disruption. And it isn't just El Salvador. That happens to be the target at the moment."[35] The words of a Cold War U.S. president are used to justify engaging in a conflict in El Salvador to keep *terrorism* out of the Western Hemisphere in the early 1980s. Kimberly Theidon writes that "the image of the terrorist is a key figure that organizes political discourse and action in our contemporary world."[36] Though spoken decades ago, Reagan's use of the word *terrorism* resembles ongoing justifications of foreign interventions abroad in the name of U.S. national security. For example, when asked about the indeterminate detention periods of prisoners in Guantanamo Bay, Defense Secretary Donald Rumsfeld stated in 2002 that "the war on terrorism is not over—the effort. These people are committed terrorists. We are keeping them off the street and out of the airlines and out of nuclear power plants and out of ports across this country and across other countries."[37] While the use of the word *terrorists* shifts across foreign landscapes as U.S. interests and strategies change with time, it is also a rallying cry that justifies acts of U.S. national security that repeatedly breach human rights and debase the securities of others elsewhere.

While agents of the state such as previous presidents or secretaries of defense can contextualize the logic of state actions enacted during the past, national historic sites actively construct and provide frameworks for nations to remember their pasts. Anthropologist Geoffrey White argues that state-sponsored memorial sites provide public affirmations, where individuals situate themselves relative to their "imagined national communities" through acts of remembrance.[38] State-sponsored national historic sites, as contrasted to memorials, are one route to understanding how the state takes an active role in structuring memories of its own history.

The U.S. nation-state has generated the Minuteman Missile National Historic Site in Philip, South Dakota. Its website claims, "The essence of history is the story of humanity, the essence of Minuteman Missile National Historic Site is a human story and how it was shaped by the forces of technology to protect freedom and democracy."[39] The site is located where an arsenal of nuclear missiles was strategically hidden in the Great Plains of the United States during the Cold War, and it includes a display of the facility that was designed to launch missiles, manned by missileers, on a moment's notice. As a national historic site, the Minuteman Missile site provides a single example of how the United States participates in the structuration of a Cold War memory of itself.

The Minuteman Missile National Historic Site establishes a timeline for the Cold War period, ranging from the bombing of Hiroshima and Nagasaki in 1945 to the 1993 deactivation of the 66th Missile Squadron[40] (a period from history that encapsulates El Salvador's 1979–1992 civil-war period). The site represents the Cold War period as a multifaceted confrontation between U.S. democratic capitalism and Soviet communist totalitarianism.[41] The site reminds visitors that the United States was engaged in protecting its citizens from communism by stockpiling the most lethal arms available on the planet at the time. The Cold War representations of history offered by the site reinforce Reagan's notion that national security threats to the United States emerge and are resolved in faraway places. Armed self-defense in response to a potential attack, deterring a threat that emerges from a faraway place, is the successful strategy that is monumentalized and collectively remembered.

The site features oral histories, which include interviews with a range of actors, including one activist, but the interviews with U.S. government employees are those that I focus on here to best understand how the U.S. state structures memories of itself. Oral history interviews with missileers who worked at the facility describe individuals sitting on alert to guard the United States. One missileer, when asked how she would like to see the Cold War interpreted through these national sites, describes how "there was a respect for the power this nation had" and that "we served as a deterrent, and that's something to be very proud of, not only as missileers but as a nation—that we were so well armed."[42] Another U.S. federal employee who worked at the facility during the Cold War said, "We had very positive feelings for the military. My friends all knew what their dads went through, and so forth, and that was maybe conveyed to me."[43] Another missileer described how, during the 1990s, she didn't "go in thinking the world was a warm and fuzzy place."[44] These employees provide insight into how the Cold War could be remembered: power, deterrence, positive feelings for the military, and conceptualizations of the world outside as hostile to the United States.

Queer theorist Judith Halberstam asks us to "suspect memorialization." She reminds us that forgetting is a "tool of dominant culture to push the past aside in order to maintain the fantasy and fiction of a just and tolerant present."[45] If we suspect what the Minuteman Missile National Historic Site asks us to remember, it is not the *denial* of wrongdoings abroad that characterizes U.S. memory but rather the building of memories around familiar themes of national security that logically extend into the present. The site does not repudiate or suppress alternative voices, and it even includes an interview with a peace activist.[46] The site does not need to condemn or suppress but rather aims to build a narrative from a position of dominance. It is not the direct repression of a counter-memory that makes power hold. Rather, it is the productive capacities of power that make power hold. Foucault writes that "if power were never anything but repressive, if it never did anything but to say no, do you really think one would be brought to obey it? What makes power hold good, what makes it accepted, is simply the fact that it doesn't only weigh on us as a force that says no, but that it traverses and produces things, it induces pleasure, forms knowledge, produces discourse."[47] The rhetoric of U.S. national security tautologically accounts for actions of state terror. U.S.-sponsored counterinsurgency efforts that provoked masses of people to emigrate from their homes can be justified in memory frameworks that project upon the past using logic that extends into present-day U.S. national security. Silence is enforced by the U.S. nation-state less through repression than it is institutionalized through a dominant narrative that is inherently forgetful. The repetition of silence in the memory field inculcates the newest memory makers with a level of ignorance that is paralleled by fantasies of self-protection.

U.S. NATIONAL SECURITY REMEMBERED

Aberrations of memory in El Norteño's diaspora in part reflect the incapacity of the U.S. government (the CIA, the DoD, and now the Department of Homeland Security) to coordinate reparative actions associated with the damages that Vietnam-era counterinsurgency efforts had in shaping campesinxs' experiences of terror and subsequent migrations out of El Salvador during the Cold War. Following the late twentieth-century conflicts in the Central American region, sociologists Cecilia Menjívar and Néstor Rodríguez wrote that "it is important to acknowledge that the U.S.–Latin American interstate regime played a key role in setting up and operating campaigns of terror to eliminate perceived 'subversives.' Perhaps acknowledging this link more clearly in truth commissions, tribunals, and the like would lead to lasting structures that would be truly conducive to peace and justice in the region."[48] Peace and justice, however, remain contested concepts. To this day, for example, the United States is not a state party to the Rome Statute of the International Criminal Court (ICC).[49] Without subjecting itself to international standards of criminal justice, checks and balances on the terror that U.S.-dominated regional systems generate to counter "terrorism" are limited as U.S. national-security concerns continue to reverberate through the U.S. government and factions of its populace.

Anthropologist Victoria Sanford, who studied state-sponsored terror in Guatemala, described how "when the overt expressions of militarization are withdrawn, internalization of encounters with terror continues to shape and define individual relationships within families and communities as well as community relationships with the nation state." Sanford describes that a living memory of terror affects community and individual capacities to reproduce democratic practices and values in the wake of state-sponsored terror.[50] There is now enough temporal distance to begin understanding the unintended long-term consequences of counterinsurgency efforts in Central America. When the Guatemalan dictator Rios Montt (who was convicted of genocide and crimes against humanity) died in 2018, Victoria Sanford publicly stated that "not only did the U.S. government know what was happening under Rios Montt's watch,

Rios Montt is a product of the U.S. school of the Americas. He had counterinsurgency training. He had officer training. He led classes for them."[51] Sanford's statements not only ask us to rethink the concept of who is a *mastermind* behind war crimes committed by Central American armies with U.S. support, but her analysis is a call for U.S. national reflection on its strategies of fighting terror with terror. National historic sites that promote narratives of self-protection in a belligerent world fail to reckon the toxicity of U.S. counterinsurgency efforts in foreign communities. Recently (in 2015), the Salvadoran Supreme Court declared Salvadoran gangs to be terrorists—a move that was perceived to draw additional aid from the United States.[52] Today, the United States needs critical periods of national self-reflection as migrants arrive in caravans, claiming to seek refuge from places where the United States has previously sponsored counterinsurgency efforts abroad.

The lasting effects of ORDEN in the memories that circulate through El Norteño's diasporic networks are a legacy of a U.S.–Latin American interstate regime that established "campaigns of terror to eliminate perceived 'subversives.'"[53] Be it state terror implemented against the terrorists of the civil war or the proclaimed "terrorists" of today (gangs), the violence, silences, and forgetting that continue to surround memories of these engagements will continue to mitigate effective strategies of reflection, reconciliation, and reparation.

CONCLUSION

In El Norteño's diasporic memory field, silences emerge regarding previous moments of violence. Everyday violence is silenced, and silences interact with the transnational distribution of power. I described one dominant memory framework employed by the U.S. nation-state to remember its Cold War self. Dominant memory frameworks are dynamic, with silences that, over time, inculcate forgetting. While I have focused on silence in this chapter, I clarify that silence is one of several dynamics implicated in a system of collective forgetting. Campesinxs navigate violence that has continued since the civil war, and silences are constantly in production as a U.S.-dominated regional system participates in the production of terror. When violence is ongoing, silence allows everyday lives to be remade while simultaneously corroding traces of culpability. Where repetitious violence can be horrifying and fatiguing, silence can be ameliorative. In the next chapter, I focus on the structuration of El Norteño's "field of violence," which I contend is one of the mediums in which traces of transnational harm are found, silenced and forgotten. I aim to show that repetition in the structuration of violence amid the distribution of silences in the memory field are ways in which collective forgetting itself is structured through strategies and disarticulated practices of the U.S. nation-state.

6 · FIELDS OF VIOLENCE

I have explored what people say they suffer from and how they attempt to
set things right.

—Kimberly Theidon, *Intimate Enemies:*
Violence and Reconciliation in Peru

There was a woman screaming. She was the anomaly. She was right
next to my car, the closest to my ears. She stomped her feet and grabbed at her
hair—inconsolable, agitated, and frantic. People were looking at her. I was looking at her. She was an image of grief that I had seen somewhere before. She realized the terror that I was experiencing right now. In front of me, there was a bus
driver, his body flopped on the pavement, his limbs and head slack. Blood and
brains rushed from a bullet hole in his head. Lots of people were running away.
When I attempted to help, I was stopped by bystanders. They instructed me to
make a U-turn and drive away. I made a U-turn and drove away.

EXPIRED BUSES, DEVALUED LIVES

In the days after the incident I described, I experienced flashbacks that left me
nauseous and disoriented as I was giving a stats lecture or standing in line to
buy coffee. As time passed, my memory of the incident changed. The most
salient aspect in my memory became and remained the screaming bystander
who was *doing everything wrong*—drawing attention to herself when she should
have been running. This perception is deeply problematic from a critical stand-
point, but then again, it was this perception that eclipsed my other memories of
the incident. "Everyday life is remade,"[1] and people form knowledge to remake
it. To this day, I have only vague and foggy recollections of the dead body,
and no matter how hard I try, I can barely visualize the abandoned bus, which
some foreigners refer to as a "chicken bus." These buses often have bright paint,
large decals, and chrome hubcaps with spiked lug-nut covers that shine in the

Pan-American highway space. The histrionics of these vehicles used to make me laugh, but now, seeing one of these buses on the road triggered nausea. They were everywhere.

The initial frameworks that I drew upon to understand my experience—namely, the rule of law and psychiatric literature on trauma—seemed to pale in comparison to the knowledge of campesinxs who had survived similar events, whose ancestors had survived (or did not survive) similar events, and the bodily logic that emerges in spaces where violent events have occurred and continue to recur. Campesinxs helped me make sense of this incident and understand what to do given the probability of its recurrence, and only in retrospect am I able to link up that sense with the silenced critiques of power that nevertheless presume its existence. I use my epistemic privilege here to help elucidate what I learned from campesinxs about violence in El Salvador and how that violence is a derivative of a U.S.-dominated regional system.

To illustrate that logic, I ground this discussion in my faded memory of that bus—an object I can hardly remember, an object that is everywhere in twenty-first-century El Salvador, and an object that made a one-way journey with cyclical migrants who traverse transnational space. Blue Bird school buses (those big yellow buses that transport children to school in the United States) were one of the first products that Mercedes, one of El Norteño's couriers, brought back from the United States in the postwar years. After the Salvadoran Civil War, Mercedes had begun flying from El Salvador to the United States with a suitcase full of parcels, delivering them throughout El Norteño's nascent diasporic networks, working for a few weeks inside the United States, and then flying back to El Salvador. She saw transnational business opportunities in North America, and she looped her husband in. North Americans were auctioning off relatively new buses, and on top of that, there were appliances for sale. During the civil war, both Mercedes and her husband survived threats of kidnapping and death, and they had family members killed by both "sides" of the conflict. But in the postwar environment, they were now entrepreneurs with U.S. tourist visas, securing bank loans that would still haunt them in the form of long-standing debts at the time I began to interview them. With time, the couple would fly from El Salvador to Denver and then *drive* used buses back to El Norteño. They would stock the Blue Bird buses full of large parcels such as washing machines and furniture for distribution and sale in the celebrated "peace" of postwar El Salvador.

During one of my interviews with Mercedes, she beckoned her husband, Chepito, over to clarify a few details, and he meandered over to where we were sitting. He was dressed in his standard outfit of working boots, pants, and a T-shirt. Now in his sixties, the age range in which he repeatedly claims campesinxs die, he was always ready for work but always waiting for death.

Through my fieldwork, Chepito had become a different kind of key informant. He was not a courier, but he had lived all his life in El Norteño, and he could patiently walk me through contexts and backstories, filling in the *detallitos* (little details) that help a foreigner understand complicated incidents in the field. In El Norteño, Chepito grew up as a campesino who did not own shoes until he was sent to work on a coffee farm as a teenager. As an adolescent during the "100 Hour War" with Honduras, Chepito was armed with a machete and instructed to protect a tower. His salient memories of that war include the coffee and pastries that his neighbors from El Norteño brought to him during his service. During the Salvadoran Civil War, Chepito drove buses. His wartime bus passengers remember Chepito as the driver who told his passengers to duck as he drove buses through shootouts where members of the guerrillas and the Salvadoran Army were shooting at each other from opposite sides of the road. One day, as Chepito hacked into sugarcane with a machete, he recalled sitting at a wartime bus terminal and observing a well-known thief remove a severed hand from his pocket—the bloody wrist and knuckles covered in jewelry that, for the thief, were worth slicing off a living human being. Chepito repeatedly claimed that for campesino men, thirty marked the middle of life, and sixty was when men die. Now, in his sixties, Chepito had little to lose. He repeatedly commented that he was living out bonus years that extended beyond the time of his expected death. Chepito was not incredibly judgmental of his neighbors who were once engaged in conflict or who are now engaged in conflict. He was a relatively forgiving person. He could easily assume multiple perspectives to explain why something happened the way it did at a given point in time, and he described his wife and children as "rangers" who could survive just about anything. Throughout the course of my fieldwork, Chepito assumed the perspective of paramilitary death-squad members, insurgents, *mareros* (gangsters), and police officers to fill in the *detallitos* that explained the *why* and *how*.

Standing beside his wife, Chepito began to remember his time in the transnational bus industry. The two of them spoke of the past interchangeably, weaving into one another's narratives to fill in details as the story moved forward. The bus industry was a family business, and memories of buses were family memories. Talking like this, the couple often brought me to tears of laughter with the curse words they casually infused into twisting and nonlinear stories that went on for hours. On this occasion, Mercedes sat still with her chin in the air as Chepito spoke, listening as though she were judging his account and clarifying the record when needed. Chepito explained, "In the USA, they only use these buses for a few years . . . but they have more life in them. . . . We can use the bus for twenty years longer after purchasing it in the United States."

Chepito was talking about the used U.S. school buses that now compose a good portion of the public transportation that runs over the pockmarked roads of twenty-first-century El Salvador. In the United States, school buses are considered to be the most stringently regulated vehicles on the road,[2] and an estimated $21.5 billion is spent on school bus transportation,[3] with the average age of school buses being less than ten years[4]. Once U.S. school buses go out of commission, some make their way to Central America, where they will be used as vehicles for public transportation.[5] In twenty-first-century El Salvador, these school buses represent the limited options of public transportation available to those with economic constraints. Ellen Moodie writes that "Salvadoran political and business leaders boast of their peace-era, free-market triumph by pointing to an astonishing upsurge of cars, pickups, and sport utility vehicles darting past the barreling, farting, often decrepit buses that the vast majority of people still must take."[6] These buses are similar to the ones that Chepito and his wife drove back from the United States—the same ones that triggered my flashbacks and nausea. When I first moved to El Salvador, I heard about a Blue Bird bus driver who was yanked from one of these buses and executed in the street near my house. Then, one day, as I was driving to lunch, I saw the same thing happen. Buses were sites of violence, and violence followed the economically constrained as they moved through El Salvador on buses.

During my interview with Mercedes, Chepito stood next to his wife and dutifully answered our questions and prompts, focusing not on the sensationally violent aspects of the bus industry but rather on facets of economic loss. Chepito remembered his first transnational journey with a bus from the United States, which he described as "shitty. When I crossed the bridge to the other side of the border, a *Federal* (member of the militarized Mexican police force) asks me where I'm going, and I tell him El Salvador. . . . He told me, 'I'm going to stop traffic, and you are going to enter the United States again.' So I went back to the United States. . . . They fined me $600 for crossing the border without permission and entering again. And I wrote a letter to the government of the United States, telling them that I had committed this error." Mercedes exhaled and sat back in her chair, shaking her head with frustration as Chepito finished remembering the $600 loss. In the 1990s, $600 easily exceeded the couple's combined monthly income in El Norteño. More than two decades later, the memory of a $600 loss was the narrative locus of attention and affect. Mercedes interjected how the Mexican Federales would rob them in Mexico, and Chepito remembered those bottles of lotion or that one lamp the Federales stole from them in Sayula. The couple's intertwined narrative and family memory were cleaving to the point that transporting buses from the United States to El Salvador resulted in them *losing money* when they were just trying to get a little bit ahead. I understood what they were talking about, but I was hung up on the violence that was missing from their stories. I was expecting the couple to tell me stories about the relative *dangers* of driving through

Mexico and Central America, as opposed to a detailed recounting of economic losses. I knew that the couple had been subject to numerous acts of violence related to their participation in the bus industry, but for the couple, state corruption and the violent events that revolved around their buses were more of an assumed backdrop to the financial setbacks that dominated the transmitted memory.

Mercedes and Chepito continued to drive buses back through Mexico until, finally, in 1998, the deadliest hurricane to strike the Western Hemisphere in two centuries hit Central America.[7] Hurricane Mitch struck immediately before Mercedes and Chepito left the United States, and it took the couple twenty-three days to make their way through the hurricane's aftermath in Mexico with a Blue Bird loaded with parcels. As she told this story, Mercedes raised her index finger in the air, as if to capture everyone's full attention, and spoke slowly, "The motor gave out. We were stranded . . . and the two of us came back eating from the same plate." Driving a bus through the aftermath of Hurricane Mitch–torn Mexico was the final straw for these rangers. The economic losses were just too much.

Chepito was dismissed, and he wandered out of the interview and went back to hacking at vegetation outside with a machete as I continued speaking with Mercedes. The couple still remained in the Salvadoran bus industry, but they stopped participating in the transport of Blue Bird buses from the United States. During my time as a participant observer, I sometimes collected bags of change from the bus drivers they managed. In 2018, this meager income was pieced together with other economic activities "that the family eats from." This income makes the family a target of jealous neighbors, who have physically threatened and even attacked the family.

In El Norteño, there are violent landmines in a postwar field that must be piloted around as one is generally doing something else—in the case of Mercedes and Chepito, the takeaway is that they are usually figuring out how to make enough money for the family to get by. As a North American who had the privileged economic option to not ride one of these buses in El Salvador if I did not want to, I once absentmindedly referred to these vehicles as "chicken buses." This is a common term in expat and tourist circles—one of those labels we sometimes use to characterize something familiar but different. I went back to Mercedes's broader family, and I asked them what they thought of that term: *chicken bus.* They didn't know what I was talking about.

It took some time to explain *chicken bus,* and I gave multiple examples. As I explained, one of the kids called Chepito and placed him on speakerphone to participate in the discussion. I tried to explain how "a foreigner will say 'I hopped on a chicken bus to go to . . .' and they are referring to *the vehicle.*" I had to reiterate that I was not talking about chicken transport, and I agreed with Chepito that a Blue Bird bus stacked full of chicken crates sounded like a ridiculous way to transport a significant quantity of chickens. We eventually arrived at a shared understanding of how the term *chicken bus* might be used by foreign interlocutors as they told their own stories about traversing twenty-first-century El Salvador. Then, with smartphone technology and growing interest, the family members collectively fed me these lines: "True, you can get on the bus and bring a pig, a cat, a dog, a chicken. But to call it a chicken bus ... it doesn't sound right. I guess in the end, it's also a way of making fun of people. I guess they think we are driving trash ... but you know what? They are benefitting because they are selling us their trash. This is one of the only economic solutions for us here. Everyone has their own way of thinking, but that's our way of living in these countries. *Chueco.*" Chepito, a healthy man in his sixties who perceived he was living out the last days of his life, provided that final word—*chueco*—to describe "our way of living in these countries." *Chueco* is frequently used in El Norteño to refer to crooked, false, and shitty fabrications or riggings or "our way of living in these countries." Even *chueco* ways of living can be normalized, made into something mundane, and fade into the background as one moves forward in life. Expired U.S. school buses are frequently sites of violence in postwar El Salvador, but they are also ways to save, or to make, a little bit of cash.

This "chicken bus" moment I've described reflects more than a semantic interest. I tell that story to explore a larger crisis regarding the devaluation of human life at the margins of transnational power.[8] While this devaluation can be conceptualized under a number of theories regarding the ways in which nations relate to one another in international space,[9] I add that the devaluation is permitted by longitudinal transnational processes of forgetting. Transnational forgetting implies the passage of time across multiple spaces, and the devaluation of human life is both temporal and transnational. Over time, in El Salvador, violence has continued from the civil war into the postwar period.[10] Ellen Moodie posits that death has actually undergone a devaluation following the country's transition into a neoliberal, postwar state that individualizes and subsequently alienates people. Moodie writes that "when Salvadorans repeat, 'It's worse than the war,' they are comparing values through a story, fashioning a narrative that reevaluates the past and runs ahead of itself to a desiccated future present."[11] In addition to temporal devaluation, there is devaluation that covaries with locations in transnational space. Chepito and Mercedes's story holds the unspoken assumption that what is no longer suitable for U.S. youth to be driven around in is suitable enough for the Salvadoran population. Inside El Salvador, it is those with comparatively large material restrictions who are relegated to ride, drive, and sometimes be executed alongside those expired U.S. school buses. The longitudinal and spatial components of devaluation are one way to map sites of violence in contemporary El Salvador. Despite inflammatory rhetoric emanating from U.S. political leaders regarding Salvadoran migrants, it is through forgetting that this devaluation is both permitted and made difficult to recognize over time. The structuration of violence in the field is being obfuscated both by campesinxs in making everyday sense of it and by the U.S.-dominated regional system that structures and restructures it.

FIELDS OF VIOLENCE

Violence is locally distributed throughout El Norteño, and its distribution can determine who lives and dies, but as I show in the introduction to this chapter, its incidents are curiously difficult to remember and subject to myriad forms of individual and collective forgetting. Paul Ricoeur writes that "forgetting boils down to a forgetting of the victims. It then becomes the task of memory to correct this systematic forgetting and to encourage the writing of the history of victims."[12] I am hesitant to assign the *victim* or *survivor* status to campesinxs who do not describe themselves as such, but I find Ricoeur's rendering of forgetting useful in thinking about ways in which power plays a role in memory, particularly when state violence is clouded by the active violence and everyday forgetting of the people. Structural violence refers to the long-standing political and economic organization of society that imposes emotional and physical distress at the individual level, being rooted in unequal and hierarchical relationships between nation-states such as El Salvador and the United States.[13] Symbolic violence refers to the reproduction of domination through the misrecognition of power structures among the dominated.[14] The memory field is one of the mediums in which symbolic violence operates, and it is the memory field that is shaped by and complicit in the reproduction of the field of violence.[15]

During the time I participated in the Salvadoran courier trade, I directly observed violence or listened to interlocutors within a diasporic network of campesinxs who described everyday violence in El Norteño and El Salvador at large. My field notes are spotted with documentation of a friend's father who attempted to kill another friend's father over a property boundary squabble. My notes include animals that were physically beaten or intentionally killed. They include human deaths where the newspapers, police, and nongovernmental organizations told stories that were discordant with the chatter that flowed between community members in the aftermath of a homicide. Friends and acquaintances received death threats and threats of sexual assault, and some of them completed suicides. My field notes include my personal experience of using my relative size to intimidate a burglar after he broke into a courier's home that was stocked with hundreds of pounds of parcels. I documented being stuck behind a national law-enforcement pickup truck in midday traffic, where in the bed of the truck, there were two men: "One of the men was wearing a black mask pulled over his face, and both were in dark-blue camouflage and black boots. The one who was wearing the mask was holding an M16 military-grade weapon with a stainless-steel lower receiver. The automatic weapon was hanging over the back of the pickup truck in front of my windshield (November 30, 2015)."

I documented masked men armed with M16 rifles like these walking along lines of shirtless men who were kneeling on the sides of highways with their hands behind their heads. I also documented conversations among my campesinx friends who were randomly stopped by the police and asked to spread their legs and place their hands behind their heads as the police asked for identification. I documented campesinx youth who were wary of walking on the street in the anticipatory anxiety of being physically assaulted not by gang members but by armed factions of the Salvadoran state. I witnessed the after-shocks that flow through a community when gang bosses are killed (presum-ably by rival gang members or by paramilitary actors), where the absence of a gang leader's place in a somewhat stable hierarchy generated anxiety among segments of the civilian population. Gang members explained that when collec-tively harassed by the police, it is better to *aguantar verga* (to endure dick) and be violently assaulted by state agents as opposed to running away, because running would mean that the police would probably shoot some of their friends dead in the name of "self-defense." I witnessed everyday abrasions on gang members' bodies that were inflicted by members of the Salvadoran state. I am not the only one who sees these. Members of kinship and friendship networks that run deep in the Salvadoran countryside also see these extrajudicially inflicted injuries that are managed by armed state security agents. These particular types of everyday and political violence occurred during my fieldwork in a rural community of campesinxs with limited access to material resources and justice.[16]

According to Pierre Bourdieu, the "field" may be understood as any struc-tured social space with its own set of laws and hierarchies. Bourdieu describes the field as consisting of "objective relations between individuals or institutions," which are regulated by organizing "laws" of experience.[17] In rural El Salvador, diverse actors including the armed factions of the Salvadoran state, its unsanc-tioned paramilitary actors/offshoots, Salvadoran gangs, and civilians regularly come into conflict with one another, and the outcomes of conflicts generated at their intersections distribute lethal acts of violence in the field. Here I focus on specific actors that distribute death, and I do not contend that the elements I focus on account for all types of violence nor all reasons for death.[18] Rather, I highlight components of the field that are repeatedly structured by what Cecilia Menjívar and Néstor Rodríguez have characterized as "a U.S.-dominated regional system."[19] This system includes armed actors who make up the Salvadoran state and components of the U.S. government, including the U.S. Immigration and Naturalization Service (INS) when it was under the U.S. Department of Justice,

U.S. Immigration and Customs Enforcement (ICE) under the Department of Homeland Security today, the U.S. State Department, and the U.S. Department of Defense. Over time, these entities have had a great deal of influence in distributing and/or investing in the human capital of actors who organize lethal violence in El Norteño, where violence is disproportionately disseminated and integrated into the everyday spaces traversed by campesinxs, who are unable to afford private security guards, private vehicles, and other solutions that could systematically reduce probabilities of victimization. Small-business owners, subsistence farmers, and day laborers may find themselves in situations where they *navigate* social situations involving actors who are engaged in ongoing conflicts.

It is through longitudinal and transnational processes that are hard to recognize, let alone narrate over time, that El Norteño's field of violence has been structured and restructured. Some individuals who work for the U.S.-backed Salvadoran state in 2018 fought the U.S.-backed Salvadoran state as insurgents in the 1980s. Some of the individuals who fled the civil-war violence in the 1980s gave birth to children who became gang members that were deported from the United States and who now participate in Salvadoran gangs in 2018. The longitudinal aspect of this structuration is what confuses culpability and implicates collective memory. With time, the actors have changed, and some of them have transmogrified, but repetitious navigational strategies reflect longitudinal similarities in the fields of violence in El Salvador.

Violence in El Salvador cannot be reduced to U.S. involvement in the region, but by that same token, the structuration of violence in contemporary El Salvador cannot be understood without accounting for U.S. involvement in the region. Here I argue that Salvadoran violence is a derivative of regulative and strategic behaviors implemented by a "US-dominated regional system" that employs knowledge, hierarchies, and operational procedures that structure lethal violence in El Salvador.[20] While the United States has historically funneled arms into the Salvadoran state and invested in the human capital of state security forces, it has also deported gang members into the same space where the eighty-fourth U.S. attorney general emphasized the importance of combatting gangs. At the 2017 International Law Enforcement Academy Graduation in San Salvador, the previous U.S. attorney general Jeff Sessions stated,

MS-13 is based here in El Salvador, but its tentacles reach across Central America, Europe, and through 40 U.S. States, and to within yards of the U.S. Capitol. With more than 40,000 members worldwide-including 10,000 in the United States-MS-13 threatens the lives and wellbeing of each and every family anywhere they exist and everywhere they infest. MS-13 members brutally rape, rob, extort, and murder. We see this here in El Salvador, in the United States, and now in many other countries worldwide. Guided by their motto: Kill, Rape, and Control, they leave misery, devastation, and death in their wake. But at the U.S. Department of Justice, we have a motto too: justice for victims and consequence for criminals.[21]

Here the attorney general generalizes ("anywhere they exist and everywhere they infest") and dehumanizes gang members, who are classified on one side of a binary reflected in the U.S. Department of Justice's "motto."[22] Missing from the attorney general's comments are acknowledgments of the criminal acts of Salvadoran security forces that also employ dehumanizing characterizations of gang members as they engage in acts such as the physical assault of minors in the countryside. The U.S. State Department, the Federal Bureau of Investigation, and ICE are invested in eliminating highly organized and powerful Salvadoran gangs that disarticulated entities of the U.S. government played a role in generating and moving between El Salvador and the United States. Today, gangs have their own justice practices that collide with justice practices of the Salvadoran state. These collisions structure new conflicts inside El Salvador.

Disarticulated justice practices are hallmarks of transnational empires. In her analysis of nineteenth-century justice systems in Peru, historian Alcira Dueñas documents the indigenous population's response to local colonial authorities' abuses, including colonizer negligence, procrastination, and inefficiency in processing indigenous claims. Dueñas illustrates how as opposed to simply assuming a passive subjectivity to colonial dominance, indigenous efforts to show colonial authorities their own abuses, using their own justice system, contributed to a constant production of interstitial spaces.[23] Critical arguments were being made that colonialists and Spanish officials were engaged in "webs of corruption that perpetuated injustice for Amerindians."[24] Over two centuries later, anthropologist Kimberly Theidon summarizes the justice practices she observed and experienced in Peru: "There were multiple justice systems interacting during the internal armed conflict and its aftermath: those of Shining Path, the armed forces, human rights organizations, the ronderos, communal authorities, and the divine. Each of these actors holds different conceptions of justice and reckoning, of what constitutes the individual and collective good, and which takes precedence when they come in tension. These different understandings of justice reverberate throughout these communities and challenge the supremacy of liberal models of justice and the dichotomy they construct between retributive and restorative forms of justice—while favoring the former."[25] The multiple justice systems characterized by Dueñas and Theidon in Peru, at two distant points in time, remind us that systems of externally deployed "justice" can be deeply flawed and dysfunctional when implemented in local contexts. In the Salvadoran case, the tensions between competing justice practices reflect external interventions and generate conflictive potentials that contribute to the reproduction of a local field of violence.

Among those living in gang-controlled territories, compliance with gang rules and expectations, not colluding with a rival gang, and not colluding with the Salvadoran police are somewhat reliable strategies that reduce the probability of death. Bourdieu described the habitus as "the system of generative schemes objectively adjusted to the particular conditions in which it is constituted." Navigating the field of violence involves using logic based on the "laws" of experience.[26] In the Salvadoran countryside, state security agents regularly break the law to fight individuals they perceive to be on the wrong side of it, thereby undermining the very rule of law they expect civilians to uphold. A few interlocutors in my networks of couriers and their clients, definitely not the majority but a substantial number nonetheless, reiterated that gang members are individuals in the community, and one must treat them with the same respect that one treats a neighbor. This includes simply greeting gang members with eye contact and some type of *saludos* such as "good day" so as to not generate micro-offenses that could later develop into larger problems. In the countryside, non-gang-involved campesinx youth are harassed by Salvadoran state security forces, and gang members (who are also community members) are subject to extrajudicial beatings and killings.[27] Gang members have described the police engaging in extrajudicial acts of physical violence while calling them "insects," which is concordant with the Trump administration's repeated reference to Salvadoran gang members as "animals"[28] and Jeff Sessions's use of the word *infest* to describe gang behavior. While the dehumanization of gang members buttresses state strategies of extermination, those strategies are generating deep vendettas against and distrust of the state across rural communities in El Salvador. The contention among the actors, who are also located within kinship networks and who have different justice practices, makes emigration from the field of violence a logical navigational strategy that reduces the probability of death.

In El Salvador, campesinxs experience the behaviors of state security agents who receive support from the U.S. government (in fiscal year 2018, the Trump administration requested $263 million for the U.S. Central American Regional Security Initiative [CARSI] and $46 million in bilateral assistance for El Salvador[29]), and campesinxs experience the behaviors of gangs that operate shadow states in rural and urban zones. In twenty-first-century El Salvador, the intersections of disarticulated justice systems are where violence is in part distributed, and this type of violence is familiar to Salvadorans who survived the Civil War (1979–1992). Much like the Civil War era, state actors engage in sanctioned and unsanctioned violence against the civilian population and those it deems deviant (today, deviants are the gangs; during the civil war, deviants were members of the guerrillas[30]), holding civilians and gang members to a rule of law that not even its security agents can follow.

It is widely assumed that a lack of security is a preoccupation of the every-day Salvadoran.[31] I add that this preoccupation is part of a historically informed bodily logic[32] that is used to navigate probabilities of lethal violence. While driving a vehicle without air conditioning in rural Chalatenango, for example, my left hand automatically hit the buttons that raise all the windows every time my right foot hit the brake pedal. This orchestration of vehicular functions and bodily responses was first taught to me by a Salvadoran courier. Like a child, I observed him smoothly repeating these actions until I began to, first with thought and now as a bodily reflex, engage in actions that resulted in the vehicle's windows rising as the car came to a stop (despite the heat). In Moodie's analysis of a crime story about a woman who was victimized at an intersection in San Salvador, she writes, "Leaving a window open, especially at a stoplight, oriented Marielena differently from before. It interrupted a collective chant, a normalizing injunction repeated again and again, about moving through space in the ever breaking-down world of end-of-century San Salvador."[33] Navigational strategies that reduce seemingly ubiquitous probabilities of violence, salient not only in observable bodily practices but also in the interlocution Moodie describes, are in and of themselves field elements that inculcate the next generation.

While I am talking about the field of violence as it pertains to death, navigating the field of violence also includes strategies that are employed to moderate the potential outcomes of everyday crime (e.g., robbery) such that the crime does not become something more violent than it needs to be. When one courier had her iPhone robbed by the same set of armed robbers who repeatedly appeared on her bus route from El Norteño to San Salvador, her children responded to the announcements of her victimizations not with sympathy, nor with a report to the police, but by repeatedly calling her a *pendeja* (dumbass). Looking at her phone on public transportation was the navigable error that she repeated at her own risk. In the multiple disarticulated justice practices of contemporary El Salvador, being perceived as assisting the police in an investigation could result in the bystander unnecessarily becoming a target of the perpetrator(s). I was once leaving a *comedor* (cafeteria) with a courier as four men in hooded sweatshirts broke into the car beside my own. The courier put out his arm out and motioned for me to be silent when the thieves noticed us. We stood still as they finished what they were doing and drove away. The courier instructed me to quickly do the same. He explained that we needed to get out of the parking lot as fast as possible and that we should not call the police, and he celebrated the fact that my car was "such a piece of shit" that the thieves chose the vehicle next to mine to rob. The takeaway lesson from this moment was that driving a substandard vehicle was a successful strategy for couriers, who frequently traverse crime-infused spaces with expensive parcels packed into their vehicles. The takeaway was *not* rectifying the practice or occurrence of robbery by engaging with law enforcement but rather recognizing and cultivating strategies that reduced probabilities of our potential victimization.

Emigration is a navigational strategy that removes the individual from their local field of violence. Campesinxs' decisions to emigrate away from El Norteño and sometimes El Salvador are inevitably multifactorial, and they are often mechanized by kin in diasporic networks and personal and family finances—a compilation of motives and imaginaries. Forces that structure campesinxs' fields of violence are ignored when, in response to the U.S. justice system's standards for refugees, asylum seekers and their advocates reduce the complexity of El Norteño (or El Salvador at large) to a unilaterally unlivable hellscape. That process is in part structured by U.S. Citizenship and Immigration Services, where an I-589 Application for Asylum and for Withholding of Removal[34] places a burden on the asylum seeker to present a convincing case, pitched at the Executive Office for Immigration Review under the U.S. Department of Justice. These applications produce narratives aimed at winning individual cases. Framing El Salvador as a hellscape does not critically elucidate the participation of the U.S. departments and agencies in the structuration of El Salvador's fields of violence. Here campesinxs come into contact with the U.S. justice system, which is concerned not with reparations for U.S. interventions abroad but rather with an alien's removability from the United States or eligibility for relief. In other words, the U.S. justice system repeatedly processes individual claims that frame violent social environments in El Salvador not as derivatives of a U.S.-dominated regional system but as risks for individuals who claim that they cannot return to foreign violence. This is one of the everyday ways in which numerous actors (legal, migrant, and academic) participate in U.S. removal proceedings that reproduce national forgetting.

EXPORTING INSECURITY AND THE FORCES USED TO FIGHT IT

I was in a taxi being driven toward what Mercedes referred to as a "little El Norteño" in Long Island. I was sitting in the back, talking with the driver about the place, when he gestured outside the window and recalled how back in the seventies and eighties, he used to refer to this area, where I was interviewing Salvadoran migrants in 2015, as the "crack city." He explained that back then, the area was predominantly black. He explained how during the eighties and nineties, all these wars were occurring in Central America. He remembered that is about the time when the Latinos started to move in, and that is when he moved in. He remembered how scary it was "to be the only brown person walking around a black neighborhood." He explained that the Latinos "fought back with their machetes, taking off legs and heads."

During that trip to "little El Norteño" in Long Island, I interviewed a woman who had just received parcels (beans) from her mother in El Norteño. As we talked about her memories of migration, we arrived at the topic of Salvadorans who "flee violence." She wanted me to understand something about Salvadoran gangs. She explained that "all of those condemned that were deported, those are the gang bosses, and they've regrouped in El Salvador . . . that wasn't born in El Salvador." The taxi driver's description of Latinos fighting against blacks with their machetes and my friend's comment about Salvadoran gangs not being "born in El Salvador" illustrate cases of symbolic violence,[35] where racialized conflicts between local "enemies" obfuscate the U.S. nation's failure to reconcile its immigration and foreign policies.

As the taxi driver described, back when all these wars were occurring in Central America, the United States was pumping arms to the Salvadoran Army—approximately 189 million over the course of the civil-war period.[36] Back then, El Norteño's residents did not remember gangs because they hadn't formed in El Norteño yet. By the mid-1980s, El Salvador had become the third largest recipient of U.S. foreign aid after Israel and Egypt.[37] Despite the United States engaging in supporting foreign conflicts abroad, the unintended consequences of those investments (e.g., the mass migration of campesinxs from that U.S.-sponsored civil-war violence to the country supporting the conflict) remained disarticulated with U.S. immigration policies. Leisy Abrego summarizes this contradiction: "Despite the U.S. government's role in the war, it did not recognize Salvadorans as political refugees. . . . Refugee status or asylum would have translated into a much more welcoming and stabilizing entrance for Salvadorans, thereby increasing their chances of thriving in the United States. Instead, the U.S. government failed to take responsibility for its role in the very violence and devastation that pushed so many Salvadorans out of their country, and it deemed Salvadorans unwanted unauthorized immigrants."[38]

The disarticulation resulted in a situation where campesinxs (and other Salvadorans migrating away from the war) were unable to receive asylum in the United States and thereby relegated to undocumented lives. In contrast to Cubans or Iraqis, who had at least a 50 percent chance of securing asylum, a refugee from El Salvador had a 5 percent chance of securing asylum during that time.[39] Some alienated Central Americans who were migrating into gang-controlled locales in Los Angeles organized into the Mara Salvatrucha and Barrio 18 gangs.[40] It was U.S. immigration policy that would mechanize the transnational movement of Salvadoran gangs when, in 1996, the United States passed the Illegal Immigration Reform and Immigrant Responsibility Act (IIRAIRA), which included two provisions that more readily facilitated the deportation of gang members back to El Salvador.[41] In 1997, the Los Angeles

Police Department (LAPD) passed a court injunction that banned all forms of communication (sitting, standing, driving, walking, appearing, gathering, whistling, or gesturing in public) between gang members, thereby making these everyday activities (which are guaranteed civil rights in the United States) criminal for U.S.-based gang members. Elana Zilberg described how "10,000 gang members on the California Gang List had been targeted for deportation, and INS and Border Patrol agents maintained a regular presence in LAPD booking and charging out facilities."[42] When gang members were incarcerated and later deported to El Salvador, they transported Los Angeles street names and territorial conflicts back with them, taking residence in war zones their parents had fled and disseminating U.S. urban gang culture into rural Salvadoran communities like El Norteño.[43]

The criminalization, deportation, and dehumanization of gang members have continued since the mid-nineties, where now, the United States simultaneously supports antigang "security" programs that are implemented in Salvadoran "communities at risk."[44] I have personally known innocent, non-gang-involved youth to be harassed and physically assaulted by armed agents of the Salvadoran state, who compose the fabric of these "security" strategies. This state terrorism enacted against campesinxs is not easily forgotten by rural youth who have been assaulted by state actors, nor by their family and community members. Recent inflammatory rhetoric pushed by right-wing political leaders in the United States has generated visions of gang members as nonhuman agents who are an external threat to the United States, and who have enjoyed a "pleasant" period that is now coming to an end. In a 2017 speech before the National Rifle Association, U.S. president Donald Trump proclaimed, "MS-13—you know about MS-13? It's not pleasant for them anymore, folks; it's not pleasant for them anymore. That's a bad group. Not pleasant for MS-13—get them the hell out of here, right? Get 'em out."[45] Despite the Trump administration repeatedly referring to Salvadoran gang members such as those in MS-13 as "animals,"[46] it is likely that MS-13 members have an overall education level that exceeds that of the general Salvadoran population.[47] In the countryside, Salvadoran gang members are also community members (sons and daughters, siblings, cousins, parents, in-laws, and friends) who, when subject to attacks by Salvadoran state security forces, respond with their own strategies of self-preservation. Their continued presence and capacity to establish control in "communities at risk" are in part an outcome of a U.S.-dominated regional system that continues to employ aggressive strategies that reproduce the foundations of transnational gang control.

Gangs are currently widespread in El Salvador, are deeply attached to communities, and wield appreciable power that is independent of nation-states. In a 2016–2017 survey of the Salvadoran population, 74 percent reported that their community was in some way affected by gangs, and 62 percent of respondents confirmed that youth/children being in gangs was a serious problem in their community.[48] I examined the statistics for El Norteño, where these percentages were lower but still quite prevalent, exceeding 60 percent of respondents reporting their community being affected by gangs and 40 percent referencing youth gang involvement. Gangs create what may be regarded as local "shadow states" within El Salvador, often replete with their own rules, enforcement mechanisms, investigations, strategies of self-preservation, and implementation of their own justice practices. Gang members or suspected gang members are also attacked by antigang forces comprising police officers and/or soldiers, who, during the daytime, wield M16 rifles and face masks. During the civil war in the 1980s, Joan Didion wrote that "these are the details—the models and colors of armored vehicles, the makes and calibers of weapons, the particular methods of dismemberment and decapitation used in particular instances—on which the visitor to Salvador learns immediately to concentrate, to the exclusion of past or future concerns, as in a prolonged amnesiac fugue."[49] Amid the prolongation of this fugue into twenty-first-century El Salvador, members of the Salvadoran state target and physically assault youth who are suspected of gang involvement for the type of hat or shoes they wear. Those same adolescents learn to develop a hate for the out-of-uniform police officers (*gallinitas ciegas* [literally, "little blind hens," but also refers to a worm that infests soil in the milpa]) and army personnel (*ranas* [frogs]), who are now targeted for the violent harm they wield against suspected gang members. Those agents sometimes engage in extrajudicial killings of gang members. The United States has been previously recognized as criticizing human rights abuses of states that it concurrently provides military aid, arms, and terror training to.[50] Today, the United States continues to back Salvadoran security forces as those same security forces participate in the extrajudicial killings of gang members.[51] This detail is not lost on the rural civilian population. The disproportionate amount of power invested into Salvadoran security forces that come into conflict with gang members the United States continues to deport to El Salvador reflects not a self-interested actor that meddles in foreign affairs but a complex bureaucratic fabric that is incapable of reconciling its unintended consequences abroad.

Longitudinal national strategies inadvertently structure ongoing harms for others elsewhere. Today, the U.S. Department of Homeland Security tracks and publishes the number of "criminals" it deports. In the cumulative criminal deportations from the United States of America to El Salvador (figure 6.1), we observe tens of thousands of criminal deportations occurring by 2016. As U.S. taxpayers pay for the law-enforcement processing, detainment, and deportations of migrants, they simultaneously invest millions into security assistance for the

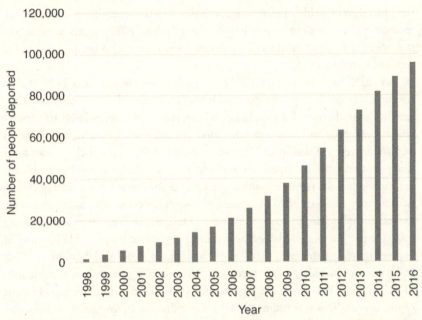

FIGURE 6.1 Cumulative criminal deportations of Salvadorans from the U.S. to El Salvador

same location to which the deported "criminals" are being sent to.[52] These are not rehabilitative or reparative strategies but conflict-generating investments that reflect an ongoing structuration of lethal violence in Salvadoran spaces.

REPETITIONS IN THE FIELD OF VIOLENCE

> The tradition of all the dead generations weighs like a nightmare on the brains of the living.
>
> —Karl Marx[53]

> And the past, in El Salvador, weighs like a nightmare.
>
> —Ellen Moodie[54]

Pumping support into a nation-state's security forces and pumping gang members into that nation-state's jurisdiction reflect a devaluation of Salvadoran life in transnational space. This devaluation is both reflected in and obfuscated by the prolonged development and existence of individual schemes that are used to make sense of and navigate fields of violence. Repetitions in navigational strategies that become normalized in the ongoing structuration of fields of violence correspond to the everyday silences in the memory field regarding culpability. The longitudinal effect of this devaluation is evident in the memories of El Norteño's residents, who continue to make sense of lethal violence.

I was in El Norteño, reclining in a hammock, when Mateo, one of El Norteño's couriers, walked through the door with packets of parcels that would be delivered in Colorado some forty-eight hours later. He was followed closely by a friend whom the family had long ago integrated into their kinship structure. Now, in her late forties, she was in El Norteño visiting her high school classmates for a thirty-year reunion. I jumped out of the hammock to help Mateo begin unloading parcels, but the family friend stopped me, as she knew I was studying collective memory. She wanted to show me a picture of her classmates today, and as we looked at the picture in 2017, she began to talk about those who were missing from the picture. She explained how during the Salvadoran Civil War, some of her teenage classmates used to fall in love with the soldiers. And then she recalled, still staring at the picture, how sometimes the guerrilla fighters would come into El Norteño and execute soldiers' girlfriends (her classmates and friends) in front of the church. This was ultimately why she didn't fall in love with soldiers, she explained, because that type of love could get you killed. Avoiding romantic alliances with actors who structure the field of violence has been and remains key to navigating probabilities of death in El Norteño, both then (during the Salvadoran Civil War) and now. The adage is that romantic involvement with a gang member / guerrilla fighter or soldier/policeman is an invitation for trouble. The actors have changed, but everyday partner choice and affect management continue to be integral to survival.

During the civil war, in El Norteño, both the army and insurgent forces were actors that regularly had confrontations with one another and relied on residents to inform them of opposing alliances. When the army was not visibly present, it used rural informants (such as ORDEN [La Organización Democrática Nacionalista] affiliates) to collect information that could result in extrajudicial killings of suspected guerrilla members or their supporters.[55] Friends and family members became *desaparecidos* (disappeared). Molly Todd writes that "distrust of the Salvadoran military ran deep in the displaced population,"[56] and she provides evidence that Salvadoran refugees in Honduras were skeptical of returning home to El Salvador, given the rising numbers of internally displaced persons, massacred civilian populations, tortures, and imprisonments by the Salvadoran military.[57] In contemporary El Norteño, gossip spreads that the Sombra Negra is active again, this time referring to paramilitary units that take out not guerrilla fighters but gang bosses. Members of Salvadoran state security forces interrogate and physically attack young people whom they suspect of gang involvement, which provokes civil-war memories of the army interrogating farmworkers suspected of being involved in the insurgency. In one campesino's narrative of his encounter with soldiers during the civil war, I can switch out the word *guerrillero* (guerrilla fighter) for *pandillero* (gangster), and the narrative nonetheless describes what happens to residents of El Norteño at two different points in time, three decades apart:

> There . . . was a pair of soldiers, and . . . I was carrying my chulita [bag] and machete. . . . They detained me. They started bothering me, saying that I was a guerrillero. . . . They were really bothering me. "No . . . I'm coming from work; I'm not coming from something else. I'm just coming back from work . . ." So the soldier told the other one, "Man, being as dumb as you are, you can't see that the man is just coming back from work. You're not looking at him, and you're thinking things that you shouldn't think. Don't be so dumb, let him go." That's how they let me go. I came right back here [to this house]. That's what happened.

In contemporary El Salvador, the army and police interrogate campesinxs who they suspect of being gang members by harassing campesinxs as they work or return from work. The rumors that the army and police are using paramilitary units to eliminate gang members are made real by these all too familiar interrogation techniques. The interrogation techniques are familiar because campesinxs have been subject to state-security-force harassment over generations. The context is updated, but the strategy of the campesinxs who navigate this field remains somewhat similar.

Campesinxs remember fearing and respecting the power of the guerrilla forces during the war in El Norteño. They also remember being kidnapped, forcefully recruited, extorted, and sexually assaulted by members of the guerrilla forces, who were supposed to be fighting in favor of the people. Working against insurgent forces could result in unwanted attention, death threats, or even being killed in wartime El Norteño. Gang control tactics vary by locale, but today, the gangs employ tactics that are not foreign to wartime survivors. Extortion, for example, is used by gangs and was used by the guerrillas during the civil war. In El Norteño, sometimes it is the same individuals who describe once paying extortion fees to the guerrillas but now paying extortion fees to the gangs. Rumors circulate throughout El Norteño about hit lists and extortion lists—not about whether they actually exist but whether the local gang bosses have actually sanctioned these lists or whether someone is trying to take advantage of the murky security situation in El Norteño. Business owners remember being extorted by the guerrilla fighters in particular ways during the Salvadoran Civil War, sometimes going straight to the guerrilla commanders to make their cases for extortion fees that are perceived to be too high. In 2018, similar extortion requests reemerge for the same business owners, who are often so savvy that they know a fake extortion request when they see one—and some go directly to the gang bosses to quell the false threats. Being suspected of talking to or aiding the police or military forces in antigang activities can also result in death threats or being killed by gang members. Weapons were and are visibly present in the field, and violence emanates from both state and antistate forces. What is notable is that the generations now navigating the current field of violence are the children of wartime survivors who navigated something similar, many of whom are still alive to navigate the updated field of violence. The actors are different, but the navigational strategies are collectively familiar.

Survivors of civil-war violence in El Norteño inculcate the subsequent generation with survival techniques honed during the civil war, even though the environment is now in a protracted "postwar" period. Marianne Hirsch's concept of postmemory, originally used to describe how trauma was transmitted to the children of Holocaust survivors, can be used to better understand strategies that endure transformed actors in Salvadoran fields of violence. Hirsch writes, "The relationship that the 'generation after' bears to the personal, collective, and cultural trauma of those who came before—to experiences they 'remember' only by means of the stories, images, and behaviors among which they grew up. But these experiences were transmitted to them so deeply and affectively as to seem to constitute memories in their own right. Postmemory's connection to the past is thus actually mediated not by recall but by imaginative investment, projection, and creation."[58] In the context of El Norteño, I would modify Hirsch's postmemory concept to specify that the "generation after" need not imagine nor create but instead live with and navigate new actors in an all too familiar field of violence—one that has been fortified with U.S. arms, human-capital investments, and deported gang members. Paramilitary forces, extortion, extrajudicial killings, interrogations by the state, and death as an outcome of multiple disarticulated justice practices were and are being navigated by wartime survivors and, now, their offspring. One Salvadoran mother who sends and receives parcels explained to me how "now they ask for money, but during the war, they asked for food," drawing an unspoken link between insurgents and gangs as the antistate actors in El Norteño, some thirty years apart. The actors have changed with time, but navigational experiences remain familiar.

CONCLUSION

I began this chapter by confessing my own personal and unheroic experience with a field of violence in El Salvador. I tried to show how the immediacy of the incident, its conditions, and the way in which I remembered it point to navigational strategies that confuse culpability for its structuration. Violence overwhelms the senses and the memories that form in its wake, and survivors learn, repeat, naturalize, and inculcate strategies to reduce probabilities of death for themselves and their loved ones.

I have explored the idea that there are multiple actors who distribute conflict in local fields of violence, with the field of violence being one of the mediums in which traces of transnational harm are reiteratively found. Disarticulated U.S. foreign and immigration practices are implicated in the structuration of El Norteño's field of violence, and these disarticulated practices are enacted by disparate institutions, agencies, and agents that over time have simultaneously contributed to the devaluation of human life in El Salvador. Disarticulated approaches to immigration and foreign policy by the U.S. government, over time, reproduce conditions that reduce life certainties and increase probabilities of death for campesinxs.

Campesinxs continue to employ emigration as a navigational strategy while the United States participates in the structuration of the fields of violence they emigrate from. In the context of El Norteño, collective forgetting obfuscates the larger forces culpable for structuring everyday harms. In the next chapter, I explore how these repetitious harms are enabled, in part, by a transnational system of forgetting that I refer to as "the U.S. fugue state."

7 · DEFERMENTS OF VOICE, MYOPIC REFLECTIONS

The U.S. mainly provided the government of El Salvador with security assistance. By following an effective strategy that linked this aid to governmental and military reform, the U.S. was able to shape the ongoing counterinsurgency and aid the government of El Salvador in defeating its insurgency.
—Field Manual, U.S. Department of the Army[1]

Why are we having all these people from shithole countries come here?
—U.S. president Donald Trump[2]

Just before the Trump administration completed a full year in office, the *Washington Post* reported that during a White House meeting to discuss an immigration deal involving foreign nationals with Temporary Protected Status and Deferred Action for Childhood Arrivals (issues that deeply implicate and affect Salvadoran migrants), the U.S. president asked the question quoted in the epigraph. Once reported, it resounded through international media. Salvadoran social media feeds were flooded with stunning pictures of El Salvador, overlaid with sarcastic yet proud "#shithole" hashtags and biting commentary regarding the U.S. president himself. The burst of media coverage that followed the "shithole" statement decried Trump as a racist, which he then denied to reporters.[3]

When I read Trump's quote, all I could do was reflect on another. What seemed more salient than ever was Bourdieu's claim that society is so difficult to understand in part because "it conceals under the most trivial appearances, those of daily banality for daily newspapers, available to any researcher, the most unexpected revelations about what we least want to know about what we are."[4] If we momentarily allow ourselves to see beyond the abrasiveness of Trump's language, beyond the sensationalism of the subsequent news coverage, and beyond the binaries generated by popular discourse that slyly confine critical thinking, we hear Trump ask a question. He wanted to know why people from "shithole" (presumably nonwhite, economically poor) countries come to the United States, specifically including El Salvador as one of those nations. He was expressing ignorance and making an interrogative statement about migration phenomena. We might wonder how, if at all, those in the room attempted to answer Trump's question. Campesinxs in El Norteño's diaspora have repeatedly provided me with numerous answers to Trump's question. Those answers include personal experiences with the reach of U.S. power long before campesinxs emigrated from El Norteño and long before Trump came to power. Those answers say something deeply critical about how the U.S. government has affected their homelands. Those answers say something about imperialism.

In chapters 5 and 6, I explored how silence surrounding violence inculcates collective forgetting over time. Here I explore the possibility that El Norteño's current diaspora is a derivative of U.S. interventions in El Salvador during the Salvadoran Civil War (1979–1992) and that the same intervening U.S. nation-state has trouble collectively recognizing and even remembering what it has done in other peoples' homelands. I contend that there is no one person, presidential administration, branch, agency, department, or political party that is individually responsible for this collective sequela. The U.S. fugue state is a transnational system of forgetting that comprises collective silences, contemporary national strategies, and practices of implementing disarticulated U.S. foreign and immigration policies. This particular manifestation of collective forgetting permits repetitious harms while simultaneously neglecting the unintended consequences of its practices, permitting the production of state ignorance (as opposed to intelligence). It is re-created by everyday practices of silence, the utterance and digestion of rhetoric, and bureaucratic inefficiencies that obscure its complexity from view. It taxes future generations, including the unborn, who have yet to collectively participate in it. In this chapter, I explore individual stories of the civil-war conflict to illustrate the forgotten *reach* of U.S. power that inadvertently stimulated campesinxs' migrations. I contend that by targeting, denigrating, and in some cases, executing knowledge managers who saw this relationship unfolding as it was occurring, the U.S. fugue state generates a collective ignorance that weighs heavy today.

CAMPESINX SILENCES

I was eating dinner with several farmers and one of El Norteño's couriers on a high-altitude coffee farm in the mountains of Chalatenango. As the sun set, our dinner conversation shifted from coffee cultivation techniques to the present-day "security situation" in El Salvador. The farmers and courier had migratory experiences, and they talked openly about the felt sense of security in the United States and the absence of that feeling in El Salvador at large. For example, they described seeing people in the United States openly looking at their phones on public transportation. In El Salvador, looking at an iPhone on a bus would make you a target for a robbery. Personal experience, family updates, and social-media feeds in diasporic networks all seemed to confirm a vision of the United States as a hypersecure environment, where one could feel safe everywhere (despite the mass shootings). The courier and the farmers continued talking about problems in El Salvador until their conversation evolved into a sharing of civil-war memories. The memory sharing and discussion kept *almost* cleaving to a point, *almost* ending with obvious conclusions, but the otherwise fluid discussion was halted by awkward pauses and forced silences. Despite the fact that I was saying very little, I started to realize from eye glances and choked smiles that my presence was underlying the discontinuities in conversation.

So I just asked what I perceived the campesinxs were not saying: "Do you think the U.S. is responsible for what has happened here in El Salvador?" The campesinxs nodded in unison, and then one of the farmers interjected that he thought the United States was interested in weapons production, and he wondered whether weapons production drives a lot of U.S. foreign interventions abroad, such as the Salvadoran Civil War. I told him that although I was a U.S. citizen, I didn't know. He seemed somewhat surprised by that—didn't the U.S. government act on behalf of its people? I explained that democracy is not perfect, and in theory, it's supposed to be an evolving process. The farmer began to explain how the United States interfered in El Salvador about thirty years ago. He remembered that the United States supplied a bunch of weapons to the Salvadoran Army during the civil war, and he explained that the particular involvement of the United States made El Salvador a more violent place than it had to be. From his perspective, U.S. power converted his homeland into a place that his community had to flee.

The farmer remembered how the aerial bombardment in El Norteño became really bad after Ronald Reagan became the president of the United States. Indeed, the Reagan administration had equipped the Salvadoran Air Force with training, helicopters, planes, and arms that the Salvadoran military used to bomb and shell civilians who remained in conflict zones such as El Norteño.[5] The farmer almost died one day when the reinforced Salvadoran Air Force dropped bombs near him and his friends as they were playing soccer. As a result of almost being killed, he decided to join the insurgents and fight the forces that would do such evil things to campesinxs who were not even engaged in the conflict. He was just an adolescent when he decided to join the insurgency. As an adolescent, his mother had enough sway to force him to travel with a *coyote* (guide) to Long Island, where she knew he wouldn't be killed fighting in the Salvadoran Civil

War. I knew where his mother sent him in Long Island—Salvadoran couriers had stiff competition in that area decades after the civil war. There, former insurgents drive minivans and wear turtleneck sweaters and work in construction jobs—and sometimes get harassed by the local police. When the war ended, the farmer returned to El Salvador to continue farming as he had always intended to do. What is unique about his story is that it was the offenses of the U.S.-backed Salvadoran military that mobilized the farmer to become an insurgent, which triggered his mother's mandate that he be sent to the United States as an undocumented migrant. His desire to join the resistance and his history of migration stemmed from his exposure to a counterinsurgency effort. He knew the United States was implicated in what happened to his country, and despite this, he was still too polite to openly say so in front of a gringo sociologist.

As a result of my conversation with a campesino in the mountains of Chalatenango, I looked into data on arms transfers to El Salvador over a sixty-five-year period. Historically, the United States has been the largest provider of arms to El Salvador, cumulatively supplying $332 million worth between 1950 and 2015. Accounting for temporal trends, U.S. arms transfers elevated significantly during El Salvador's civil-war period, reaching approximately 189 million arms (see figure 7.1).[6] The farmer was right: in comparison to the other countries providing arms to El Salvador during the civil war, the United States stood apart as the largest arms provider, even when comparing the minuscule transfers that were received by the insurgents (approximately 1.6 percent of the size of the U.S. transfer to the Salvadoran Army).

The farmer's question about whether U.S. interventions abroad are driven by weapons production corresponds to statistics that illustrate that the United States is currently the world's largest military spender. In 2017, the estimated $610 billion in U.S. military expenditures represented 35 percent of the world total.[7] These military expenditures produce outcomes that bleed far beyond the tautological boundaries of "national security," and as I aim to show in the case of El Norteño's diaspora, the investment in counterinsurgency warfare was an integral component of what stimulated El Norteño's mass migrations. Anthropologist David Graeber writes that "violence, particularly structural violence, where all the power is on one side, creates ignorance. If you have the power to hit people over the head whenever you want, you don't have to trouble yourself too much figuring out what they think is going on, and therefore, generally speaking, you don't."[8] In this chapter, I admit my own initial ignorance that there might be a relationship between my country's national security strategies of yesterday and the migrants arriving to the doors of the United States today.

Social forgetting in this context is manufactured through means of institutionalization by which states regulate violence, replete with its consequent manifestations of silence. As I argued in chapter 5, that silence thickens with the intensity of

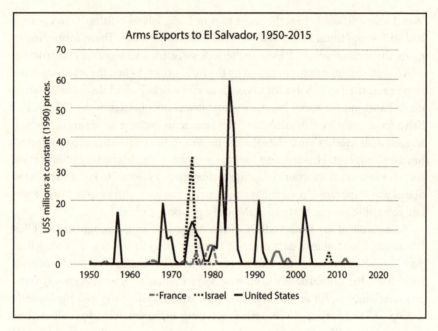

FIGURE 7.1 Arms Transfers to El Salvador by nation and year

power in the hierarchy of the memory field. In the following section, I illustrate an extent of U.S. national forgetting, along with the enforced silences that generate U.S. national ignorance in the name of its own security. I begin with excerpts from an interview I conducted with one North American woman who was deployed to Central America as part of her service to the U.S. Department of Defense (DoD). Our interview was shrouded in secrecy, code words, written messages uncaptured by my tape recorder, and inaudible whispers. These "deferments of voice" are indicative of both collective forgetting and collaborative remembering that speak to what the oral historian Alexander Freund refers to as "the incompleteness of the ostensibly complete, archived record."[9] These deferments of voice, some thirty years after they happened, reproduce forgetting in the memory field.

DEFERMENTS OF VOICE FROM "THE FORGOTTEN GROUP"

I sat bundled up in winter clothes on a couch in a veteran's living room in the United States, when she surprised me by describing El Norteño's landscape: "You've been in El Salvador . . . you know those lovely mountains that go from zero to two thousand? My body has taken a few of those. The good, the bad, and the ugly." Those are the mountains where high-altitude coffee is cultivated by farmers whose sons and daughters, now living in far-off places like Nueva York, don't really speak Spanish anymore. She was deployed into a Central American combat zone as part of her service to the people of the United States in the 1980s. She remembered how, in the early 1980s, "they were having these little pop-up incidents going on. You had El Salvador, you had Honduras, you had Nicaragua . . . because we, in our infinite wisdom, want to control everything. . . . We needed forces to be able to do that. So they created these Rapid Deployable Units that have anywhere from twenty-four to seventy-two hours to be in country." She was talking about U.S. history, and she was using the words *we* and *they*. By *we*, she was referring to *we the people of the United States*. By *they*, she was referring to *the U.S. government*. Her distinction as a U.S. war veteran speaks to a perceived distance from U.S. government actions and decision-making. It is an important detail to denote because the manifestation of the U.S. fugue state implicates more than the individuals who remember and forget it. The Cold War veteran was telling me that as U.S. citizens, we, the people of the United States, wanted to control everything, and the government thus created Rapid Deployable Units so that *we the people* could control everything. Without explicitly saying so, she was mocking the imperialist overtones of U.S. Cold War national-security rhetoric.

While she had memories of particular experiences, she explained that her experiences would be difficult to map out with documents or to even look for. She explained that during the Cold War days, there was always an "official" version of what DoD personnel were doing, and then there was the real version. Her official reason for being in Central America was banal—she was there to build a road. She explained how "if there's a new highway . . . the military is involved. . . . It took four times as many of us as it probably needed to, which meant they were just rotating us in and out wherever they needed. . . . If you're building a road, you can bring everybody in; it's a temporary duty assignment that doesn't have anything to do with anything bad. We're building a road. Again, how do you mask thousands of troops? Build a road." She was monitoring the construction of a road in Honduras, a country that bordered El Salvador. During this part of the interview, she carefully chose what to say into the tape recorder and what was scribbled on paper. Despite the Salvadoran Civil War having ended some twenty-three years prior to our interview, I remain perplexed by the specificity with which she chose to speak on and off the record. Officially, she never entered El Salvador. Nowhere in her military records is there evidence that she entered El Salvador in uniform. I asked if she personally entered El Salvador during the Salvadoran Civil War. She nodded: "I went twice. . . . Basically, you just kept your head down and kept moving."

This Cold War veteran's experiences in El Salvador aren't available to the U.S. public for remembering or reflection. Her armed and uniformed body served the United States in El Salvador in the name of keeping terrorism out of El Salvador, but there is no documentation of what she did (which I, too, must not disclose so as to avoid disclosing potential links to her identity). But as she spoke, I began to realize that some records of U.S. involvement in El Salvador were nonexistent and that living memories of those experiences were systematically silenced. Tine Gammeltoft writes that "silence weaves together psychic lives and social institutions, enabling individuals to endure and social order to persist."[10] Perhaps the social order of imperialist interventions has persisted, but during the war, there would have been major disruptions to the silence that enables the persistence of the social order—namely, injuries and even deaths among U.S. military personnel. I assumed those incidents generated sufficient noise that would have to be documented, as they involved her colleagues as they provided service to the U.S. DoD in a place they were not supposed to be. She responded by explaining how "any time you have a fire incident, you have to record it; even if you're in a place you're not supposed to be, it gets recorded. So that was their way of making sure nothing got recorded. There would be a training accident where a helicopter went off site or there was something *else* that happened." She was explaining "their way" of recording data such that it would be distorted when archived, presumably to cover the fact that U.S. troops were being asked to do something in places they should not have been. The official record did not reflect her truth: what could be excavated would be a distortion of the truth. Everything she said made sense, but little of what she said could be cross-validated. It seemed that the documentation practices employed by the U.S. DoD in and around El Salvador at that time eliminated auto-evaluative possibilities for the next generation of U.S. taxpayers.

This particular veteran had experience at Fort Benning, Georgia, where the U.S. Army School of the Americas was relocated in 1984, a DoD institute known for graduating Latin America's worst human-rights abusers and some of the most notorious dictators in the region.[11] I asked the Cold War veteran where I could find more information on what Cold War veterans were asked to do, both with the School of the Americas and during their deployments to Central America. She explained to me that it would be difficult because "you were always constantly in motion. Anybody who says that they were stationed at, say, Fort Benning—were they really stationed at Fort Benning? Yes. Were there bodies there? . . . Out of three years, only about six to eight months—because we rotated. You also didn't have to classify it as a real deployment if you do it that way because it's just temporary duty, so there's no real record of it ever occurring. . . . Nowhere in my record does it show those." There are U.S. soldiers who served in Central America who are alive today, and their status and work as combat veterans, much less their physical and mental traumas, remain largely unacknowledged. The Cold War veteran explained to me that "the Cold War veterans were the forgotten group. We are the ones not talked about, 'cause what we did. . . . We weren't in the war. We weren't wartime. We got our hands dirty because they told us to, without any recognition. So when people talk about heroes, how do you define that? Is it only wartime? . . . People still shoot bullets, whether it's Cold War or not, and so I think that the next group of 'Cold War' soldiers is in for a rude awakening, and those are the ones that are coming out now. . . . They're all deployed; it's just not a war."

As I discussed in the previous chapter, the Salvadoran field of violence comprises actors who participate in the distribution of conflicts within that field, and the United States has historically had a role in structuring actors, providing them with resources and fortifying them with human capital as they participate in foreign fields of violence. This structuration is poorly acknowledged and largely forgotten, in part due to the way in which "the record" is altered as it is being produced. The oral histories of U.S. Cold War veterans thwart these distortions, but the silences that emerge even in those oral histories reflect power in the memory field. Edna Lomsky-Feder writes that "the personal narrative of war veterans should be read as a 'cultural text' that interweaves private experiences with collective representations that constitute the memory field of war," and she reminds us that accessibility to particular memories is regulated by social and cultural criteria.[12] U.S. national security is a framework that regulates accessibility to memories of the U.S. nation-state. As I showed in chapter 5, one dominant U.S. memory framework for remembering the Cold War involves a narrative of national security that naturalizes U.S. military interventions of the past as they inform the present. A rare narrative provided by a Cold War veteran who served in Central America was still subject to auto-censorship that was dynamic with the weight of power in the memory field. The social forgetting buttressed by power in the memory field has a way of generating a degree of collective ignorance so great that powerful actors in the memory field experience a narrowing in capacities of auto-evaluation.

In a twenty-first-century U.S. Army Field Manual publication on counterinsurgency, a breakout box concerning security cooperation in El Salvador explains that "the mid-1980s saw a massive U.S. aid effort, and considerable civilian and military reform. Congressionally constrained to an initial limit of no more than 55 military advisors and no combat troops, U.S. aid consisted of arms, military trainers, and reform and civic action programs. Several of these programs made slow progress because many in the Salvadoran military resented their imposition by an outside power."[13] The U.S. DoD, both through its own field manual and through the oral histories of its veterans, provides evidence of irreverence for U.S. power, despite the presumption of U.S. power. What interests me is the underlying narrative that is absent from national memories in the face of this power, which reflects a type of social forgetting. A Cold War veteran spoke of warped documentation practices and, decades after her service, continued to scribble notes on scraps of paper so as to avoid the record. Her deferments of voice reflect the power of the U.S. nation-state in the memory field. The U.S. Army Field Manual publication on counterinsurgency recognizes the Salvadoran military's resentment of the imposition of an outside power, without elaborating on the social phenomena that occur when an outside power imposes itself on others. Social forgetting renders the U.S. nation-state incapable of evaluating the unintended consequences of programs it has implemented elsewhere, and its current leader wants to know why all these people are leaving "elsewhere."

I am not arguing that the U.S. government is a single actor responsible for the entirety of the Salvadoran migration phenomena, but I am highlighting that the U.S. fugue state buttresses the mechanisms of forgetting in transnational space that would otherwise allow for a more thorough auto-evaluation of its impact. War veterans, scholars like myself, and campesinx migrants participate in the suppression of memories. A Salvadoran farmer who perceived that his country has been harmed by the United States maintained silence so as to not offend a U.S. citizen. A Cold War veteran who served the U.S. nation-state experienced deferments of voice in remembering her government service. I, after listening to the narrative of a Cold War veteran, was too freaked out to audio-record interviews with more of them. Pierre Bourdieu writes that "submission to the established order is the product of the agreement between the cognitive structures that collective history (phylogenesis) and individual history (ontogenesis) has inscribed in bodies and the objective structure of the world to which they are applied. The self-evidence of the injunctions of the State imposes itself so powerfully because the State has imposed the cognitive structures through which it is perceived."[14]

Today, the U.S. nation-state finds itself concerned with influxes of immigrants whose movement toward the United States gives rise to discussions of strategies regarding how to keep migrants out. That discourse unnecessarily criminalizes and dehumanizes migrants as their human rights are undermined. Absent from discourse about keeping migrants out is a reckoning of how the United States has structured the diasporas underlying transnational movements. Historian Paul Kramer writes that "in different ways and to varying degrees, many immigrants to the US can be recognized as already internal to US-centered fields of power and interaction before they cross US national-territorial borders."[15] This is particularly true in the case of El Salvador.

Understanding how U.S.-sponsored counterinsurgency efforts stimulated migration can be illustrated in the particularity of everyday lives. In chapter 5, I discussed ways in which U.S.-sponsored counterinsurgency efforts produced pre-civil-war and civil-war terror in El Norteño. While terror may seem like an abstract reason to migrate, I will now provide an everyday example of how a decision to migrate manifested in a campesina and then provided the basis for intergenerational migration in her family.

THE MIGRATION OF A SALVADORAN CIVIL WAR VETERAN

Historian Erik Ching highlights the absence of campesinx soldiers who opposed the guerrilla insurgents in the memory communities that provide collective narratives of the civil war in El Salvador.[16] During my fieldwork, I encountered a Salvadoran Army veteran who fought the insurgents and who today sends beans from El Norteño to her daughter in Long Island. Her narrative illustrates one of the ways in which an army backed by millions of dollars in U.S. aid[17] destroyed social relationships and made enemies of community members who had to migrate away from each other to live.

Graciela was a Salvadoran Army veteran who lived high up in the mountains of El Norteño. To get to her house, I ascended a mountain in a friend's pickup truck, the pavement disappearing into dirt as pine trees and coffee farms began to surround us on all sides. There were sweeping views of the Rio Lempa and the San Salvador volcano in the far distance. My friend explained how guerrilla forces occupied these mountains during the civil war, which allowed them to see the army advance by land. As we drove farther up the mountain, we passed swaths of coffee beans spread out on the cement to dry under the intense sunlight. We were near the border of Honduras, where the U.S. Cold War veteran I interviewed described being stationed some thirty years ago.

We came to a point where the road turned to mud. The truck could drive no farther. We hopped out and began walking. Chickens ran freely around the path, and *aguacateros* (mutt dogs) barked as we passed the properties they protected. We arrived at Graciela's small home, which was surrounded by an orange grove, the smell of citrus drifting in and out of her porch. Her kitchen was dimly lit by a woodstove. Graciela served me a cup of unfiltered coffee, sweetened with artisanal chocolate, and she killed one of a dozen game hens that were running around her backyard to make soup.

Graciela began telling me her memory of migration by gesturing toward the mountain behind her house. She told me that when she was just a girl, "the Armed Forces came here and said that if we weren't going to give them food, they were going to bomb the place." Graciela's family did not have any food to give them: "So my dad said, 'Daughter, you go.'" Graciela remembered how in the army, "they obliged us to work. When I was mad, crying that I couldn't come back here, I told them, 'I wasn't looking for work, you all made me come here to work.' And I couldn't return to this place because the guerrillas would kill me. That's how I entered the army." Graciela was forcibly recruited into the U.S.-backed counterinsurgency effort in El Salvador. Graciela was just a teenager when Reagan came to power, and she served in the Salvadoran Army during the Reagan administration. She spoke of no ideological motives. She spoke of hunger and threats.

Graciela's forced recruitment into the Salvadoran Army instantly transformed her into an enemy of the insurgents (her neighbors), whom her family was trying to protect from being bombed by handing over their daughter to Salvadoran state security forces. During her time in service, Graciela survived a mine blast that killed several of her colleagues. The shooting pain associated with her physical injuries continued to overwhelm her the year I interviewed her (nearly three decades after the blast). She remembered her husband dying in the war while she was pregnant, and she remembers giving birth to her daughter during active duty. She remembers that her daughter was born very thin.

When Graciela finally decided to leave the army, she could not return to her rural home because she feared being killed by her ex-insurgent neighbors. The same was true for several of her coworkers. She recounted, "We say, in the army, there are no rich people—there are farmworkers. All the soldiers are farmworkers. . . . They were poor more than anything . . . so when they left, they didn't have any other option but to emigrate." Graciela left El Salvador as an undocumented migrant with a coyote; she borrowed money from family members to pay the coyote, and she was granted asylum after she made it to New York. She stayed in the United States until one of her parents in El Salvador fell ill. If she returned to El Salvador, she would lose her legal status and risk being killed by her neighbors, but the war was far enough in the past that she decided to risk it to see her parents before they died. On her last day in the United States, Graciela clocked out of work and informed her boss that she was not coming back the next day because she only had one set of parents, and one of them was about to die. She returned to El Salvador and found that, following the peace accords, her neighbors no longer intended to kill her for her time served in the Salvadoran Army. They understood enough of her situation to allow her to live in peace.

When Graciela's daughter reached her teenage years, she told Graciela that she, too, wanted to go to the United States just like her mom did. Graciela's migratory behavior oriented her daughter toward *more innovative possibilities*[18] that included emigrating from El Norteño. Graciela told her daughter to test her luck, and Graciela's daughter now lives with her family in Long Island. Graciela and her daughter send parcels to one another using one of El Norteño's couriers, who Graciela's daughter described to me as the "one we know the best who brings the majority of parcels from my village." The everyday intimacy that is cultivated between mother and daughter, the intergenerational migrations within Graciela's family, and Graciela's impetus to leave El Salvador stem from Graciela's forced recruitment into a U.S.-funded counterinsurgency effort.

Graciela's ability to earn asylum was a rarity in the United States, as it was granted to less than 3 percent of Salvadorans prior to 1990.[19] Her time in the U.S.-backed army certainly helped her case, but here, I do not want to chalk up Graciela's life experience to her being a "lucky" recipient of asylum. Consider

Graciela's life course: it involved forced recruitment into the Armed Forces during her teenage years; she became an enemy of the neighbors she grew up with; she carried painful symptoms of physical injuries experienced during her time in service; she had to pay a coyote to get to the United States so that she could apply for asylum from within the United States; and she was unable to pay him with all the money she had to her name. In the end, she renounced the asylum she was "granted" to see her parents before they died, and now, she remains separated by national boundaries from her daughter. Graciela's being granted asylum was anomalous for a Salvadoran at that time, but in the end, the costs were on Graciela.

THE STIMULATION OF DIASPORIC MOVEMENT

It is well documented that the migration of Salvadorans to the United States began to increase dramatically during El Salvador's civil war.[20] This migration phenomenon developed until Salvadorans in the United States represented approximately one-fifth of the total population of El Salvador.[21] Today, one of the leading Salvadoran newspapers, La Prensa Gráfica, has a section titled "Department 15," recognizing the United States as El Salvador's fifteenth department (El Salvador comprises fourteen departments).

In the Community Population Survey (CPS) of the United States, one can examine where immigrant respondents came from and when. In the January 1996 results[22] of the CPS, for example, one can examine respondents who reported their birthplaces as Northern Triangle countries.[23] When I examined the 1996 results, the five highest values occurred for Salvadorans who reported entering the United States during the Salvadoran period of the Salvadoran Civil War.

It is important to acknowledge that the mass migration of Salvadorans out of El Salvador began at the same time U.S. taxpayers made several significant investments into the Salvadoran Civil War. The United States helped develop intelligence apparatuses that terrorized campesinxs, transferred millions in arms to the wartime government(s) of El Salvador,[24] and trained military personnel who would go on to become human-rights abusers.[25] By the mid-1980s, El Salvador had become the third largest recipient of U.S. foreign aid after Israel and Egypt.[26] In total, the United States contributed $4 billion to El Salvador in an effort to defeat the insurgency and implant democracy.[27] An investment of these proportions into a violent conflict in a relatively small country will carry proportionately large unintended consequences that need to be evaluated and understood. Admitting this is not anti-American. Admitting this should and could be part of interagency and interdepartmental improvement practices, moments of national acknowledgment and reflection, and government accountability projects that aim to examine not only the damaging effects of U.S. counterinsurgency efforts abroad but their long-run cost effectiveness for U.S. taxpayers.

In a study of Salvadoran migration conducted *during* the Salvadoran Civil War, a social anthropologist documented that over three-fourths of Salvadoran migrants arrived in the United States following the political crisis and that migrants from the eight most conflict-ridden departments were overrepresented.[28] That is to say, civil-war violence was already being recognized by a scholar, in real time, as a factor causing migration. The author of the report, Segundo Montes, was executed along with several of his colleagues shortly thereafter by Salvadoran security forces that received training from the U.S. DoD in Panama.

When Salvadoran refugees began arriving en masse to the United States during the 1980s, 97 percent of those who applied were denied political asylum,[29] reflecting the Reagan administration's contention that Salvadoran immigrants were economic immigrants.[30] At that time, in the United States, there was already a public consciousness regarding the fact that the U.S. government had played a role in the displacement of Salvadorans. Groups that worked for change engaged in lobbying, protests, and involved the U.S. justice sector in legal issues surrounding asylum. Meanwhile, nongovernmental organizations such as Americas Watch and Amnesty International that held contentions with the actions of the Reagan and Bush administrations were surveilled by the FBI and audited by the Internal Revenue Service.[31] In 1985, religious and refugee advocacy organizations had to file a class action lawsuit in federal court against the U.S. government in *American Baptist Churches v. Thornburgh* (known as the ABC lawsuit) for discriminatory treatment of asylum claims made by Guatemalans and Salvadorans. A settlement agreement was reached in 1991.[32] There were numerous administrative and legal-sector accessibility challenges with these cases, including disparities in lawyer/client understandings of what was being filed along with the government's capacity to process the applications. The experience is one of the ways in which immigration law established the terms through which Salvadoran immigrants negotiated their legal statuses[33] and set the stage for the myriad statuses, settlements, and related policy decisions that inform U.S. Salvadoran immigration today.[34] Historian Maria Cristina Garcia writes that "despite the lessons learned from the Central American refugee crisis and from the subsequent international efforts to exchange information, coordinate policies, and share responsibility for the accommodation of displaced persons, US interests have dominated these regional discussions and policies. Safeguarding civil liberties, due process, and human rights is often trumped in the name of national security. Once again, it is the non-governmental actors that remain the asylum seekers' most vocal advocates, trying to force nations to examine difficult issues that in the post-9/11 era many are reluctant to examine."[35]

The mass denial of political asylum claims and the subsequent need for the ABC lawsuit points to a lack of reparative actions taken by the United States for the role it played in the Salvadoran diaspora. Susan Bibler Coutin writes that "recognizing Salvadorans as refugees during the 1980s could have led to a reduction in US aid to El Salvador, which in turn could have affected the course of the Salvadoran Civil War."[36] The disarticulation between U.S. foreign and immigration policies over time not only creates the conditions in which experiences of injustice are lived, but the disarticulation weighs on U.S. taxpayers along with what it is that they can collectively remember about where their tax dollars have gone. Strategies that occupy public attention and national debate today include keeping migrants out by building a border wall, which has been projected to cost $25 billion.[37] The link between the billions spent on aid to El Salvador during its civil war and the estimated billions that the United States spends to maintain immigrant detention centers[38] is not the focus of public outrage concerning migration. This type of outrage is not popular in part because it is difficult to recognize, and social forgetting makes it difficult to recognize.

PROBLEMS OF RECOGNITION

The U.S. fugue state is a transnational manifestation of collective forgetting that is buttressed by its strategic frameworks (i.e., national security) that inform how the U.S. national past is gazed upon. Through structured silences and social forgetting, the U.S. fugue state generates a collective ignorance that reproduces support for its strategies, which will inevitably produce effects that will be paid for by future generations. The collective ignorance that is cultivated is a shadow of its disarticulated strategies, which continue to generate knowledge gaps in transnational space.

Prior to the start of the Salvadoran Civil War, the broader U.S. Cold War confrontation with the USSR shaped academic scholarship in the United States. In *Cold War University*, Matthew Levin describes how social-science scholarship "was notable for its lack of fundamental criticism of mainstream American policies and values. As the United States engaged in an ideological war with the Soviet Union and radicalism was largely discredited, it was assumed by most scholars that the essential questions about American society had been answered."[39] William Stanley has described that in theories of political development in the 1950s and 1960s, "even to raise questions about violence would place a researcher outside the intellectual mainstream."[40]

In the 1980s, social psychologist Ignacio Martín-Baró was teaching at La Universidad Centroamericana (the Central American University, or UCA) in El Salvador and developing scholarship on "liberation psychology," which was conversant with the liberation theology that was being digested by factions of

Salvadoran freedom fighters / insurgents / "terrorists"[41] (depending on who was talking about them during Cold War conflicts in Central America). From a state security perspective, liberation theology during the Cold War in Central America represented something similar to *jihad* in the contemporary conflicts in the Middle East. In Martín-Baró's work, he directly calls out transnational hierarchies of power. Shortly before his execution, he wrote that liberation theology constituted an antithesis of Latin American fatalism and that "the attacks against this popular movement of faith exhibit the point to which the dominant social classes in Latin America and the hegemonic interests articulated in Washington resent not only insurgent movements or revolutions of the Latin American pueblos, but also all thinking which supports a praxis that helps to break the shackles of conformity and social domination."[42] In 1989, Martín-Baró was executed along with Segundo Montes (author of the exploratory study that showed civil-war violence was a factor causing migration),[43] four other Jesuits, and two of their housekeepers at the UCA in El Salvador. They were executed by members of the Atlacatl Battalion, one of the first rapid-deployment infantry battalions of the Salvadoran Armed Forces that was created to destroy the rural support base for the insurgents.[44]

The Atlacatl Battalion received training by the U.S. military's SOUTHCOM (Southern Command) in Panama and was reportedly equipped with the latest North American M16 rifles, M-60 machine guns, 90mm cannons, and 60mm and 81mm mortars. They were responsible for the 1981 Mozote Massacre in the Department of Morazán, killing hundreds of campesinxs.[45, 46] On November 16, 1989, members of the Atlacatl Battalion entered the campus of the UCA and executed six Jesuits, their housekeeper, and her sixteen-year-old daughter.[47] The intellectual authors of the murders avoided prosecution, given their support from conservative politicians and a dysfunctional right-wing judiciary.[48] Twenty-nine years after their execution, at the alumni meeting of the Graduate School of UCA El Salvador, various speakers remembered and acknowledged the deep impacts these executions had on higher education and thinkers in El Salvador.

State-sponsored targeting of scholars was not particular to El Salvador. During the civil war, anthropologist Philippe Bourgois directly observed and ran from a 1981 attack by the Salvadoran Army in Morazán. Bourgois spoke out about how U.S. military aid and military trainers were assisting with the killing of civilians in El Salvador. In response, the CIA circulated a report to members of Congress to discredit him by portraying him as a communist propagandist. He later wrote that "the killing of some 75,000 people in El Salvador during the 1980s was directly attributable to US military, economic and logistical support for the Salvadoran army."[49] The discreditation of Bourgois harkened back to the U.S. domestic anticommunist fervor associated with the McCarthyism of the late 1940s and 1950s.[50] Social forgetting is one of the numerous ways in which the tradition of previous generations weighs on the brains of the living.

The denigration of knowledge managers, in this case, critical scholars who recognized and wrote about the deleterious impacts of U.S. counterinsurgency efforts in El Salvador, illustrates the extent to which ignorance was managed by the United States as it provided counterinsurgency security assistance to the Salvadoran state. Absent from evaluations of U.S. counterinsurgency efforts abroad are analyses, for example, of their unintended effects on the production of knowledge and the development of higher education in El Salvador.

CONCLUSION

In the previous two chapters, I examined the development and inculcation of forgetting as it relates to violence and the silence that emerges in its ongoing aftermaths. Here I explored ways in which previous U.S. counterinsurgency efforts implicated the emigration of select individuals who compose El Norteño's diaspora today. Campesinx memories illustrate unintended consequences of U.S. intervention in El Salvador's civil war.

The U.S. fugue state today is a system of forgetting that is re-created through practices of silence, the repetition of national security strategies, and practices of implementing disarticulated U.S. immigration and foreign policies. It permits unintended consequences of its previous actions abroad to forego critical evaluation, even when those consequences undermine the national securities of others and threaten the "national security" of itself and its future generations. Social forgetting generates collective ignorance, which makes social forgetting all the more difficult to see.

CONCLUSION

I have tried to tease out the machineries that have distorted and colonized our collective memory. I am interested in sabotaging them in any way possible.

—Penny Coleman[1]

Factions of the U.S. populace doubt whether all Salvadoran migrants deserve to be referred to as human, while some campesinx migrants doubt the integrity of what U.S. Americans call food. Both of these renderings of the Other raise questions about what is forgotten and remembered in transnational space, and they bring into relief the possibilities of memory studies for making sense of human and nonhuman dimensions of the present.

Teasing out the various ways in which collectives gaze upon and forget the past is both an elucidating and deceiving endeavor. Collective present experiences inform the way in which the past is accessed,[2] and it is possible to learn new things about present social arrangements through an examination of memories. But the scholarly acts of dissecting the ways in which collectives remember and forget can quickly lead us to power. In its presence, we risk developing metanarratives of truths and countertruths that might be too binary, too epistemically distant, and perhaps too unrecognizable to those who are doing the remembering. In this book, I have highlighted elements of collective remembering that inform, silence, preserve, project, obfuscate, and forget in the context of a rural diaspora and some of the nation-states that diaspora involves. These manifestations of social memory are interactive and multiplicative. They are implicated in everyday acts of recall that people use to make sense of multiple pasts across multiple borders.

In this book, I focused on some of the ways and dimensions in which campesinxs in one rural Salvadoran diaspora collectively remember, grounding my participation and observation in everyday practices that move nonhumans and humans across diasporic divides. In the microeconomies of El Norteño's

couriers, who transmit parcels between kin, I found that memory practices transnationally mobilize, assign values, and generate risks associated with the transport
of nonhuman objects in transnational space. Campesinx memories of migration
continue to be a medium in which knowledge regarding hazards associated with
the Mexican state, the Mexican cartels, coyotes, and the U.S. nation's border-
protection strategies are transmitted. Those transmitted memories inform the
basis of youths' imaginaries, governing their near and possible futures. Among
El Norteño's campesinxs, who transcend diasporic divides, collective forms of
nostalgia both reveal and suture sites of discontinuity. Campesinx restorative
nostalgia preserves traditional knowledge regarding milpa cultivation techniques that illustrate what Virginia Nazarea has poignantly described as "irreverence, possibly more than resistance"[3] to the hegemony of modern agriculture.
Campesinx remembering made me not interrogate a truth or countertruth
that feeds into a justice framework but rather ask critical questions about biodiversity and food. Collective memories are loaded with so much more than
narratives conducive to developing arguments about conflict and justice, and
grounded theoretical and ethnographic approaches should continue to take
the full possibilities of collective remembering into account—even when the
topics of interest concern power and its deleterious effects. Campesinxs taught
me to abandon the categories and frameworks that I initially used to understand collective memory and opened my mind to the expansive possibilities of
the collective memory cosmos.

That said, I cannot ignore the immense stress experienced by Salvadoran
couriers, particularly when they are directly affected by U.S. national security
strategies. In a recent get together with my courier friend Mateo, he showed me
a certificate he received from a San Salvador training regarding laws on money
laundering, terrorist financing, and narcotics. He told me the U.S. Drug Enforcement Agency (DEA) was present at the training because couriers could be used
to smuggle drugs into the United States, but their presence as part of the U.S.
governmental fabric he interfaces with was and remains mysterious to him. The
U.S. DEA arrived to a training of ANGEC (National Association of Parcels and
Culture Managers in El Salvador) couriers in El Salvador who service the Salvadoran diaspora, while U.S. Customs and Border Protection (CBP) agents
suspect ANGEC couriers on tourist visas of being drug smugglers as they enter
the United States with hundreds of pounds of food. ANGEC couriers may be
deemed unworthy of being spoken to in Spanish by Spanish-speaking CBP
agents inspecting their cargo, and U.S. Immigration and Customs Enforcement
(ICE) captures and deports some of ANGEC couriers' clientele. Despite his
best efforts to maintain his professional conduct with ANGEC, to comply with
what he learned from the DEA training, and to meticulously fill out the prior-
notice forms with the U.S. Food and Drug Administration (FDA), Mateo will

have an entire load of food parcels misclassified and confiscated upon entry into the United States as this book goes to press. This economically disastrous outcome for Mateo does not reflect novelties in his business practices but rather the discretion of the CBP agent who chose to call his parcels merchandise and then confiscate them at this one moment in time. The attention and energy usurped by the confrontations between couriers, their clients, and different departments and entities of the U.S. government seem to overshadow the much larger question of why U.S. citizens demand so many narcotics. Mateo asks me if Trump has it out for Salvadoran couriers. I consider Trump's "shithole" question, and I tell Mateo that the U.S. president is most likely unaware that Salvadoran couriers exist. He laughs. A few moments later, he agrees.

In the U.S. fugue state, where agents interfacing with the outside world operate under national security frameworks to interpret the Other, it seems that the terrorist, gang member, criminal, animal, and narco-trafficking fantasies of what the Other could be overshadow capacities for critical national reflection. That type of reflection is necessary not because Salvadoran couriers feel stress at U.S. ports of entry but because migrant children were forcibly removed from their parents by the U.S. Department of Homeland Security. Migrants are conflated with criminals and animals by the U.S. president. The border patrol has launched tear gas in the direction of children. The fugue allows for monstrous generalizations to metastasize in consciousnesses across the United States.

REMEMBERING IN A U.S. FUGUE STATE

The unintended consequences of U.S. counterinsurgency efforts abroad during the Cold War are interpreted as potential national security threats in 2018. There is no one person, presidential administration, branch, agency, department, or political party that is individually responsible for the collective sequela of U.S. interventions abroad and the collective experience of the U.S. fugue state. The complexity of the U.S. fugue state, particularly as reflected in its institutionalized practices (disarticulated policies and actions) and overarching strategies (national security), perhaps poses the greatest challenge to finding meaningful ways to collectively remember. In the post-9/11 era, the Immigration and Naturalization Service became U.S. CBP, U.S. Citizenship and Immigration Services (USCIS), and U.S. Immigration and Customs Enforcement (ICE). Shifting from the U.S. Department of Justice to the U.S. Department of Homeland Security, U.S. immigration policies and practices have become increasingly hostile toward immigrants, where immigrants, refugees, and asylum seekers are being conflated with potential terrorist threats. Finding alternative ways to remember moving forward is going to be challenging, particularly given that I have only highlighted one of multiple manifestations of social forgetting.

What I am calling the U.S. fugue state is a type of social forgetting that specifically concerns a particular period in time regarding U.S. relations with one country (El Salvador), but there are numerous collective fugue states being practiced in the United States and across the globe. I have shown one way in which forgetting interacts with national strategies and disarticulated policies that translate into contemporary collective actions, but there is social forgetting surrounding conflicts such as the establishment of the Virginia slave codes, the war in Vietnam, and the Guatemalan Civil War. It seems that with so much forgetting and collective culpability over generations, remembering might not be worth it. Sociologist Jeffry Olick writes that "we are all guilty. The challenge is to maintain the productive impulse in this acknowledgment rather than to let ourselves slip into the conclusion that because we are all guilty, we need not worry about it too much."[4] We citizens, scholars, students, migrants, government employees, gang members, resisters, and upholders of the system re-create the U.S. fugue state, and it is important to acknowledge that contemporary forgetting will lead to future ignorance. This is not a collective condition that can be resolved by name-calling, shaming, dichotomizing, and demanding that forgetters be subject to the same styles of domination they practice. That approach will reproduce the fugue. I see great potential for memory studies in elucidating pathways out of states of national oblivion.

One complicating aspect of the U.S. fugue state is that it has metastasized into national security strategies that have logic, which buttresses forgetting itself. This is a complex problem that requires complex solutions, and we need to find ways to deconstruct strategies that tautologically mitigate auto-evaluative endeavors. At the beginning of 2017, I wrote to my senators in Florida regarding my concern for the protection of immigrants during the Trump administration. Both provided generic responses, but Marco Rubio's response in particular provided exemplary rhetoric. In his response to my letter, Rubio juxtaposed the nation's historical role as a safe haven for refugees escaping foreign conflicts with the conjecture that "we must balance this honorable tradition of America's generosity with the recognition that the federal government's first responsibility is to protect the safety and security of American citizens. This is a duty I take very seriously, and that's why I have supported enhanced vetting to ensure we are not granting refugee status to terrorists."[5] My use of this quote is intended not to say anything about Senator Rubio himself but rather to illustrate some popular rhetoric circulating through U.S. consciousnesses today, where terrorism counterbalances the idea of immigrant sanctuary. This cognitive link has become so naturalized that it is almost too frightening to contradict. If we were to invert the logic behind that rhetoric, where we are concerned instead with state terror committed against indigenous peoples and immigrant benevolence, we might encounter deeper sources of the U.S. fugue state.

In the most recent census of the U.S. population, 0.9 percent identified as American Indian and/or Alaska Native alone.[6] This implies that 99.1 percent of the U.S. population descends in some form or another from immigrants, refugees, asylum seekers, or potential "terrorists" entering North America. The structured genocides, forced removals of children from their homes during the "boarding-school era,"[7] systematic sexual assaults, confinement to reservations, and quantitative reduction of indigenous North American communities reside within an imperial epicenter of U.S. national forgetting. On the five-hundredth anniversary of Columbus's discovery of the "New World," the late Vince Tucker wrote that international development work and planning are heirs to the tradition of indigenous degradation and domination:

> The language used to name others, as Columbus named the "Indians," has changed but the underlying assumptions of superiority and inferiority, of accomplishment versus deficiency, rationality versus superstition and ignorance, remain the same. In Columbus' time non-Europeans were described as "savages" while the European conquerors saw themselves as "civilized." Later the terms "advanced" and "backward" came into use, followed by "modern" and "traditional," and more recently "developed" and "underdeveloped." The superior have always seen it as their right and even duty to intervene in and transform the lives of those whom they decide need "developing." This is sometimes done with frank brutality while in other cases it operates under altruistic sounding names such as "aid."[8]

By the mid-1980s, El Salvador had become the third largest recipient of U.S. foreign *aid*.[9] Aid is now provided by the United States to help countries fight incessantly emergent threats of "terrorism," but the state terror the U.S. government has structured for its indigenous communities, slaves, and foreign communities that contain "insurgents" is repeatedly subject to forgetting. Violence begets more violence, regardless of whether terms such as *terrorism* or *national security* are used to justify it. We may be tempted to address the complexity of the issue using justice frameworks, but those frameworks alone are not sufficient.

CULPABILITY

In 2016, there was a Supreme Court ruling in El Salvador that overturned the postwar amnesty law guaranteeing impunity for civil-war crimes. In El Salvador, where the state calls the same people "terrorists" that the Trump administration calls "animals,"[10] the Salvadoran ruling offers a critical moment for reflection and reconciliation. However, I am skeptical about the possibilities for true reconciliation and reparation when U.S. culpability in the Salvadoran conflict is not adequately addressed. If war criminals leveraged human capital garnered from the U.S. School of the Americas to commit their crimes, who is the true *mastermind* of Salvadoran war crimes?[11] Further, the first warrants issued since the 2016 repeal of the Salvadoran amnesty law were for former guerrilla fighters who killed American soldiers.[12] I wonder what these justice practices will reveal and if they will do anything to alter the disillusionment of Salvadorans who say things such as "*The Truth Commission*—that was just another political thing" or "We live in the shadow of the U.S." or the individual who sprayed graffiti near Boulevard de los Héroes in San Salvador (see figure C.1).

Perpetrators and survivors alike practice the evasion of culpability through silences that produce forgetting. As Salvadorans prepare to move forward with prosecutions following the repeal of the Supreme Court ruling, as disillusioned campesinxs remain disillusioned, and as the current U.S. president refers to the newest members of a state security threat as "animals," the need for acknowledgment and reconciliation regarding the role of the U.S. government in El Salvador's conflict is ever more imperative. I am less concerned with the prospects of prosecuting individuals than finding ways to acknowledge and reconcile the complex ways in which U.S. intervention in El Salvador has structured and restructured tiring and harmful conflicts.

Taking symbolic violence seriously means holding power accountable. Cecilia Menjívar and Néstor Rodríguez write that "the United States does not bear sole responsibility for every act of state terror in Latin America. . . . Yet, it is important to acknowledge that the U.S.–Latin American interstate regime played a key role in setting up and operating campaigns of terror to eliminate perceived 'subversives.' Perhaps acknowledging this link more clearly in truth commissions, tribunals, and the like would lead to lasting structures that would be truly conducive to peace and justice in the region."[13] But who holds a U.S.-dominated regional system accountable for such actions? At the formal inauguration of the International Criminal Court (ICC), Erna Paris observed that "one country is conspicuously not represented in this room. The absence of the United States is glaring."[14] While the U.S. DoD may not be prone to leaving trace evidence at the scene of war crimes, we have learned from El Salvador that the United States nonetheless trains and arms those individuals who go on to commit them. It is likely that meaningful reconciliations for actions where the U.S. government was culpable may never be adequately addressed in tribunals and truth commissions that target perpetrators who were equipped by powerful agents that remain outside of these justice arenas. Outside of justice frameworks, scholars and students can engage in memory studies not only to generate findings but also to educate the next generation of citizens, government employees, and institution makers on the complexity and importance of memory to national governments.

FIGURE C.1 Graffiti appearing near Boulevard de los Héroes, San Salvador, more than two decades after the Salvadoran Civil War (2018). It equates the Armed Forces of El Salvador (FAES) with assassins; the guerrilla resistance (FMLN) with traitors.

THE PROMISE OF MEMORY STUDIES

In the United States, current immigration discourse suggests that a physical barrier along the U.S. southern border with Mexico is a logical next step worth investing in. Indeed, there are advantages to be gained by acknowledging and remembering what the United States did in places like El Salvador before spending money on those types of projects. Irina Carlota Silber questions the ways in which modes of U.S.-funded counterinsurgency techniques used in El Salvador emerge as possibilities for the war in Iraq, and she notes that the legacies of that option are still unfolding in El Salvador.[15] Within the memory field of campesinxs from one rural Salvadoran diaspora, I found that the legacies of that option included emigration. Memory studies can be much more than a way to retell stories or antagonize truths—memory studies can inform program evaluations of U.S. interventions abroad, particularly in screening for *unintended consequences* of past interventions (particularly counterinsurgency efforts). The United Nations Evaluation Group writes that "the purposes of evaluation are to promote accountability and learning. Evaluation aims to understand why—and to what extent—intended and unintended results were achieved."[16] Beyond tweaking counterinsurgency programs over time (e.g., Vietnam, El Salvador, Iraq), there is a larger need to understand the long-term and unintended impacts of such programs, particularly in cases where the U.S. DoD explicitly acknowledges findings such as "these programs made slow progress because many in the Salvadoran military resented their imposition by an outside power."[17] In my analysis of the memory field in El Norteño's diaspora, I found that counterinsurgency techniques generated vague renderings of the past, where the details underlying the murder of family members by living neighbors cannot be recalled or reconciled and where emigration is a continued navigational strategy from a field of lethal violence that is ongoing, with no end in sight. Considering the relative size of the Salvadoran diaspora, one wonders what other social phenomena will unfold decades from now, following the U.S. interventions in the Middle East.

In addition to having a utility for program evaluation, memory studies can and should have a growing role in higher education. Upcoming generations are those that will encounter the unintended consequences stemming from the U.S. fugue state. Legal scholar Martha Minow suggests that scholars can focus on the history of responses to atrocity versus atrocity alone and that "education, teaching materials, books, exhibits, and events, for adults and for children—all of these are vital responses to mass violence."[18] While I do not expect that the U.S. government will one day erect a monument to honor its Cold War veterans, and nor do I expect that the United States will sign on to statutes that hold it accountable for war crimes any time soon, I do think that the burgeoning field of memory studies has a productive place in both U.S. and Salvadoran education. It is one of the ways we can work to educate future generations of government employees and U.S. citizens to navigate us out of the fugues we collectively participate in. I see the desire for it when I run into Texas school teachers who are touring El Salvador in an effort to understand the country that so many of their students come from. I see it in Salvadoran university students when they intuitively include criminal deportations from the United States as an independent variable in longitudinal models of Salvadoran homicides. I see it when disparate teams of U.S. government employees ask for a tour of the Centro Monseñor Romero at the Central American University, where the clothes of Jesuits executed by U.S.-trained special forces are displayed behind glass. Despite the weight of the U.S. fugue state, in all its complexity, there is a latent curiosity among U.S. citizens and Salvadorans that turns attention to transnational pasts. The curiosity stems not only from confused and crystal-clear memories of the recent past but from imaginaries of how different the future could be.

APPENDIX

RESEARCH METHODS

Here, I explain my core data-collection methods, analytic strategy, and the reiterative procedures I used to eventually write this book. Grounded-theory methods are flexible yet systematic guidelines that researchers sometimes use to collect and analyze data, typically qualitative, to construct theories grounded in data.[1] Grounded-theory methods tend to rely on constructivist epistemological frameworks in contrast to positivistic approaches that use deductive logic to evaluate theories tested on people. In grounded theory, *who* produces knowledge in the collapsing space of researcher and informant remains a central, salient question throughout data collection and analysis. It is also an approach that emphasizes the interplay between data collection and analysis, where the theory "emerges" from data that are reiteratively visited and collected.[2] I personally chose to use grounded-theory methods to better reconcile my own work with epistemological critiques that have emanated from critical indigenous scholarship regarding the extraction of knowledge from local communities and ways that research can instead involve, honor, and be shaped by individuals in the field.[3] I also use grounded theory given my interests in the epistemological critiques that emanate from the "ontological turn" in the social sciences, particularly where the productive processes for generating theory are being decentered,[4] and where the natures of nonhuman actors (such as parcels) are being conceptualized as contributing to knowing in an interactive manner.[5]

I used a mixed-methods approach to collect data under a grounded-theory framework. In particular, I used participant observation with field notes, collected *testimonios* (testimonies), and conducted intensive interviews. On several occasions, I examined secondary quantitative data that were relevant to emergent themes identified from my core qualitative research strategies, allowing for a "back-and-forth interplay" between qualitative and quantitative data, "with qualitative data affecting quantitative analyses and vice versa."[6] I tried to avoid letting the logic of quantitative explanatory modeling exert power over emergent theories in this book, and I instead attempted to treat the scarce amount of quantitative modeling evident in this final work as "monster slang"[7] that can here assume a passive and secondary role to the abductively reached conclusions.

I used theoretical sampling to collect data, where I focused on collecting data related to parcels, the memories associated with parcels, and the emergent findings generated from the data itself.

PARTICIPANT OBSERVATION

Participant observation was a core method that helped me immerse myself, for a brief moment in time and to a certain extent, in El Norteño's diasporic communities. Anthropologists who have experience working in Chalatenango have emphasized the utility of participatory observation techniques. In writing about doing memory research in Chalatenango, the Salvadoran anthropologist Carlos Benjamín Lara Martínez emphasizes that researchers should have an understanding of the values and conceptions of the local culture that is used to construct discourse.[8] To better understand the memory discourse that emerged in the field, I intermittently worked with couriers from El Norteño in the northern Department of Chalatenango over a three-year period (2015–2018). While I spent most of my time with couriers, I regularly interacted with their clients located in El Norteño, Colorado, and Long Island. I participated in couriers' business operations and attended trips that moved parcels between individuals located in these diasporic networks, beginning in the countryside of Chalatenango and ending in enclaves of campesinxs located inside the United States. Anthropologist Irina Carlota Silber writes that "I learned early that tagging along and getting a lay of the land would be a critical aspect of my fieldwork methodology. For Chalatecos war was everyday and rooted in territory."[9] I also learned that tagging along with Chalatecos, participating in their work and spending ample amounts of time doing everyday activities, was a critical way for me to understand objects, both gazed upon and transferred, in a diasporic memory field that was not my own.

Because couriers typically leverage their homes and family members to conduct business, I lived with two couriers (my key informants) for an intensive four-month period to orient myself to their everyday lives and to better understand everyday aspects of their profession that I could not obtain by simply arriving to work during daytime hours. Living with couriers allowed me to be present for the endless and sporadic phone calls and emergencies that needed to be resolved at the last minute, at all times of the day and night. I received on-the-job training and spent ample time collecting, inspecting, weighing, and repackaging parcels delivered by Salvadoran campesinxs to couriers. I had the privilege of talking to couriers about this study as we relaxed in hammocks at the end of each evening. Over the course of this study, I spent a total of three years participating in sections of courier travel sequences (e.g., being present at collection only or distribution only), and I fully participated in transnational collection-to-delivery sequences on six occasions. I participated in the U.S.-based distribution of parcels in Colorado (including Boulder County and the Metro Denver area) and Long Island, New York (Suffolk and Nassau counties).

My field notes were first written by hand and then typed into a computer. After typing up my field notes with aliases and pseudonyms, I burned the handwritten notes so as to further eliminate potential links to the identities of campesinxs who had spent a great deal of energy avoiding documentation by the state, only to then be documented by a gringo sociologist. While I am hesitant to use the epistemologically patriarchal notion of "protecting" research subjects, I have also spent ample time talking with key informants about their views on the need to remove links to personal identities from this final work.

My field notes were thematically centered—focused primarily on parcels and memory practices associated with parcels. I often wrote down details of my environments. I took notes as I was collecting parcels from peoples' homes or as they delivered them to us, as I sat at kitchen tables, and as individuals dictated stories or information to me, and I also wrote field notes in private in various trailer-park parking lots, bathroom stalls, fast-food restaurants, and bedrooms located throughout El Salvador and the United States. I felt that it was important for people to know what I planned to do with the work (write a book). While one might say that openly taking field notes biased my observations, I would also add that it was more of an interactionist (versus representational) way of knowing that often produced unexpected recruitments of storytellers who had time (often the older generations) and who wanted their stories documented. On other occasions, the overwhelming burden of courier labor did not allow me the time or space to write notes at the time something was occurring because I was busy doing something else (e.g., packaging and moving parcels). I was also conscious of whether the situation called for field-note taking. For example, when individuals first expressed "conversational testimonios" regarding sexual assault or other human-rights abuses, I often did nothing but listen. Depending on the situation, I might ask if the individual felt comfortable repeating the story in front of a tape recorder or if it was all right if I wrote about it.

With time, I started to become recognizable in my key informants' networks and became increasingly more involved in the transport of more sensitive parcels. I could become involved in transporting parcels such as papers for child custody cases, where family members split by diasporic divides trusted me with sensitive information that was to be relayed between El Salvador and the United States. With time, I developed my own relationships with couriers' clientele, many of which have turned into friendships. Working in this manner provided me with ample context for understanding not only the parcels, actors, and places in campesinxs' memories but the diurnal deviations, the implicit temporalities, and the significance of narrative devices used to relate memories of migration.

TESTIMONIOS

Sometimes campesinxs (more often, those living in the United States) wanted to provide a *testimonio* (testimony) of their migration experiences. A testimonio is different from an interview. During a testimonio, the speaker structures the telling of a personal or collective truth. Testimonios disrupt epistemological distances between interviewer and interviewee in mainstream research,[10] reissuing some power back to the speaker. In Latin American contexts, the testimonio has become one of the methods used for making sense of oral histories and the political narrative of oppression.[11] Testimonios "involve witnessing" and are expressed in the first-person, marked by interested voices that speak with "urgency and involvement."[12] Further, testimonios can be used to structure histories that are poorly recognized. The queer theologian Marcella Althaus-Reid wrote that "in Spanish, the words 'story' and 'history' are written with the same word: historia. This means that as a Spanish speaker, my notion of the boundaries between interpreting a story and the meaning of history, is somehow blurred. Stories are historical events. History is made up of stories."[13] I collected both recorded and unrecorded testimonios from campesinxs who chose to share them during my fieldwork in order to better understand powerful memories regarding movement, the diaspora, and migration.

My general style of receiving an individual's testimonio (be it recorded or unrecorded) was to be quiet and listen to an unstructured presentation of a narrative, interjecting questions only at the end of a story. I perceived that the political climate of the United States increased the general urgency of testimonios provided to me, particularly as xenophobic rhetoric toward Central American migrants seemed to be salient in the United States at the time I was collecting data (both prior to and following the election of Donald Trump as the president of the United States). Testimonios more often than not came from migrants inside the United States, often from individuals who wanted to clarify a record—ultimately about them—to which they had to regularly listen but had rarely been asked to contribute. The testimonios that I documented with audio recordings typically involved campesinxs who expressed an interest in wanting to say something for the record, often as the result of a felt experience of injustice.

Testimonios also generated moments of critical reflection.[14] The substance of testimonios challenged my ignorance of certain aspects of speakers' circumstances and histories, and I examined my own ignorance, in part as a symptom of collective forgetting. As such, this project allowed me the space to acknowledge and then resolve erroneous assumptions I held and to think about where those assumptions came from. In this sense, my attempt to decenter epistemic privilege in the methods I used highlights campesinxs as some of my most patient, favorite, and trusted teachers. Often, the speaker of a recorded testimonio was remembering a painful event: a traumatic war memory, a clandestine trip through Mexico, a sexual assault during the civil war, an unexpected detention in a windowless cell in the United States, or abuse by an immigration law-enforcement official. Recorded testimonios that I documented were often spoken in front of other people. The grisliest of testimonios always seemed to be told in front of children and at dinner tables (this has implications for both intergenerational trauma and for memory as an informative strategy). Storytelling in campesinx kinship networks was a locus of remembering, and testimonios that emerged from these spaces highlight the collective dynamics of *historias* (stories/histories) as they are remembered in El Norteño's diaspora.

INTENSIVE INTERVIEWS

I did carry with me, almost at all times, an evolving semistructured interview instrument that I generally administered to campesinxs who had experience with undocumented migration to the United States. The instrument included probes regarding events in Salvadoran history (e.g., *La Matanza*, the Civil War) that have played a role in Salvadoran migration, as well as questions that could provoke everyday memories relevant to migration. I had questions about the civil war in El Salvador that varied by age of the interviewee at the time of the interview and questions about experiences in Mexico, the Salvadoran economy, violence, detention and deportation, rural folklore, and parcels. The basic interview instrument was reviewed, edited, and partially structured with the help of my courier key informants. It provided ample probes regarding the mass exodus of Salvadorans, and there were generally points of departure that could stimulate particular memories of migration for a single individual who was being recorded.

Being a participant observer helped me pay attention to the importance of memories that some oral historians describe as forms of remembering "that are unadorned with adversaries and heroes, that are not about nationally salient events with compelling plots or violent struggles."[19] While I was certainly attentive to the fact that the Salvadoran Civil War was an index period for many family memories of migration, my time spent as a participant observer helped me hone in on memories that were not historically spectacular. Instead of showing up for a "cold" interview about a past that I could frame (through questions and approach) as being "traumatic," I often had a deeper context and knowledge of the individual I was going to interview before an audio-recorded interview or testimonio occurred. Often, interviews were referred to me within families or generated as a result of individuals sharing memories that intersected with historically significant events (e.g., a migration memory corresponding to known moments of violence in Chalatenango during the Salvadoran Civil

War). By working as a participant observer in an occupation that was familiar to campesinxs in El Norteño's diasporic communities, I was able to use context and family networks to generate and understand recorded interviews.

While I personally prefer the collection of unstructured testimonios over semistructured interviews, it was the structured portion of the semistructured interview that sometimes helped a memory maker share her/his story. While campesinxs had much to say about the diaspora, some froze in front of a tape recorder. The first time this happened, I was trying to take a testimonio from a friend who had spent days telling me tales about his undocumented journeys through Mexico. He agreed to have his stories recorded, but when I finally turned on the tape recorder, he did not speak. He asked me to shut off the tape recorder, and after I did so, he explained that he wasn't sure that he had anything important to say, and he was worried about saying it in an uneducated manner. We talked a bit more about the research project, and he said it would be helpful if I could instead treat this as an interview and ask him questions so he knew what I was interested in. I took out my semistructured interview instrument and began asking the migration-centered questions in the instrument, which quickly provoked a testimonio, and I then abandoned the instrument. These types of interactions are documented issues in the oral history methods literature, where the questioning of the interviewer can help evoke a testimony.[20] In the context of this diasporic network, I had to be flexible and switch methods if the audio recording became an issue (usually regarding issues of epistemic authority).

Limited formal schooling and illiteracy were not major barriers to collecting data. Campesinxs preserve knowledge in collective memory, theorizing and communicating about the effects of larger forces on everyday lives (such as the weather—a cosmic force that could result in abundance or loss). Irina Carlota Silber writes that "ultimately, many Chalatecos have ample practice thinking and living through the larger structures that constrain their lives."[21] My findings coincide with Silber's, in that much like the weather, campesinxs' perceptions of transnational power and violence were often direct and concise, honed using collective knowledge, oral history transmission, and accumulated observation. Their observations often put me to shame as a sociologist, and I frequently followed their leads to obtain more historical information or statistics that provided context for their claims about life in El Norteño and its diaspora. While I maintained a distinction between field notes and interviews, I was careful about the level of importance I assigned to transcribed text, keeping in mind that I was "consuming a constructed artefact"[22] when analyzing transcribed interview data. Transcribed interviews were useful, but in having a familiarity with a small network of individuals who were selected for an interview, I was usually surprised by how much someone changed his or her style of speaking in front of a tape recorder to sound "more educated." The central weight of my data collection was thus my experience in writing field notes, which helped me make the most sense of the multiple forms of data I collected and analyzed to write this book.

I should finally mention that I obtained informed consent prior to recording any testimonio or intensive interview, and I redacted records to eliminate identifiers. I burned the initial written drafts of my field notes in order to eliminate various links to specific people and parcels and the times and places associated with them. Characteristics and identities located in this work have been changed and altered with the explicit purpose of honoring privacy.

ANALYSIS

In practicing grounded theory, I underwent two major phases of data collection and analysis. After the first seven months of data collection, I analyzed all my field notes and interview data for emergent themes. I used Atlas.ti software[15] to conduct the first round of coding on field notes, testimonios, and interview transcripts. I did line-by-line coding of the field notes and interview text to develop "open codes,"[16] where I generally expressed these codes in present-progressive summaries of the text. Next, I linked open codes to develop "axial codes" based on my identification of emergent themes in the data. Finally, I developed "theoretical codes" that correspond to the chapters that structure this book. As it concerns "theoretical saturation," I followed Charmaz's suggestion that one needs to "be open to what is happening in the field and be willing to grapple with it."[17] After coding, I reentered the field to resample individuals, guided by the emergent theoretical findings derived from round one of data collection.

The second round of participant observation and interviewing occurred over an eight-month period, where I lived in El Salvador but spent less time with couriers' everyday business operations and more time conducting theoretical sampling, where I sought out data that were specifically focused on emergent findings from round one. During round two, I shared my initial findings with couriers and their campesinx clientele in El Salvador and the United States, who often provided depth regarding the round-one themes I had identified. After this second phase of data collection, I again coded all my round two field notes and interview data using the open, axial, and theoretical coding sequence described prior. During round two of theoretical coding, I reconciled, altered, and changed my original theoretical codes. I maintained close contact with couriers as I did this, often calling them on the phone or meeting with them in person as I attempted to sort and make sense of codes.

As I developed the "theory" presented in this book, I aimed less to fit my findings into existing theoretical frameworks, and I aimed more for "low theory," which Judith Halberstam describes as "theoretical knowledge that works at many levels at once, as precisely one of these modes of transmission that revels in the detours, twists, and turns through knowing and confusion, and that seeks not to explain but to involve."[18] I found, for example, that using real-life examples of symbolic violence seemed to appeal to couriers, whereas theories of stigma did not. This does not mean that stigma is not implicated in the field, but it does mean that I was more prone to importing social theories such as symbolic violence that key informants could recognize in their communities. After two rounds of data collection and analysis, I began to engage in a period of intensive writing in El Salvador that spanned 2017 to 2018. During the writing period, I regularly encountered lingering questions, holes in my knowledge, and doubts regarding representation as I aimed to finish a chapter of text. Writing "in the field" as opposed to outside the field helped me patch together (versus gloss over) the presentation of data in this work. It was normal for me to bring my laptop computer into the homes of key informants and sometimes their campesinx clientele, where I translated sections of text and expressed my questions and concerns. While my methods inevitably produced errors that plague all research projects, my use of reiterative data collection and analysis, theoretical sampling, and writing in the field were ways in which I attempted to stay grounded in the memories of campesinxs connected to El Norteño's diaspora.

ACKNOWLEDGMENTS

As I worked on this project, I encountered people who helped me learn, theorize, and reflect. I am forever grateful to the Salvadoran couriers "Mercedes" and "Mateo." They took an interest in what I was doing, and they were engagingly involved in the research methods and many dialogues that formed the foundation of the theorizing process for this project. They shared their resources, food, medicine, and time. They provided me the opportunity to learn about what it is that they do, and they expanded my vocabulary such that it now includes a wide range of creative curse words that I will forever treasure. I am deeply thankful to their family members, friends, and clients in transnational space. Chalatecxs throughout Chalatenango, Colorado, and New York generously shared their resources, houses, time, and memories with me. I am particularly thankful to one family in Colorado that repeatedly fed and housed me every time I arrived. After discussing the matter at length with key informants and several interview participants, I have changed names and other characteristics to remove potential links to identities throughout this work.

Over the past four years, my colleague Hope Ferdowsian provided me with the personal mentorship I needed to write a book. She introduced me to my private editor, Lauren Chopin, who provided sharp criticism and substantive intellectual feedback and dialogue. Victoria Sanford supported the development of the thinking that went into this book and paved a way to publicly talk about the legacy of U.S. counterinsurgency efforts in Central America. I am deeply grateful to Molly Todd for feedback on an earlier version of this manuscript, as she has helped me shape, refine, and expand my thinking. Leah Schmalzbauer reviewed some of my earliest plans for this work, and she kindly guides me in new directions at key moments when I need guiding. I am particularly thankful to Irina Carlota Silber for the numerous anthropological insights that she shared (and continues to share) with me during just about any conversation we have. Two of my students at UCA (Universidad Centroamericana) El Salvador, Blanca Estela Vindel Sandoval and Carlos Alberto Echeverría Mayorga, took a particular interest in chapter 2 and stimulated my quantitative imagination as they developed their own models of nonhuman actors. Lorena Rivas de Mendoza provided me with the space and breath to think at the UCA when I needed it the most. Leslie Mitchner and Nicole Solano at Rutgers University Press showed an enthusiasm for this project that made it possible.

As I wrote this book, I reached out to numerous thinkers whose work I deeply respect, and I was delighted when they responded with indispensable information and resources. I am grateful to Amparo Marroquín Parducci, Alisa Garni, Jason De León, Kimberly Theidon, Alcira Dueñas, Elizabeth Kennedy, John Mark Robeck, Carmen Molina Tamacas, Purcell Carson, and Virginia Nagy for stimulating my thinking during long stretches of writing.

My parents, Carol Wheeler and Frank Anastario, were encouraging through this process and did not pass judgment as I broke away from the everyday rhythms of North American life to collect data and write this book. I am ultimately mindful of and quite personally thankful to them for being so open and accepting. I am finally thankful to my grandmothers, Maria and Viola, for taking so much time to talk with me about their memories of migration and of migrants. Those stories taught me that there was always something more to be learned by listening to memories of migrations.

NOTES

INTRODUCTION

1. "What You Need to Know about the Violent Animals of MS-13," The White House, May 21, 2018, https://www.whitehouse.gov/articles/need-know-violent-animals-ms-13/, accessed July 3, 2018.
2. M. Anastario, K. Barrick, D. Gibbs, W. Pitts, R. Werth, and P. Lattimore, "Factors Driving Salvadoran Youth Migration: A Formative Assessment Focused on Salvadoran Repatriation Facilities," *Children and Youth Services Review* 59 (2015): 97–104.
3. N. Hamilton and N. S. Chinchilla, "Central American Migration: A Framework for Analysis," *Latin American Research Review* 26, no. 1 (1991): 75–110; Segundo Montes and Juan José García Vásquez, *Salvadoran Migration to the United States: An Exploratory Study* (Washington, D.C.: Georgetown University, Hemispheric Migration Project, Center for Immigration Policy and Refugee Assistance, 1988); Molly Todd, *Beyond Displacement: Campesinos, Refugees, and Collective Action in the Salvadoran Civil War* (Madison: University of Wisconsin Press, 2010), 51.
4. Tim Golden, "Accord Reached to Halt Civil War in El Salvador," *New York Times*, 1992; Scott Wallace, "You Must Go Home Again: Deported L.A. Gangbangers Take Over El Salvador," *Harper's Magazine* 301, no. 1803 (2000): 47–56, http://scottwallace.com/PDF2010/HarpersGangs.pdf.
5. "Illegal Alien Apprehensions from Countries Other Than Mexico by Fiscal Year (Oct. 1st through Sept. 30)," U.S. Customs and Border Protection, https://www.cbp.gov/sites/default/files/assets/documents/2017-Dec/BP%20Total%20Apps%2C%20Mexico%2C%20OTM%20FY2000-FY2017.pdf, accessed June 14, 2018.
6. Summaries are for fiscal years (FY2000–FY2019). See also "Southwest Border Deaths by Fiscal Year (Oct. 1st through Sept. 30th)," U.S. Customs and Border Protection, https://www.cbp.gov/sites/default/files/assets/documents/2017-Dec/BP%20Southwest%20Border%20Sector%20Deaths%20FY1998%20-%20FY2017.pdf, accessed June 14, 2018.
7. Amparo Marroquín Parducci is a professor of communications at the Universidad Centroamericana (UCA) José Simeón Cañas in El Salvador. See Marroquín Parducci, "All Roads Lead North: A Reading of News on Migration through the Figure of the Coyote," trans. Miguel Winograd, *E-misférica* 8, no. 2 (2010).
8. See the work of Annette Georgina Hernández Rivas, "Cartografía de la memoria: Actores, lugares, prácticas en El Salvador de posguerra (1992–2015)" (PhD diss., Universidad Autónoma de Madrid, December 2015); and Carlos Benjamín Lara Martínez, "La hora de Sofía: Memoria histórica del movimiento campesino de Chalatenango" (PhD diss., Universidad Nacional Autónoma de México, November 2016).
9. Jeffrey K. Olick, "From Collective Memory to the Sociology of Mnemonic Practices and Products," in *Cultural Memory Studies: An International and Interdisciplinary Handbook*, ed. Astrid Erll and Ansgar Nünning (Berlin: Walter de Gruyter, 2008), 159.
10. *Courier* is also the term that my key informants chose to be identified as in this book.

11. Alisa Garni, "Transnational Traders: El Salvador's Women Couriers in Historical Perspective," *Sociological Forum* 29, no. 1 (March 2014), doi:10.1111/socf.12074.

12. Aldo Lauria-Santiago writes, "More than 50 percent of those killed were peasants, while this group accounted for only 12 percent of those arrested in 1981. This finding is explained in part by the fact that most massacres, especially after 1979, took place in the countryside." See Lauria-Santiago, "The Culture and Politics of State Terror and Repression in El Salvador," in *When States Kill: Latin America, the U.S., and Technologies of Terror*, ed. Cecilia Menjívar and Néstor Rodríguez (Austin: University of Texas Press, 2005), loc. 2031–2033, Kindle.

13. Erik Ching, *Stories of Civil War in El Salvador: A Battle over Memory* (Chapel Hill: University of North Carolina Press, 2016), 11, Kindle.

14. Here I am specifically referring to Ramón Grosfoguel's analysis of epistemicide as part of the larger conquest process in the Americas, where "religious racism" was used to assume that people without a religion were people without a soul. Epistemic privilege (the capital/patriarchal, Western-centric/Christian-centric modern/colonial world system) and epistemic inferiority (the knowledge of indigenous peoples) are rooted in imperial dynamics. See Grosfoguel, "The Structure of Knowledge in Westernized Universities: Epistemic Racism / Sexism and the Four Genocides / Epistemicides of the Long 16th Century," *Human Architecture: Journal of the Sociology of Self-Knowledge* 11, no. 1 (2013), https://scholarworks.umb.edu/humanarchitecture/vol11/iss1/8/.

15. Sarah J. Mahler, *American Dreaming: Immigrant Life on the Margins* (Princeton, N.J.: Princeton University Press, 1995), 191.

16. I use the term *campesinx* in order to be gender/sexuality inclusive and gender/sexuality expansive in referring to rural farming peoples of Salvadoran descent. That said, as a nonnative speaker, I realize the use of the *x* suffix can be interpreted as an imperialist, neocolonial practice. I spoke with several Salvadoran peers about my use of the term, and *campesinx* was the end result of those discussions. Another suggestion that was considered, but was ultimately tabled, was to use gender-inclusive suffixes such as *es* in place of *x*; however, this was viewed as being perhaps too confusing for some readers given the implied plurality of the *es* suffix. There are also moments where I speak about individual actors without using the *x* suffix. In this case, I am referring to individuals who have a female or male gender identity. I ask the reader to speak the word *campesinx* aloud from time to time, changing the gender that is demarcated by the traditionally male or female *o* or *a* suffix, respectively, and to move beyond the allure of classification and demarcation in preconceptualized renderings of "rural people." I ask the reader to pause when speaking the word *campesinx* and consider who s/he is thinking about; whether limits have been placed on even thinking about the gender or sexualities of campesinxs; whether s/he feels a call to advocacy, an impulse to "speak for" the predefined oppressed, an impulse to classify the other in a larger framework; and the epistemic power dynamics implicated in those frameworks. For more discussion on the use of the *x* suffix, I recommend that readers look to Ed Morales's commentary in "Why I Embrace the Term Latinx," *Guardian*, January 8, 2018, https://www.theguardian.com/commentisfree/2018/jan/08/why-i-embrace-the-term-latinx, accessed July 4, 2018.

17. K. Charmaz, *Constructing Grounded Theory: A Practical Guide through Qualitative Analysis* (Los Angeles: Sage, 2010), 133.

18. In addition to conflicts with local law enforcement practices, the conflicts also stemmed from ongoing experiences of racial discrimination, education accessibility, economic restructuring, and unemployment. See Thomas Sugrue and Andrew Goodman, "Plainfield Burning: Black Rebellion in the Suburban North," *Journal of Urban History* 33, no. 4 (May 2007): 568–601.

19. My key informants came up with and suggested the pseudonym "El Norteño" to remove links to the identities of individuals throughout this book. "La Norteña" is also a nickname for "La Troncal del Norte," which is a highway connecting Chalatenango with San Salvador.

20. In the most recent Salvadoran census, 37.3 percent of the population was reported as living in rural areas. Within the northern Department of Chalatenango, 66.7 percent were reported as living in rural areas. See Dirección General de Estadística y Censos, *Población por área y sexo*, Censo de Población y Vivienda, San Salvador, El Salvador, 2007. According to a report by the Salvadoran secretary of culture (reference not included so as to not reveal location/identities), the municipality where I conducted this study is more than 99 percent rural.

21. To not reveal the identities of the people I interviewed and documented, I aim to respect their undocumented strategies by not naming the core municipalities where they are located.

22. In the context of studying memories of migration in a location that was foreign to me, I aimed to obtain depth over breadth (hence the small sample size). Becoming familiar with the migration circumstances surrounding a small number of families from this region allowed me to gain a deeper understanding of ways in which El Norteño's residents participated in the Salvadoran Civil War, ways in which they migrated to and established themselves in the states, and ways in which they remained connected across diasporic divides. The more familiar I became with individuals in El Norteño's diasporic networks, the more textured the stories (and correspondingly, memories) became. Particular details surrounding violence and clandestine movement did not emerge in stories that were told to me until later in my fieldwork, once I became a repeat presence in the field. In my absence, individuals I would eventually interview often asked my key informants about me, which also helped me establish mutual trust and more detail that might otherwise be lost if I aimed for breadth with a larger sample size.

23. Centro Nacional de Tecnología Agropecuaria y Forestal (CENTA), "Enrique Álvarez Córdova." Colecta de Germoplasma criollo de maíz, frijol y sorgo a nivel nacional, CENTA Banco de germoplasma, Ciudad Arce, La Libertad, El Salvador, 2010.

24. Fifteen hundred pounds of parcels is not much in comparison to the number of pounds that a single courier transports annually. My primary key informant moved approximately 16,800 pounds of parcels between the United States and El Salvador in a single year.

25. These experiences were invariably skewed given my presence as a white North American citizen with a U.S. passport. I further discuss this privilege in the context of couriers leveraging it as human capital in chapter 1.

26. I do this to familiarize readers with the everyday circumstances of individuals who remember pasts in ways that are replete with details and logics that may seem unfamiliar, just as they were at first unfamiliar to me. This may frustrate some readers who wish to see more sociological nuance from the author, but I would propose that in focusing on depth and dimension, I am trying to write while keeping the risk of "equivocation" salient in this work of grounded theory. Eduardo Viveiros de Castro proposes

> equivocation as a means of reconceptualizing, with the help of Amerindian perspectivist anthropology, this emblematic procedure of our academic anthropology. The operation I have in mind is not the explicit comparison of two or more sociocultural entities external to the observer, done with the intention of detecting constant or concomitant variations having a nomothetic value. While that has certainly been one of anthropology's most popular modes of investigation, it remains just one among others at our disposal, and is merely a "regulative rule" of the discipline's method. Comparison as I conceive it, on the contrary, is a "constitutive rule" of method, the procedure

involved when the practical and discursive concepts of the observed are translated into the terms of the observer's conceptual apparatus. So when I speak of comparison, which is more often than not implicit and automatic—making it an explicit topic is an essential moment of anthropological method—the anthropologists' discourse is included as one of its terms, and it should be seen as being at work from the first moment of fieldwork or even of the reading of an ethnographic monograph.

See Viveiros de Castro, *Cannibal Metaphysics*, ed. and trans. Peter Skafish (Minneapolis: Univocal, 2014), 85–86.

27. The Central American Minors program provided an alternative to undocumented land migration through Mexico in order to reunite children under the age of twenty-one with their parents in the United States. See also "In-Country Refugee/Parole Processing for Minors in Honduras, El Salvador and Guatemala (Central American Minors–CAM)," U.S. Citizenship and Immigration Services, https://www.uscis.gov/CAM, accessed July 13, 2017.

28. Nina Lakhani, "Thousands of Young Central Americans at Risk as Refugee Ban Halts Key Program," *Guardian*, February 2, 2017, https://www.theguardian.com/us-news/2017/feb/02/central-america-young-refugees-cam-trump-travel-ban, accessed July 13, 2017.

29. Judith Halberstam, *The Queer Art of Failure* (Durham, N.C.: Duke University Press, 2011), loc. 205–207, Kindle.

30. Viveiros de Castro, *Cannibal Metaphysics*, 84.

31. American Psychiatric Association, *Diagnostic and Statistical Manual of Mental Disorders*, 5th ed. (Washington, D.C.: American Psychiatric Association, 2013).

32. I build here on historian Yael Zerubavel's conceptualization of "state amnesia" as periods or events "that remain unmarked in the master commemorative narrative." See Zerubavel, "Recovered Roots: Collective Memory and the Making of Israeli National Tradition," in *The Collective Memory Reader*, ed. Jeffrey Olick, Vered Vinitzky-Seroussi, and Daniel Levy (New York: Oxford University Press, 2011), 239. See also the full quote in chapter 5.

In addition to suppressed narratives and master narrative construction, the idea of the U.S. fugue state includes reconciling contemporary national strategies and practices of implementing disarticulated U.S. foreign and immigration policies as part of the collective forgetting I examine in this book.

33. Amparo Marroquín Parducci, "El Salvador, una nación, muchas narrativas: contrapunto y fuga de la patria chica," in *Entre Saberes Desechables, y Saberes Indispensables: agendas de país desde la comunicación*, documento 9-FES-C3, Centro de Competencia en Comunicación para América Latina, C3, FES, Bogotá, 2009, 69–98.

34. Marroquín Parducci, "All Roads Lead North."

CHAPTER 1   *ES BARATA Y ES CARA*

1. The Chapultepec Peace Accords were signed in mid-January 1992, and on the last day of January, leaders from the FMLN and Armed Forces were ordered to stand down. See "El Salvador: Government," Department of Peace and Conflict Research, Uppsala Conflict Data Program, http://ucdp.uu.se/#conflict/316, accessed August 1, 2017.

2. The number of ANGEC-registered couriers fluctuates each year. When I began working with couriers, there were 640 registered members. At the time this chapter is being written, there were 767. Through personal communication with an ANGEC-approved courier and ANGEC administration, it was estimated that approximately 2,080 couriers had been registered as parcel managers with Salvadoran customs over time, with the majority being inactive or no longer registered with ANGEC.

3. Alisa Garni, "Transnational Traders: El Salvador's Women Couriers in Historical Perspective," *Sociological Forum* 29, no. 1 (March 2014), doi:10.1111/socf.12074.

4. A. Terrazas, "Salvadoran Immigrants in the United States," Migration Policy Institute, January 5, 2010, https://www.migrationpolicy.org/article/salvadoran-immigrants-united-states, accessed October 14, 2017.

5. Garni, "Transnational Traders."

6. When couriers have asked me to do personal favors, including communicating with CBP agents, I have done so. In comparison to the amount of data I have collected on couriers, courier requests of me have been rare, and I have tried my best to honor their requests to the best of my ability when they arise.

7. Otis Mason, "The Beginnings of the Carrying Industry," *American Anthropologist* A2, no. 1 (January 1889): 21–46, doi:10.1525/aa.1889.2.1.02a00030.

8. Garni, "Transnational Traders."

9. An ANGEC-registered courier will typically pay a 13 percent tariff on a parcel, whereas an unregistered courier would be asked to pay 30 percent on the unregistered parcel.

10. "Quienes Somos?," Asociación Nacional de Gestores de Encomiendas y Cultura, El Salvador, http://www.angec.net/somos.html, accessed July 26, 2017.

11. Sarah Gammage, "Viajeros y Viajeras in El Salvador: Connecting Worlds, Cementing Ties," Centro de Estudios Ambientales y Sociales para el Desarrollo Sostenible, report to the Inter-American Foundation, September 2003.

12. Garni, "Transnational Traders."

13. ANGEC specifically hoped to secure E-1 or E-2 visas for couriers, which are types of visas offered to traders and capital investors from any countries with which the United States maintains treaties of commerce and navigation. See Gammage, "Viajeros y viajeras"; and "Temporary Workers," U.S. Citizenship and Immigration Services, https://www.uscis.gov/working-united-states/temporary-nonimmigrant-workers, accessed December 3, 2018. Over a twelve-year period (from the 2004 CAFTA negotiations to 2016, when this chapter was being written), the United States has granted one E-1 visa and ten E-2 visas to Salvadorans. See "Nonimmigrant Visa Issuances by Visa Class and by Nationality, FY1997–2016," United States Department of State, Bureau of Consular Affairs, https://travel.state.gov/content/travel/en/legal/visa-lawo/visa-statistics/nonimmigrant-visa-statistics.html, accessed August 29, 2017.

14. Mateo, my primary key informant, perceived that my being a gringo and of the same nationality as customs inspectors affected the experience. He added that the experiences in U.S. customs when I accompanied him "always allowed for a good environment at the time of the inspection, including being able to get the inspectors to laugh—inspectors who are normally really serious. Your presence smoothed out the experience, because in customs, they are really rigid. This was probably the result of you being a gringo, and I think that the connection within people of the same nationality allowed for a better experience."

15. A major component of this variation includes local histories and economies, the relative volume of remittances sent to a location, and courier competition internal to a diasporic community. El Norteño's couriers provide services to a population of campesinx clientele, many of whom live in an area where subsistence agriculture is still practiced. Further, El Norteño's couriers do have competition in Colorado and Long Island, but that competition is likely much less intense than couriers who fly between larger sending and receiving enclaves (e.g., San Miguel and Los Angeles).

16. Jason De León, *The Land of Open Graves: Living and Dying on the Migrant Trail*, California Series in Public Anthropology (Berkeley: University of California Press, 2015), Kindle.

17. Irina Carlota Silber, *Everyday Revolutionaries: Gender, Violence, and Disillusionment in Postwar El Salvador* (New Brunswick, N.J.: Rutgers University Press, 2011), 196.

18. Cecilia M. Rivas, *Salvadoran Imaginaries: Mediated Identities and Cultures of Consumption* (New Brunswick, N.J.: Rutgers University Press, 2014), 136.

19. These were the general price ranges I heard referenced among ANGEC couriers in El Salvador from 2015 to 2018. These price ranges do not include costs for documents, identity cards, or photographs. Those items have separate costs that are more variable between couriers, and I have found that these prices vary in relation to whether the courier is also a participant in transactions (e.g., legal transactions that include getting documents notarized with the presence of disparate individuals) as opposed to simply delivering a parcel.

20. Pierre Bourdieu, "Structures, Habitus, Power: Basis for a Theory of Symbolic Power," in *Outline of a Theory of Practice* (New York: Cambridge University Press, 1977), 186.

21. Garni, "Transnational Traders."

22. Based on personal communication received by the CBP Information Center on January 20, 2016, in response to an email I sent to the U.S. center after a Salvadoran ANGEC courier had luggage confiscated by a CBP agent in Houston, Texas.

23. Indeed, English-language speaking ability is a component of human capital that couriers can leverage to get through customs or to navigate intra-Latinx racism when a Spanish-speaking CBP officer refuses to speak Spanish. While my U.S. citizenship is helpful, I am unaware of any courier from El Norteño who has U.S. citizenship. I would add that the ease of the interaction was also facilitated by awareness and education—once the agent had context for what Mateo was doing, obtained through communication in English, she approached him differently. In this sense, my own direct observations are biased because of my privileged position as a white U.S. citizen conducting research with a Salvadoran courier at the time of CBP inspection.

24. Garni, "Transnational Traders."

25. Lesley Bartlett, "Women Teaching Class: Emotional Labor in Brazilian Literacy Classes," *Anthropology of Work Review* 22, no. 3 (2001): 22–26; Arlie Russell Hochschild, *The Managed Heart: Commercialization of Human Feeling* (Berkeley: University of California Press, 1983).

26. Hochschild, *Managed Heart*, 7.

27. Hillary Rodham Clinton, *What Happened* (New York: Simon & Schuster, 2017).

28. Amy S. Wharton, "The Sociology of Emotional Labor," *Annual Review of Sociology* 35 (2009): 147–165, doi:10.1146/annurev-soc-070308-115944.

29. Pierre Bourdieu, "Symbolic Violence and Political Struggles," in *Pascalian Meditations* (Palo Alto, Calif.: Stanford University Press, 1997), 233.

30. Garni, "Transnational Traders."

31. Sarah Gammage notes that Salvadoran migrants were some of the first to be eligible for temporary protective status (TPS) in 1990, a status that does not confer permanent rights to residency, granting work authorization but making TPS holders ineligible for public cash or medical assistance. See Gammage, "Viajeros y viajeras."

32. I declined to translate curses at the airline employees, although in retrospect, I feel that Mateo probably wanted me to vehemently argue for those two pounds, which I failed to do.

33. While this is the formal process, the entire process can be sped up and made easier by paying out cash bribes. Mateo does not pay bribes but passes through the free and official—albeit tedious and bureaucratized—processes to leave the airport.

34. U.S. Department of Health and Human Services, Office of the Secretary, *Annual Update of the HHS Poverty Guidelines*, 82 FR 8831, document no. 2017-02076, January 31, 2017.

CHAPTER 2   A SEQUENCE OF UNDOCUMENTED MIGRANT MEMORIES

1. U.S. Government Accountability Office, *Illegal Immigration: Border-Crossing Deaths Have Doubled since 1995: Border Patrol's Efforts to Prevent Deaths Have Not Been Fully Evaluated*, report to Hon. Bill Frist, Majority Leader, U.S. Senate, August 2006.

2. Jason De León, "'Better to Be Hot Than Caught': Excavating the Conflicting Roles of Migrant Material Culture," *American Anthropologist* 114, no. 3 (2012): 477–495.

3. Excerpt translated by the author (one of many potential translations and by no means a final translation) from Roque Dalton's "Poema de Amor" (1974), in *Ruta transnacional: A San Salvador por Los Ángeles: Espacios de interacción juvenil en un contexto migratorio*, ed. Narváez Gutiérrez and Juan Carlos (México, D.F.: Editorial Miguel Ángel Porrúa, 2007), ProQuest. While I was hesitant to even translate this excerpt of Dalton's poem into English, I wanted to illustrate a consciousness of transnational harms for a non-Spanish-speaking audience.

4. Anthropologist Susan Bibler Coutin writes that "coyotes have been known to rape clients (some suggest that this is part of the price that coyotes charge), hold clients hostage, abandon clients, force clients to carry illicit goods, and otherwise endanger clients' lives." See Coutin, "Being En Route," in "Migration and Immigration," special issue, *American Anthropologist* 107, no. 2 (2017): 195–206.

5. Amparo Marroquín Parducci, "All Roads Lead North: A Reading of News on Migration through the Figure of the Coyote," trans. Miguel Winograd, *E-misférica* 8, no. 2 (2010).

6. I refer the reader to the works of anthropologists such as Jason De León, *The Land of Open Graves: Living and Dying on the Migrant Trail*, California Series in Public Anthropology (Berkeley: University of California Press, 2015), loc. 4435–4438, Kindle; and Wendy Vogt, "Crossing Mexico: Structural Violence and the Commodification of Undocumented Central American Migrants," *American Ethnologist* 40, no. 4 (2013): 764–780, doi:10.1111/amet.12053.

7. In referring to state power, I am referencing a historically situated regional political structure where U.S. interests weigh heavily and U.S. support for state tactics of terror in Latin America continues to be a relevant issue. See Cecilia Menjívar and Néstor Rodríguez, eds., *When States Kill: Latin America, the U.S., and Technologies of Terror* (Austin: University of Texas Press, 2005), loc. 88–98, Kindle.

8. M. Gaborit, M. Zetino, L. Brioso, and N. Portillo, *La esperanza viaja sin visa: Juventud y migración indocumentada en El Salvador* (San Salvador: United Nations Population Fund [UNFPA], Salvadoran Ministry of Foreign Affairs, University of Central America [UCA], 2012).

9. Amparo Marroquín Parducci writes about how coyotes strike deals with Mexican cartel members. She describes findings from an interview with a coyote:

> The "deal" is that you have to pay to cross; there is a fee you have to pay to cross through Mexico. They outline the routes for you and provide you the safe-passes themselves. Then, even if you encounter a narco-trafficker, you won't face any danger. They give you a phone number, a password, a . . . a safe-pass, as they call it, a code word, as they call it. But it's not always the same, because sometimes they tell you, "Hey, call the boss, this is his number." They give you the number, but they're changing it constantly so that even if you think you're clever, you won't get away with it.

See Marroquín Parducci, "All Roads Lead North."

10. "Donald Trump Announces a Presidential Bid," *Washington Post*, June 16, 2015, https://www.washingtonpost.com/news/post-politics/wp/2015/06/16/full-text-donald-trump-announces-a-presidential-bid/?utm_term=.6a739c9483b3, accessed September 14, 2017.

11. De León, *Land of Open Graves*, loc. 4435–4438.

12. Jonathan Daniel Rosen and Roberto Zepeda Martínez, "La guerra contra el narcotráfico en México: Una guerra perdida," *Reflexiones* 94, no. 1 (2015): 153–168.

13. Vogt, "Crossing Mexico," 764–780.

14. Daniel Rosen and Zepeda Martínez, "Guerra contra el narcotráfico," 153–168.

15. Daniel Rosen and Zepeda Martínez, 153–168.

16. A description of the Merida Initiative is located on the U.S. Embassy and Consulates in Mexico website, https://mx.usembassy.gov/our-relationship/policy-history/the-merida-initiative/, accessed September 14, 2017.

17. Daniel Rosen and Zepeda Martínez, "Guerra contra el narcotráfico," 153–168.

18. Marroquín Parducci, "All Roads Lead North."

19. Vogt, "Crossing Mexico," 764–780.

20. E. Nadelmann and L. LaSalle, "Two Steps Forward, One Step Back: Current Harm Reduction Policy and Politics in the United States," *Harm Reduction Journal* 14, no. 37 (2017), https://doi.org/10.1186/s12954-017-0157-y.

21. Congressional Research Service, *Border Security and the Southwest Border: Background, Legislation, and Issues,* report RL33106, September 28, 2005.

22. De León, *Land of Open Graves,* loc. 1590.

23. Congressional Research Service, *Border Security.*

24. De León uses the theory of the "hybrid collectif" to make the argument that "people or objects don't act in isolation, but instead have complex relationships at different moments across time and space that sometimes create things or make things happen. It is these relationships that 'perform agency,' not isolated humans or solitary objects." See De León, *Land of Open Graves,* loc. 783–796.

25. Congressional Research Service, *Border Security.*

26. National Centers for Environmental Information, Climate Data, Station WBAN:53131, National Oceanic and Atmospheric Administration, 2017, https://www.ncdc.noaa.gov/cdo-web/datasets#LCD.

27. Coalición de Derechos Humanos, "Remembering the Dead," https://derechoshumanosaz.net/coalition-work/remembering-the-dead/, accessed September 8, 2017.

28. Adam Isacson, Maureen Meyer, and Hannah Smith, "Increased Enforcement at Mexico's Southern Border: An Update on Security, Migration, and U.S. Assistance," Washington Office on Latin America (WOLA), November 2015, https://www.wola.org/files/WOLA_Increased_Enforcement_at_Mexico%27s_Southern_Border_Nov2015.pdf, accessed September 14, 2017.

29. "The Math of Immigration Detention," National Immigration Forum, August 22, 2013, http://immigrationforum.org/blog/themathofimmigrationdetention/, accessed September 28, 2017.

30. Immigration Detention Transparency and Human Rights Project, National Immigrant Justice Center, *Freedom of Information Act Litigation Reveals Systemic Lack of Accountability in Immigration Detention Contracting,* August 2015 report.

31. "A Toxic Relationship: Private Prisons and U.S. Immigration Detention," Detention Watch Network, December 2016, https://www.detentionwatchnetwork.org/sites/default/files/reports/A%20Toxic%20Relationship_DWN.pdf.

32. "Toxic Relationship."

33. "Fatal Neglect: How ICE Ignores Deaths in Detention," American Civil Liberties Union, Detention Watch Network, and the National Immigrant Justice Center, February 2016, https://www.immigrantjustice.org/sites/immigrantjustice.org/files/Fatal%20Neglect_ACLU%2C%20DWN%2C%20NIJC.pdf, accessed December 3, 2018.

34. Immigration Detention Transparency and Human Rights Project, *Freedom of Information Act Litigation*.

35. Jorge Rivas, "ICE Seeks Permission to Destroy Records of Sexual Assaults and Deaths," *Splinter Magazine*, August 29, 2017, https://splinternews.com/ice-seeks-permission-to-destroy-records-of-sexual-assau-1798541263?rev=1504036289614, accessed September 21, 2017.

36. James Grossman, "Letter from Executive Director of the American Historical Association to the National Archives and Records Administration," American Historical Association, Washington, D.C., July 25, 2018.

37. Dara Lind, "The Trump Administration's Separation of Families at the Border, Explained," *Vox News*, updated June 15, 2018, https://www.vox.com/2018/6/11/17443198/children-immigrant-families-separated-parents, accessed July 16, 2018.

38. Karl A. Hoerig, "Remembering Our Indian School Days: The Boarding School Experience," *American Anthropologist* 104, no. 2 (2002): 642–646.

39. "Donald Trump Announces."

CHAPTER 3   DIASPORIC INTIMACY AND *NOSTOS* IMAGINARIES

1. Svetlana Boym, *The Future of Nostalgia* (New York: Hachette, 2008).

2. By referring to transnational chasms, I mean undocumented campesinxs who can get on a plane to go back to El Salvador but cannot return to their U.S. homes with reasonable fluidity. These state-imposed limitations on bodily movement through space lead to the development of "transnational chasms," where kin remain connected through actors like couriers but cannot physically reunite with frequency or ease.

3. Cecilia M. Rivas, *Salvadoran Imaginaries: Mediated Identities and Cultures of Consumption* (New Brunswick, N.J.: Rutgers University Press, 2014).

4. Svetlana Boym, "Nostalgia and Its Discontents," in *The Collective Memory Reader*, ed. Jeffrey Olick, Vered Vinitzky-Seroussi, and Daniel Levy (New York: Oxford University Press, 2011), 456.

5. Boym, 456.

6. Boym, 457.

7. Boym, *Future of Nostalgia*.

8. There are certainly other ways to conceptualize nostalgia, particularly in the context of migration and food (a topic addressed in this chapter). Anthropologist David E. Sutton analyzes various mass-marketed nostalgia cookbooks and describes types of nostalgia that include "nostalgia for an imaginary lost Eden, nostalgia for that which was destroyed as part of modernization, and nostalgia for the immigrant/regional extended family at the table." While elements of these types of nostalgia overlap with findings in this chapter, my foci are different from Sutton's. For a more in-depth analysis of the ways in which nostalgia surfaces in relation to food, see Sutton, *Remembrance of Repasts: An Anthropology of Food and Memory* (New York: Berg, 2001), esp. 155.

9. Svetlana Boym, "On Diasporic Intimacy," in *Future of Nostalgia*.

10. The Nazi slogan *Blut und Boden* stresses ethnic identity based on blood descent and territory. The violence exhibited at such protests illustrates the ways in which restorative nostalgia can be invoked to justify racism and policies of exclusion. See also Meg Wagner, "'Blood and Soil': Protesters Chant Nazi Slogan in Charlottesville," *CNN*, August 12, 2017, http://edition.cnn.com/2017/08/12/us/charlottesville-unite-the-right-rally/index.html, accessed December 17, 2017.

11. E. P. Köster, "Diversity in the Determinants of Food Choice: A Psychological Perspective," *Food Quality and Preference* 20 (2009): 70–82.

12. J. A. Gottfried and R. J. Dolan, "The Nose Smells What the Eye Sees: Crossmodal Visual Facilitation of Human Olfactory Perception," *Neuron* 39, no. 2 (July 2003): 375–386.

13. Jon D. Holtzman, "Food and Memory," *Annual Review of Anthropology* 35 (2006): 361–378.

14. Factory Farm Nation, *Food & Water Watch*, 2015 ed., May 2015, http://www.foodandwaterwatch.org/sites/default/files/factory-farm-nation-report-may-2015.pdf, accessed May 22, 2017.

15. Jonny Frank, "Factory Farming: An Imminent Clash between Animal Rights Activists and Agribusiness," *Boston College Environmental Affairs Law Review* 7, no. 3 (1979); Evelyn B. Pluhar, "Meat and Morality: Alternatives to Factory Farming," *Journal of Agricultural and Environmental Ethics* 23, no. 5 (2010): 455–468, doi:10.1007/s10806-009-9226-x; Doug Gurian-Sherman, *CAFOs Uncovered: The Untold Costs of Confined Animal Feeding Operations* (Cambridge, Mass.: Union of Concerned Scientists, 2008).

16. Paul B. Thompson, "The GMO Quandary and What It Means for Social Philosophy," *Social Philosophy Today* 30 (2014).

17. Secretaría de Cultura de la Presidencia, *Dirección nacional de espacios de desarrollo cultural*, Casa de la Cultural de (name redacted to protect anonymity of location), El Salvador, report accessed in 2017.

18. "Color Additive Status List," U.S. Food and Drug Administration, U.S. Department of Health and Human Services, December 2015, http://www.fda.gov/ForIndustry/ColorAdditives/ColorAdditiveInventories/ucm106626.htm, accessed May 22, 2017.

19. Casper Bruun Jensen, "A Nonhumanist Disposition: On Performativity, Practical Ontology, and Intervention," *Configurations* 12 (2004): 229–261.

20. Chalatenango was sometimes historically referred to in El Salvador as the *tierra olvidada* (the forgotten land). See Molly Todd, "Remapping the Tierra Olvidada," in *Beyond Displacement: Campesinos, Refugees, and Collective Action in the Salvadoran Civil War* (Madison: University of Wisconsin Press, 2010).

21. Virginia Nazarea, "Potato Eyes: Positivism Meets Poetry in Food Systems Research," *Culture, Agriculture, Food and Environment* 36, no. 1 (2014): 4–7.

22. P. Barlow and J. Fisahn, "Lunisolar Tidal Force and the Growth of Plant Roots, and Some Other of Its Effects on Plant Movements," *Annals of Botany* 110, no. 2 (2012): 301–318, https://doi.org/10.1093/aob/mcs038.

23. René Edgardo Vargas Valdez, *Realidad nacional*, 2nd ed. (San Salvador: Editorial Multilibros, 2013).

24. E. Eckwall, "Slash and Burn Cultivation: A Contribution to the Anthropological Terminology," *Man* 55 (1955): 135–136.

25. Several campesinxs remember practicing a fire-farming method where a forest was burned to clear land, and then the remainder of the organic waste from the first cultivation cycle (the *huatal*) was burned once again prior to rotating the land in two-year cycles (sometimes longer but rarely more than five years). In El Norteño, farmers remember that this style of cultivation did not require pesticides, herbicides, or synthetic fertilizers and that weed growth was managed with a sickle. Farmers remember synthetic fertilizers first being introduced to El Norteño in the 1960s. See also Peter Harrison, "Maya Agriculture," in *Maya: Divine Kings of the Rain Forest*, ed. Nikolai Grube (China: Tandem Verlag GmbH, 2007), 71.

26. Secretaría de Cultura de la Presidencia, *Dirección nacional*.

27. Francisco Metzi, *Por los caminos de Chalatenango: Con la salud en la mochila*, 2nd ed. (San Salvador: UCA Editores, 2013), 67.

28. George Foster, "On the Origin of Humoral Medicine in Latin America," *Medical Anthropology Quarterly* 1, no. 4 (1987): 355–393.

29. Michael Anastario, "Seven Things You Need to Know about Amoxicillin: An Interview with Dr. Hope Ferdowsian," *Mike Anastario, PhD* (blog), July 28, 2016, http://mikeanastario.com/2016/07/28/amoxicillin/, accessed December 3, 2018.

30. Michel Foucault, "Truth and Power," in *Power/Knowledge: Selected Interviews and Other Writings 1972–1977*, ed. Colin Gordon (New York: Vintage, 1980), 119.

CHAPTER 4   WE DO NOT HAVE TO LEARN TO BE WHAT WE ARE NOT

1. Amparo Marroquín Parducci, "All Roads Lead North: A Reading of News on Migration through the Figure of the Coyote," trans. Miguel Winograd, *E-misférica* 8, no. 2 (2010).

2. Anna Lowenhaupt Tsing, *The Mushroom at the End of the World: On the Possibility of Life in Capitalist Ruins* (Princeton, NJ: Princeton University Press, 2015), viii.

3. Anna Holmes, "The Underground Art of the Insult," *New York Times Magazine*, May 14, 2015, https://www.nytimes.com/2015/05/17/magazine/the-underground-art-of-the-insult.html?_r=0, accessed October 12, 2017.

4. Brian Keith Axel, "The Diasporic Imaginary," *Public Culture* 14, no. 2 (2002): 411–428.

5. It is particularly easy to rely on a linear development framework when comparing rural social environments in El Salvador to the environments where rural diasporic communities are located inside the United States. Casual conversations and researcher unfamiliarity can make a linear development framework (like that proposed by W. W. Rostow) alluring, particularly given the way in which high mass consumption in the United States contrasts with rural living in El Salvador. See W. W. Rostow, *The Stages of Economic Growth* (New York: Cambridge University Press, 1963). I try to avoid characterizing differences between El Norteño and Colorado or Long Island as such, particularly given that campesinxs in El Norteño do not envision—or in some cases, even desire—to "achieve" North American levels of "development" in their own environments.

6. Pierre Bourdieu, *The Field of Cultural Production* (London: Polity Press, 1993), 183.

7. *Hybridity* has been used in theories of diaspora "that emerged out of Black British cultural studies in the 1980s and 1990s," emphasizing impure and inauthentic notions in contrast to religious and ethnic absolutism used by nationalist projects. See Gayatri Gopinath, *Impossible Desires: Queer Diasporas and South Asian Public Cultures* (Durham, N.C.: Duke University Press, 2005), 6–7, Kindle.

8. Censo de población y de vivienda 2007, "Población por área de residencia y sexo, según departamento, grupos de edad y edades simples, Cuadro 2. Departamento Chalatenango," Ministerio de economía, Dirección general de estadística y censos (DIGESTYC), San Salvador, 2009.

9. Gustavo López, "Hispanics of Salvadoran Origin in the United States, 2013," Pew Research Center: Hispanic Trends, September 15, 2015, http://www.pewhispanic.org/2015/09/15/hispanics-of-salvadoran-origin-in-the-united-states-2013/ph_2015-09-15_hispanic-origins-el-salvador-04-2/, accessed October 14, 2017.

10. Aaron Terrazas, "Salvadoran Immigrants in the United States," Migration Policy Institute, January 5, 2010, https://www.migrationpolicy.org/article/salvadoran-immigrants-united-states, accessed October 14, 2017.

11. Note that these migration-based class mobilities do not apply to all Salvadoran migrants. For example, urban Salvadoran lawyers who move to San Francisco and become sanitation workers while in the United States, only to return to El Salvador to work in law, have much different transnational class mobility experiences than subsistence agricultural laborers who migrate to the United States and work in jobs (such as fast-food drive-through restaurants) that were not comparatively present in El Norteño.

12. In El Salvador in 2007, the average age at first marriage was estimated at 21.9 for women; in 2008, it was estimated at 25.5 for men. In the United States in 2009, it was estimated at 26.9 for women and at 28.8 for men. These differences are likely to be larger for the Salvadoran countryside. See "Age at First Marriage, El Salvador," World Bank Development Indicators, Data Bank, Gender Statistics, http://databank.worldbank.org/data/reports.aspx?source=world-development-indicators, accessed October 30, 2017.

13. John Morton, "Civil Immigration Enforcement: Guidance on the Use of Detainers in the Federal, State, Local, and Tribal Criminal Justice Systems," memorandum, U.S. Immigration and Customs Enforcement, December 21, 2012.

14. "How ICE Uses Local Criminal Justice Systems to Funnel People into the Detention and Deportation System," National Immigration Law Center, March 2014, https://www.nilc.org/wp-content/uploads/2015/11/state-local-enforcement-and-ice-2014-03-25.pdf, accessed October 19, 2017.

15. Morton, "Civil Immigration Enforcement."

16. Noelle Phillips, "ICE Includes Denver in Immigration Sweep That Targeted Sanctuary Cities," *Denver Post*, September 28, 2017, http://www.denverpost.com/2017/09/28/denver-immigration-sweep-arrest-sanctuary-city-ice-hancock/, accessed October 19, 2017.

17. Leisy Abrego, *Sacrificing Families: Navigating Laws, Labor, and Love across Borders* (Palo Alto, Calif.: Stanford University Press, 2014).

18. Obergefell v. Hodges, 135 S. Ct. 2584 (2015), https://www.supremecourt.gov/opinions/14pdf/14-556_3204.pdf, accessed October 20, 2017.

19. Scott Gessler, "Statement of Sufficiency: Proposed Initiative 2011–12 #30," Colorado Department of State, February 27, 2012, http://www.sos.state.co.us/pubs/elections/Initiatives/ballot/Statements/2012/SufficiencyProp30.pdf, accessed October 20, 2017.

20. Colorado Constitution, article 18, section 16, "Personal Use and Regulation of Marijuana."

21. Asamblea Legislativa, Indice Legislativo, decreto no. 153, http://www.druglawreform.info/images/stories/LeyReguladora-Drogas.pdf, accessed October 30, 2017.

22. James W. Loewen, *Lies My Teacher Told Me: Everything Your American History Textbook Got Wrong* (New York: New Press, 2008), Kindle.

23. Molly Fox, Zaneta Thayer, and Pathik Wadhwa, "Accultural and Health: The Moderating Role of Sociocultural Context," *American Anthropologist* 119, no. 3 (September 2017): 405–421.

24. Irina Carlota Silber, "Mothers/Fighters/Citizens: Violence and Disillusionment in Postwar El Salvador," *Gender & History* 16, no. 3 (November 2004): 561–587.

25. Cecilia M. Rivas also notes that "since the numbers of emigrants increased in the 1980s, shifts in taste and patterns of consumption have become more apparent in urban as well as rural areas. . . . Sneakers, cell phones, and jeans connote a familiarity with the United States and its brands, and remittances are sometimes spent in many of the country's fast food franchises or in other forms of recreation. While transnational ties between migrants and their families are not the sole cause of the shifting consumption patterns found in postwar El Salvador, their importance in contemporary Salvadoran society lends predominance to this idea." See Rivas, *Salvadoran Imaginaries: Mediated Identities and Cultures of Consumption* (New Brunswick, N.J.: Rutgers University Press, 2014), 129–130.

26. Dinah Volk, "'Contradictions, Clashes, Cominglings': The Syncretic Literacy Projects of Young Bilinguals," *Anthropology & Education Quarterly* 44, no. 3 (2013): 234–252.

27. Rivas, *Salvadoran Imaginaries*, 119.

28. Kimberly Adilia Helmer, "A Twice-Told Tale: Voices of Resistance in a Borderlands Spanish Heritage Language Class," *Anthropology & Education Quarterly* 44, no. 3 (2013): 269–285.

29. Statistics were derived from an analysis of the U.S. Census Bureau data from the 2014 American Community Survey (ACS) and the 2008 Survey of Income and Program Participation (SIPP). See James Bachmeier and Jennifer Van Hook, "Profile of the Unauthorized Population: Colorado," Migration Policy Institute (MPI), https://www.migrationpolicy.org/data/unauthorized-immigrant-population/state/CO, accessed on October 19, 2017.

30. This, too, could reflect that Salvadoran women using the word *puta* can be perceived to be particularly "strong" in El Norteño, and *pinche* might be a softer (although Mexican) alternative to *puta* that would otherwise be replaced by words like *puchica* in the Salvadoran countryside to soften the strength of *puta* when used as an adjective. That said, the use of words like *puta* to indicate the English-language *fucking* also have inherently sexist/*machista* implications.

31. Jane H. Hill, "Syncretism," *Journal of Linguistic Anthropology* 9, no. 1–2 (2000): 244–246.

32. Leonardo Boff and Clodovis Boff, *Introducing Liberation Theology*, trans. Paul Burns (Maryknoll, N.Y.: Orbis, 2005).

33. G. Deleuze and F. Guattari's principle of asignifying rupture includes the idea that "a rhizome can be broken, shattered at a given spot, but it will start up again on one of its old lines, or on new lines." See Deleuze and Guattari, *A Thousand Plateaus: Capitalism and Schizophrenia* (Minneapolis: University of Minnesota Press, 1987), 9.

34. Irina Carlota Silber, *Everyday Revolutionaries: Gender, Violence, and Disillusionment in Postwar El Salvador* (New Brunswick, N.J.: Rutgers University Press, 2011), 34.

35. Marcella Althaus-Reid, *Indecent Theology: Theological Perversions in Sex, Gender and Politics* (New York: Routledge, 2000); Boff and Boff, *Introducing Liberation Theology*.

36. Molly Todd, *Beyond Displacement: Campesinos, Refugees, and Collective Action in the Salvadoran Civil War* (Madison: University of Wisconsin Press, 2010), 226.

37. Todd, 42.

38. While in the Salvadoran context, I am focusing on class, sexuality, and gender, it is worth mentioning that in the United States, liberation theology has also been widely applied in the context of race. It was historically important to the Black Power movement in the late 1960s, but there has been more recent criticism from within the Black Liberation Theological tradition. Elonda Clay writes, "In our contemporary material context, the term liberation is increasingly used in ways that increase the social capital of the Black theologian, who often deploys the word in conjunction with historically significant events, but not active theological praxis. The latter requires the continual process of what liberation purports to mean, do, and for whom it is invoked, in the various contexts across many historical conjunctures." See Clay, "A Black Theology of Liberation or Legitimation? A Postcolonial Response to Cone's *Black Theology, Black Power* at Forty," *Black Theology* 8, no. 3 (2010): 307–326; and Boff and Boff, *Introducing Liberation Theology*.

39. Althaus-Reid, *Indecent Theology*.

40. Note that queer diasporic remembering can provide maps for alternative renderings of nostalgia and mainstream remembering. Gayatri Gopinath writes, "If conventional diasporic discourse is marked by this backward glance, this 'overwhelming nostalgia' for lost origins, for 'times past,' a queer diaspora mobilizes questions of the past, memory, and nostalgia for radically different purposes. Rather than evoking an imaginary homeland frozen in an idyllic

moment outside history, what is remembered through queer diasporic desire and the queer diasporic body is a past time and place riven with contradictions and the violences of multiple uprootings, displacements, and exiles." See Gopinath, *Impossible Desires*, 4.

41. Althaus-Reid, *Indecent Theology*, 146.

42. Note that the rural-to-urban and transnational experiences of "liberation" associated with sexuality have also been documented elsewhere and are increasingly made complex by *who* is going *where*. Alexander Freund, for example, writes about a German man from a small midwestern town who felt great liberty when he came out of the closet in Germany, which conflicted with the emotional experiences of his Jewish partner. See Alexander Freund, "Toward an Ethics of Silence? Negotiating Off-the-Record Events and Identity in Oral History," in *The Oral History Reader*, Routledge Readers in History, 3rd ed., ed. Robert Perks and Alistair Thomson (Boca Raton, Fla.: Taylor & Francis, 2016), xiii, Kindle.

43. Rivas, *Salvadoran Imaginaries*.

44. Gopinath, *Impossible Desires*, 20.

45. Anthropologist Tine Gammeltoft reminds us that while imaginaries reflect our creative capacities, "these capacities are shaped through politically inflected structures that extend conscious awareness of self, stimulating the imagination yet operating at more subdued levels of life." See Gammeltoft, "Toward an Anthropology of the Imaginary: Specters of Disability in Vietnam," *Ethos* 42, no. 2 (2014): 153–174.

CHAPTER 5   SILENCE AND SYSTEMATIC FORGETTING

1. UN Security Council, *From Madness to Hope: The 12-Year War in El Salvador*, report of the Commission on the Truth for El Salvador, S/25500, March 15, 1993, 5–8.

2. Here I am referring to longitudinal processes of structural violence. Anthropologist Philippe Bourgois writes, "Structural violence refers to the political-economic organization of society that imposes conditions of physical and emotional distress, from high morbidity and mortality rates to poverty and abusive working conditions. It is rooted, at the macro-level, in structures such as unequal international terms of trade and it is expressed locally in exploitative labor markets, marketing arrangements and the monopolization of services." See Bourgois, "The Power of Violence in War and Peace: Post–Cold War Lessons from El Salvador," *Ethnography* 2, no. 1 (2001): 5–34.

3. Edna Lomsky-Feder, "Life Stories, War, and Veterans: On the Social Distribution of Memories," *Ethos* 32, no. 1 (2004): 82–109.

4. Tine Gammeltoft, "Silence as a Response to Everyday Violence: Understanding Domination and Distress through the Lens of Fantasy," *Ethos* 44, no. 4 (2016): 427–447.

5. Jeffrey Gould and Aldo Lauria, *To Rise in Darkness: Revolution, Repression and Memory in El Salvador, 1920–1932* (Durham, N.C.: Duke University Press, 2008); Erik Ching, *Authoritarian El Salvador: Politics and the Origins of the Military Regimes, 1880–1940* (Notre Dame, Ind.: University of Notre Dame Press, 2014).

6. In contrast, journalist Joan Didion interviewed the grandson of General Maximiliano Hernandez Martínez, who was the dictator of El Salvador through the 1930s and the political author of La Matanza. During the interview, the grandson remembers his grandfather as a man "capable of inspiring great loyalty." Didion also describes an eighteen-year-old campesinx from Chalatenango who sat at the table during her interview, unable to speak English:

> "If he were cutting cane in Chalatenango, he'd be taken by the Army and killed. If he were out on the street here he'd be killed. So. He comes every day to my studio,

he learns to be a primitive painter, and I keep him from getting killed. It's better for him, don't you agree?"

I said that I agreed.

See Didion, *Salvador* (New York: Vintage International, 1983), 56, Kindle.

7. In order to demonstrate that there was no need for a Yankee intervention, General Martínez, the political architect of La Matanza, sent a message to the captains of the "four ships anchored off Acajutla that the Communists 'had been totally beaten and dispersed' and would be 'entirely exterminated.'" One of the generals even went ashore to verify that the killings were occurring, and he was invited to lunch and a few executions. See William Stanley, *The Protection Racket State: Elite Politics, Military Extortion, and Civil War in El Salvador* (Philadelphia: Temple University Press, 1996), 56.

8. Kimberly Theidon, *Intimate Enemies: Violence and Reconciliation in Peru* (Philadelphia: University of Pennsylvania Press, 2012), 6.

9. Post-traumatic stress disorder (PTSD) is a trauma- and stressor-related disorder that includes exposure to a traumatic event with the development of symptoms that include reexperiencing/reliving the trauma, avoidance, arousal and reactivity, and cognition and mood symptoms. While PTSD is the most widely known and referenced chronic post-traumatic psychiatric disorder, there are numerous other types of chronic post-traumatic psychiatric disorders that can be diagnosed. See Y. Auxéméry, "Post-traumatic Psychiatric Disorders: PTSD Is Not the Only Diagnosis," *Presse Med* 47, no. 5 (2018): 423–430; and American Psychiatric Association, *Diagnostic and Statistical Manual of Mental Disorders*, 5th ed. (Washington, D.C.: American Psychiatric Association, 2013).

10. Judith Halberstam, *The Queer Art of Failure* (Durham, N.C.: Duke University Press, 2011).

11. Gammeltoft, "Silence as a Response," 427–447.

12. Transitional justice includes memorials, war-crimes prosecutions, tribunals, reparations, and truth commissions. See Theidon, *Intimate Enemies*.

13. The PDC was a center-left party directed / led by José Napoleón Duarte Fuentes, who visited Antonio Rivas before he was executed.

14. Aldo Lauria-Santiago, "The Culture and Politics of State Terror and Repression in El Salvador," in *When States Kill: Latin America, the U.S., and Technologies of Terror*, ed. Cecilia Menjívar and Néstor Rodríguez (Austin: University of Texas Press, 2005), loc. 6630–6633, Kindle.

15. Annette Georgina Hernández Rivas, "Cartografía de la memoria: Actores, lugares, prácticas en El Salvador de posguerra (1992–2015)" (PhD diss., Universidad Autónoma de Madrid, December 2015).

16. Lauria-Santiago, "Culture and Politics," loc. 6630–6633.

17. William Stanley, "Self-Defense, Class Oppression, and Extortion: Alternative Views of State Violence," in *Protection Racket State*, 81.

18. Leigh Binford, *The El Mozote Massacre: Human Rights and Global Implications*, rev. and expanded ed. (Tucson: University of Arizona Press, 2016), Kindle.

19. Lauria-Santiago, "Culture and Politics," loc. 6630–6633.

20. Binford, *El Mozote Massacre*, loc. 1403–1408.

21. Binford, loc. 1378–1380; Lauria-Santiago, "Culture and Politics," loc. 6630–6633; Didion, *Salvador*, 63–64.

22. Hernández Rivas, "Cartografía de la memoria." See also Lauria-Santiago, "Culture and Politics," loc. 6630–6633.

23. Matthew Levin, *Cold War University: Madison and the New Left in the Sixties*, Studies in American Thought and Culture (Madison: University of Wisconsin Press, 1973), loc. 1901–1905, Kindle.

24. UN Security Council, *From Madness to Hope*, 5–8.

25. Nina Lakhani, "El Salvador Issues Warrants for Guerrillas Who Killed US Soldiers during Civil War," *Guardian*, July 25, 2017, https://www.theguardian.com/world/2017/jul/25/el -salvador-guerrilla-fighters-us-soliders-helicopter-killings, accessed November 17, 2017; Elisabeth Malkin and Gene Palumbo, "Salvadoran Court Overturns Wartime Amnesty, Paving Way for Prosecutions," *New York Times*, July 14, 2016.

26. Margarita S. Studemeister, ed., *El Salvador: Implementation of the Peace Accords*, Peaceworks 38 (Washington, D.C.: United States Institute of Peace, 2001).

27. Hernández Rivas, "Cartografía de la memoria."

28. Irina Carlota Silber, *Everyday Revolutionaries: Gender, Violence, and Disillusionment in Postwar El Salvador* (New Brunswick, N.J.: Rutgers University Press, 2011), 185.

29. Broader discussions of sexism and gender inequality within the FMLN during the civil war have since arisen. See Erik Ching, *Stories of Civil War in El Salvador: A Battle over Memory* (Chapel Hill: University of North Carolina Press, 2016), 158–159, Kindle; and Lorena Peña, *Retazos de mi vida: Testimonio de una revolucionaria salvadoreña* (Querétaro: Ocean Sur, 2009).

30. Irina Carlota Silber writes that "many Chalatecos experience the postwar as full of deceit and disillusionment. They seek to identify what is true (verdad) and what is a lie (mentira) about a postwar world that many interpret as a constant battle against deception (engaño). For a call to 'rescue the past' circulates across Chalatenango, in contradistinction to a national rebuilding policy predicated on amnesia." See Silber, *Everyday Revolutionaries*, 15.

31. Yael Zerubavel, "Recovered Roots: Collective Memory and the Making of Israeli National Tradition," in *The Collective Memory Reader*, ed. Jeffrey Olick, Vered Vinitzky-Seroussi, and Daniel Levy (New York: Oxford University Press, 2011), 239.

32. "Transcript of Address by President on Lebanon and Grenada," *New York Times*, October 28, 1983, http://www.nytimes.com/1983/10/28/us/transcript-of-address-by-president-on -lebanon-and-grenada.html, accessed November 20, 2017.

33. The United States has a long history of intervention in Latin America, launching its first intelligence training and gathering effort in Latin America as twelve countries (El Salvador being one) interned and eventually sent approximately three thousand Axis nationals to the United States. The Special Intelligence Service (SIS) was sanctioned by President Roosevelt and represented "the first U.S.-led program for the comprehensive monitoring and neutralizing of suspects across Latin America through bureaucratic coordination with national and local police forces." See Cecilia Menjívar and Néstor Rodríguez, eds., *When States Kill: Latin America, the U.S., and Technologies of Terror* (Austin: University of Texas Press, 2005), loc. 209–215, Kindle.

34. Anna Lowenhaupt Tsing, *The Mushroom at the End of the World: On the Possibility of Life in Capitalist Ruins* (Princeton, NJ: Princeton University Press, 2015), 27.

35. Ronald Reagan, interview by Walter Cronkite, CBS News, March 3, 1981, http://www .presidency.ucsb.edu/ws/?pid=43497, accessed December 6, 2016.

36. Theidon, *Intimate Enemies*, 325.

37. "Secretary Rumsfeld and Gen. Pace," U.S. Department of Defense news briefing, January 22, 2002, http://archive.defense.gov/transcripts/transcript.aspx?transcriptid=2254, accessed November 20, 2017.

38. Geoffrey White, "Emotional Remembering: The Pragmatics of National Memory," *Ethos* 27, no. 4 (2000): 505–529.

39. "Stories," Minuteman Missile, https://www.nps.gov/mimi/learn/historyculture/stories .htm, accessed November 9, 2017.

40. "Cold War Timeline," Minuteman Missile, https://www.nps.gov/mimi/learn/history culture/cold-war-timeline.htm, accessed November 10, 2017.

41. "Stories."

42. Wendy McNiel, interview by Michael Hosking, January 29, 2007, Minuteman Missile National Historic Site, National Park Service, U.S. Department of the Interior.

43. Gary Overby, interview by Michael Hosking, February 10, 2003, Minuteman Missile National Historic Site, National Park Service, U.S. Department of the Interior.

44. Wendy McNiel, interview by Eric Pogany, February 10, 2003, Minuteman Missile National Historic Site, National Park Service, U.S. Department of the Interior.

45. Halberstam, *Queer Art of Failure*.

46. Incidentally, I was unable to download the lone interview with the one peace activist whose oral history was on record. I emailed the site, and with time, they delivered the oral history to me. It was the peace activist who highlighted the unintended and understated health consequences of the Cold War: "If the Russians lost it, well so did we because we have something on the realm of 300,000 cubic meters of high level radioactive waste and nothing to do with it except spread cancer and leukemia to future generations for the rest of time. This is called losing the Cold War and so I would hope that there'd be some segment of this museum that would reflect, you know, embarrassment, shame, outrage, you know, the protest against these weapons that is still going on today. And that needs to succeed in bringing about complete elimination of these devices." John LaForge, interview by Mary Ebeling, January 3, 2003, Minuteman Missile National Historic Site, National Park Service, U.S. Department of the Interior.

The peace activist's suggestion that the site reflect embarrassment, shame, and outrage stands in contrast to the site's representation of itself, valorizing "the forces of technology to protect freedom and democracy" (see "Stories"). The inclusion of the peace activist's voice at the historic site does offer an alternative perspective. However, his is clearly not reflective of the dominant framework/voice.

47. Michel Foucault, "Truth and Power," in *Power/Knowledge: Selected Interviews and Other Writings 1972–1977*, ed. Colin Gordon (New York: Vintage, 1980), 119.

48. Menjívar and Rodríguez, *When States Kill*, loc. 6665–6667.

49. "The States Parties to the Rome Statute," International Criminal Court, n.d., https://asp.icc-cpi.int/en_menus/asp/states%20parties/Pages/the%20states%20parties%20to%20the%20rome%20statute.aspx, accessed August 2, 2018.

50. Victoria Sanford, "The Phenomenology of Terror," in *Buried Secrets: Truth and Human Rights in Guatemala* (New York: Palgrave Macmillan, 2003).

51. "Efrain Rios Montt, Former Guatemalan Dictator, Dies at 91," NPR, April 3, 2018, https://www.npr.org/2018/04/03/599240693/efrain-rios-montt-former-guatemalan-dictator-dies-at-91, accessed April 5, 2018.

52. La Sala de lo Constitucional, "Sala declara como grupos terroristas a pandillas denominadas MS y 18," press release, August 24, 2015, http://www.csj.gob.sv/Comunicaciones/2015/AGO_15/COMUNICADOS/42.%20Comunicado%2024-VIII-2015%20terrorismo.pdf, accessed August 3, 2018; Azam Ahmed, "They Will Have to Answer to Us," *New York Times*, November 29, 2017.

53. Menjívar and Rodríguez, *When States Kill*, loc. 6665–6667.

CHAPTER 6   FIELDS OF VIOLENCE

1. Kimberly Theidon, *Intimate Enemies: Violence and Reconciliation in Peru* (Philadelphia: University of Pennsylvania Press, 2012), 394.

2. "The Yellow School Bus Industry," National School Transportation Association, 2013, http://www.schoolbusfleet.com/whitepaper/89/the-yellow-school-bus-industry, accessed July 30, 2018.

3. "Quick Facts and Stats," Safe Routes to School National Partnership, n.d., http://www
.saferoutespartnership.org/healthy-communities/101/facts, accessed July 30, 2018.

4. *School Bus Fact Book* 61, no. 11 (2016), http://digital.schoolbusfleet.com/2016FB/Default/
16/1/2918502#&pageSet=23, accessed July 30, 2018.

5. The documentary film *La Camioneta* illustrates the transformation of a yellow school bus
that makes its way from the United States into the Guatemalan system of public transport.
The film reminds viewers to consider their interconnectedness in the world. Mark Kendall,
dir., *La Camioneta*, 2012, http://www.lacamionetafilm.com/.

6. Ellen Moodie, "Microbus Crashes and Coca-Cola Cash: The Value of Death in 'Free-
Market' El Salvador," *American Ethnologist* 33, no. 1 (2006): 63–80.

7. Jon Hellin, Martin Haigh, and Frank Marks, "Rainfall Characteristics of Hurricane Mitch,"
Nature 399 (May 1999): 316.

8. This devaluation is evidenced by behaviors of the current Trump administration, which
includes separating Salvadoran migrant children from their parents and administration
officials referring to MS-13 gang members as "animals." See Nelson Renteria, "El Salvador
Demands U.S. Return Child Taken from Deported Father," *Reuters*, June 21, 2018, https://
www.reuters.com/article/us-usa-immigration-el-salvador/el-salvador-demands-u-s-return
-child-taken-from-deported-father-idUSKBN1JH3ER, accessed July 28, 2018; and Oliver
Laughland, "Trump's Focus on MS-13 Risks Bolstering Gang's Fearsome Image, Study Says,"
Guardian, February 12, 2018, https://www.theguardian.com/us-news/2018/feb/12/trump
-ms-13-gang-fearsome-image-study-us-immigration, accessed July 28, 2018.

9. For example, using transnational feminist practice and/or world systems theory. See
Chandra Talpade Mohanty, "'Under Western Eyes' Revisited: Feminist Solidarity through
Anticapitalist Struggles," *Signs: Journal of Women in Culture and Society* 28, no. 2 (2002); and
Immanuel Wallerstein, *The Modern World-System I: Capitalist Agriculture and the Origins of the
European World-Economy in the Sixteenth Century* (New York: Academic Press, 1974).

10. Irina Carlota Silber, *Everyday Revolutionaries: Gender, Violence, and Disillusionment in
Postwar El Salvador* (New Brunswick, N.J.: Rutgers University Press, 2011), 13; Ellen Moodie,
El Salvador in the Aftermath of Peace: Crime, Uncertainty, and the Transition to Democracy (Phil-
adelphia: University of Pennsylvania Press, 2010).

11. Moodie, "Microbus Crashes," 63–80.

12. Paul Ricoeur, "Memory-History-Forgetting," in *The Collective Memory Reader*, ed. Jeffrey
Olick, Vered Vinitzky-Seroussi, and Daniel Levy (New York: Oxford University Press, 2011),
480.

13. Philippe Bourgois, "The Power of Violence in War and Peace: Post–Cold War Lessons
from El Salvador," *Ethnography* 2, no. 1 (2001): 5–34; P. E. Farmer, B. Nizeye, S. Stulac, and
S. Keshavjee, "Structural Violence and Clinical Medicine," *PLoS Med* 3, no. 10 (2006): e449,
https://doi.org/10.1371/journal.pmed.0030449; J. Galtung, "Violence, Peace and Peace
Research," *Journal of Peace Research* 6 (1969): 167–191.

14. Theoretically, Pierre Bourdieu's concept of "the law of the conservation of violence" is
useful in thinking about how structural violence is *conserved*, or paid for, by the active violence of the people (e.g., crime, suicide, alcoholism, self-destructive behaviors). See Pierre
Bourdieu, *Pascalian Meditations* (Palo Alto, Calif.: Stanford University Press, 1997), esp. 233.

15. Throughout this chapter, I refer to the dynamics of a theoretical "field" of violence and
a local "field" of violence, with the understanding that multiple "fields" of violence may exist
within a nation-state. Further, I do not assume that the memory field and the field of violence
as autonomous. The way in which power transects both affects how violence is remembered,
forgotten, and reimplemented.

16. Relevant concepts of everyday and political violence have been further developed by anthropologists. In an extension of Nancy Scheper-Hughes's concept of everyday violence (which includes rumors, imaginings, and enactments that bring people into contact with the state), Philippe Bourgois seeks to identify "the routine practices and expressions of interpersonal aggression that serve to normalize violence at the micro-level such as domestic, delinquent and sexual conflict, and even substance abuse." Violence within families, between neighbors, or inflicted on oneself or even animals can be classified as a form of everyday violence that normalizes the experience of violence itself. Bourgois usefully distinguishes everyday violence from other types of violence—political, structural, and symbolic—in producing a framework for thinking through the larger forces that organize violence (and simultaneously obscure their organization from view) in the enactment of everyday harms. In the transnational spaces and temporal renderings of imperial forgetting, I assume that expressions of violence (everyday or political, for example) populate an everyday "field of violence" that is experienced by campesinxs who survive, participate in, manage, navigate, and eject themselves from it. Thus while particularly manifestations of the violence I observed can be classified as *everyday* or *political*, I focus here on how actors are structured to produce and reproduce the field itself. See Nancy Scheper-Hughes, *Death without Weeping: The Violence of Everyday Life in Brazil* (Berkeley: University of California Press, 1993), 230; and Bourgois, "Power of Violence," 5–34.

17. Pierre Bourdieu, *Outline of a Theory of Practice* (New York: Cambridge University Press, 1977).

18. Further, I am hesitant to use statistics to describe this distribution as the homicide rate in San Salvador, as the homicide rate has been shown to vary relative to electoral periods, which raises several questions about the validity of the numbers reported. See J. A. Mendoza Posada, L. B. Orellana Herrera, and G. S. Pocasangre Portillo, "Modelado multivariable de homicidios y hurtos en el Departamento de San Salvador" (PhD diss., Universidad Centroamericana José Simeón Cañas, El Salvador, 2016).

19. Cecilia Menjívar and Néstor Rodríguez, eds., *When States Kill: Latin America, the U.S., and Technologies of Terror* (Austin: University of Texas Press, 2005), loc. 95–98, Kindle.

20. Cecilia Menjívar and Néstor Rodríguez write that states implement terror using different terror tactics, and these tactics "have in common their institutionalization. They are regulated through norms, tasks, statutes, hierarchies, knowledge, and procedures of operation. Tactics involve defining objectives, selecting techniques, training staff, and finding locales to practice. Those in charge of carrying out terror campaigns are usually state personnel or subcontracted agents, which means they have occupations and salaries that are regularized by statutes and training." See Menjívar and Rodríguez, loc. 362–365.

21. "Attorney General Jeff Sessions Delivers Remarks at the International Law Enforcement Academy Graduation," U.S. Department of Justice (DOJ), July 28, 2017, https://www.justice.gov/opa/speech/attorney-general-jeff-sessions-delivers-remarks-international-law-enforcement-academy, accessed July 30, 2018.

22. The DOJ website describes that the actual motto appearing on the organization's seal, *Qui Pro Domina Justitia Sequitur*, "refers to the Attorney General (and thus to the Department of Justice), '*who prosecutes on behalf of justice* (or *the Lady Justice*).'" "DOJ Seal—History and Motto," DOJ, https://www.justice.gov/about/history/doj-seal-history-and-motto#foot25, accessed August 7, 2018.

23. Alcira Dueñas, *Indians and Mestizos in the "Lettered City": Reshaping Justice, Social Hierarchy, and Political Culture in Colonial Peru* (Boulder: University Press of Colorado, 2010).

24. Alcira Dueñas, "The Lima Indians Letrados: Remaking the República de Indios in the Bourbon Andes," in "Indigenous Liminalities: Andean Actors and Translators of Colonial Culture," special issue, *The Americas* 72, no. 1 (January 2015): 55–75.

25. Theidon, *Intimate Enemies*, 99.

26. Bourdieu, *Outline of a Theory*.

27. Clare Ribando Seelke, *El Salvador: Background and U.S. Relations*, Congressional Research Service, R43616, November 3, 2017, 9.

28. "What You Need to Know about the Violent Animals of MS-13," The White House, May 21, 2018, https://www.whitehouse.gov/articles/need-know-violent-animals-ms-13/, accessed July 3, 2018.

29. Seelke, *El Salvador*, 15.

30. Ignacio Martín-Baró, *Sistema grupo y poder: Psicología social desde Centroamérica (II)* (San Salvador: UCA Editores, 2014).

31. Cecilia M. Rivas, *Salvadoran Imaginaries: Mediated Identities and Cultures of Consumption* (New Brunswick, N.J.: Rutgers University Press, 2014).

32. Pierre Bourdieu, *Distinction: A Social Critique of the Judgement of Taste*, trans. Richard Nice (Cambridge, Mass.: Harvard University Press, 1984).

33. Moodie, *El Salvador in the Aftermath*, 118–119.

34. Available through the U.S. Citizenship and Immigration Services, https://www.uscis.gov/i-589, accessed December 15, 2017.

35. Pierre Bourdieu defines symbolic violence as

> the coercion which is set up only through the consent that the dominated cannot fail to give to the dominator (and therefore to the domination) when their understanding of the situation and relation can only use instruments of knowledge that they have in common with the dominator, which, being merely the incorporated form of the structure of the relation of domination, make this relation appear as natural; or, in other words, when the schemes they implement in order to perceive and evaluate themselves or to perceive and evaluate the dominators (high/low, male/female, white/black, etc.) are the product of the incorporation of the (thus naturalized) classifications of which their social being is the product.

See Pierre Bourdieu, *Pascalian Meditations*, 170.

36. Information from the Stockholm International Peace Research Institute (SIPRI), "Importer/Exporter TIV Tables," n.d., http://armstrade.sipri.org/armstrade/page/values.php, accessed September 13, 2016.

37. Scott Wallace, "You Must Go Home Again: Deported L.A. Gangbangers Take Over El Salvador," *Harper's Magazine* 301, no. 1803 (2000): 47–56, http://scottwallace.com/PDF2010/HarpersGangs.pdf.

38. Leisy Abrego, "Salvadoran Transnational Families," in *Sacrificing Families: Navigating Laws, Labor, and Love across Borders* (Palo Alto, Calif.: Stanford University Press, 2014), 13–14.

39. Maria Cristina Garcia, *Seeking Refuge: Central American Migration to Mexico, the United States, and Canada* (Berkeley: University of California Press, 2006), 162, Kindle.

40. Albert De Amicis, "Mara Salvatrucha (MS-13) and Its Violent World" (independent study, University of Pittsburgh, Graduate School for Public and International Affairs, October 9, 2010), https://www.ncjrs.gov/pdffiles1/239226.pdf, accessed December 6, 2017.

41. Mary Helen Johnson, "National Policies and the Rise of Transnational Gangs," Migration Policy Research Institute, April 1, 2006, http://www.migrationpolicy.org/article/national-policies-and-rise-transnational-gangs, accessed May 16, 2017.

42. Elana Zilberg, "A Troubled Corner: The Ruined and Rebuilt Environment of a Central American Barrio in Post-Rodney-King-Riot Los Angeles," *City and Society* 14, no. 2 (2002): 185–210.

43. Wallace, "You Must Go Home Again"; Moodie, *El Salvador in the Aftermath.*

44. This takes place through efforts such as the U.S. Central American Regional Security Initiative (CARSI), which has funneled millions of dollars into Central American security forces to combat illegality, crime, smuggling, and trafficking through funding, supplies, and training. See Wendy Vogt, "Crossing Mexico: Structural Violence and the Commodification of Undocumented Central American Migrants," *American Ethnologist* 40, no. 4 (2013): 764–780, doi:10.1111/amet.12053.

45. "Violent Gang MS-13 Is Believed to Be Linked to Several Recent Long Island Killings," ABC News Radio, April 28, 2017, http://abcnewsradioonline.com/national-news/violent -gang-ms-13-is-believed-to-be-linked-to-several-recen.html, accessed December 12, 2017.

46. "What You Need to Know."

47. Karla Arévalo, "¿Cuántos pandilleros en las cárceles tienen título universitario?," Elsalvador.com, December 15, 2016, https://www.elsalvador.com/noticias/nacional/210629/ cuantos-pandilleros-en-las-carceles-tienen-titulo-universitario/, accessed July 27, 2018.

48. Data were derived from the Latin American Public Opinion Project (LAPOP), "Barómetro de las Américas 2016 Cuestionario El Salvador, version 14.0.2.2, 2016–2017," https://www.lapopsurveys.org, accessed November 17, 2017.

49. Joan Didion, *Salvador* (New York, Vintage International, 1983), 56, Kindle.

50. Menjívar and Rodríguez, *When States Kill*, loc. 95–98.

51. "Murderous Latin American Police Need to Start Policing Themselves," *The Economist*, October 26, 2017.

52. Seelke, *El Salvador*, 15.

53. Karl Marx, "The Eighteenth Brumaire of Louis Bonaparte," in *The Marx-Engels Reader*, 2nd ed., ed. Robert C. Tucker (New York: W. W. Norton, 1978), 595.

54. Ellen Moodie, "Big Stories and the Stories behind the Stories," in *El Salvador in the Aftermath*, 22.

55. I refer the reader to chapter 5 for a more in-depth discussion of ORDEN.

56. Molly Todd, *Beyond Displacement: Campesinos, Refugees, and Collective Action in the Salvadoran Civil War* (Madison: University of Wisconsin Press, 2010), 213.

57. Todd, 194.

58. Marianne Hirsch, *The Generation of Postmemory: Writing and Visual Culture after the Holocaust* (New York: Columbia University Press, 2012).

CHAPTER 7   DEFERMENTS OF VOICE, MYOPIC REFLECTIONS

1. Department of the Army (DOA), *Insurgencies and Countering Insurgencies*, FM 3-24/ MCWP 3-33.5, May 2014, pp. 11-1–11-2.

2. Josh Dawsey, "Trump Attacks Protections for Immigrants from 'Shithole' Countries," *Washington Post*, January 11, 2018, https://www.washingtonpost.com/politics/trump-attacks -protections-for-immigrants-from-shithole-countries-in-oval-office-meeting/2018/01/11/ bfc0725c-f711-11e7-91af-31ac729add94_story.html?utm_term=.59e117038a7e.

3. The president stated, "No, no, I'm not a racist. I'm the least racist person you have ever interviewed." See Brent D. Griffiths, "Trump: 'I Am the Least Racist Person You Have Ever Interviewed,'" *Politico*, January 14, 2018, https://www.politico.com/story/2018/01/14/trump -least-racist-person-340602, accessed January 25, 2018.

4. Pierre Bourdieu, *Pascalian Meditations* (Palo Alto, Calif.: Stanford University Press, 1997), 8.

5. Leigh Binford summarizes that the planes and helicopters included "mainly subsonic A-37 jets, O-2 spotter planes, and Huey UH-1H transport helicopters" and that the armaments included "2.75-inch rockets, machine guns, and bombs of 250-, 500-, and 750-pound size." See Binford, *The El Mozote Massacre: Human Rights and Global Implications*, rev. and expanded ed. (Tucson: University of Arizona Press, 2016), loc. 3778–3785, Kindle.

6. I used the Prais-Winsten regression estimator, where $y_t = x_t\beta + u_t$ and where the errors satisfy $u_t = \rho u_{t-1} + e_t$ to account for potential autocorrelation in the errors and to assess changes in U.S. transfers during the 1979–1992 civil-war period. The Prais-Winsten estimate of the coefficient of the civil-war period (beta = 9.8; SE = 3.9) was statistically significant (p = 0.014), with a Durbin-Watson statistic of 1.98. See also Stockholm International Peace Research Institute (SIPRI), "Importer/Exporter TIV Tables," n.d., http://armstrade.sipri.org/armstrade/page/values.php, accessed September 13, 2016.

7. Tian Nan, Fleurant Aude, Kuimova Alexandra, Wezeman Pieter, and Wezeman Siemon, "Trends in World Military Expenditure, 2017," SIPRI Fact Sheet, May 2018.

8. David Graeber, *Fragments of an Anarchist Anthropology* (Chicago: Prickly Paradigm Press, 2004), 72.

9. Alexander Freund, "Toward an Ethics of Silence? Negotiating Off-the-Record Events and Identity in Oral History," in *The Oral History Reader*, Routledge Readers in History, 3rd ed., ed. Robert Perks and Alistair Thomson (Boca Raton, Fla.: Taylor & Francis, 2016), 255–256, Kindle.

10. Tine Gammeltoft, "Silence as a Response to Everyday Violence: Understanding Domination and Distress through the Lens of Fantasy," *Ethos* 44, no. 4 (2016): 427–447.

11. Cecilia Menjívar and Néstor Rodríguez, eds., *When States Kill: Latin America, the U.S., and Technologies of Terror* (Austin: University of Texas Press, 2005), loc. 381–382, Kindle.

12. Edna Lomsky-Feder, "Life Stories, War, and Veterans: On the Social Distribution of Memories," *Ethos* 32, no. 1 (2004): 82–109.

13. DOA, *Insurgencies and Countering Insurgencies*, p. 11-2.

14. Bourdieu, *Pascalian Meditations*, 176.

15. Paul A. Kramer, "The Geopolitics of Mobility: Immigration Policy and American Global Power in the Long Twentieth Century," *American Historical Review* 123, no. 2 (April 2018): 393–438.

16. Erik Ching's analysis of memory communities includes grouping individuals who talk about the same events, who use similar narrative structures and styles, whose claims are roughly identical, who approach Salvadoran history in a similar manner, and who have similar assessments of certain organizations and people. See Ching, *Stories of Civil War in El Salvador: A Battle over Memory* (Chapel Hill: University of North Carolina Press, 2016), 11, Kindle.

17. Government of El Salvador, Uppsala Conflict Data Program, Department of Peace and Conflict Research, 1979–1991, http://ucdp.uu.se/, accessed December 3, 2018. See also Raymond Bonner, "Time for a US Apology to El Salvador," *Nation*, April 15, 2016, https://www.thenation.com/article/time-for-a-us-apology-to-el-salvador/, accessed August 7, 2018.

18. Pierre Bourdieu, *The Field of Cultural Production* (London: Polity Press, 1993), 183.

19. Maria Cristina Garcia, *Seeking Refuge: Central American Migration to Mexico, the United States, and Canada* (Berkeley: University of California Press, 2006), 11, Kindle.

20. Historian Molly Todd writes that 1980 was "when mass displacements began in earnest." See Molly Todd, *Beyond Displacement: Campesinos, Refugees, and Collective Action in the Salvadoran Civil War* (Madison: University of Wisconsin Press, 2010), 51. See also N. Hamilton and N. S. Chinchilla, "Central American Migration: A Framework for Analysis," *Latin American Research Review* 26, no. 1 (1991): 75–110; and Segundo Montes and Juan José García Vásquez,

Salvadoran Migration to the United States: An Exploratory Study (Washington, D.C.: Georgetown University, Hemispheric Migration Project, Center for Immigration Policy and Refugee Assistance, 1988).

21. M. Anastario, K. Barrick, D. Gibbs, W. Pitts, R. Werth, and P. Lattimore, "Factors Driving Salvadoran Youth Migration: A Formative Assessment Focused on Salvadoran Repatriation Facilities," *Children and Youth Services Review* 59 (2015): 97–104.

22. The Salvadoran Civil War ended in 1992; thus the 1996 survey allows for the migrants through the full war period to arrive (and to have been surveyed) to illustrate the temporal trend corresponding to the civil-war period. Note that these trends are likely to appear differently in future years given deportations and subsequent waves of new migrants.

23. "Current Population Survey (CPS)," U.S. Census Bureau for the Bureau of Labor Statistics, microdata for January 1996 downloaded through DataFerret.

24. SIPRI, "Importer/Exporter TIV Tables."

25. Menjívar and Rodríguez, *When States Kill*, loc. 381–382.

26. Scott Wallace, "You Must Go Home Again: Deported L.A. Gangbangers Take Over El Salvador," *Harper's Magazine* 301, no. 1803 (2000): 47–56, http://scottwallace.com/PDF2010/HarpersGangs.pdf.

27. Tim Golden, "Accord Reached to Halt Civil War in El Salvador," *New York Times*, 1992.

28. Montes and Juan Jose, *Salvadoran Migration*.

29. Garcia, *Seeking Refuge*, 11; A. Mountz, R. Wright, I. Miyares, and A. Bailey, "Lives in Limbo: Temporary Protected Status and Immigrant Identities," *Global Networks* 2, no. 4 (2002): 335–356.

30. S. C. B. Coutin, "From Refugees to Immigrants: The Legalization Strategies of Salvadoran Immigrants and Activists," *International Migration Review* 32, no. 4 (1998): 0901–0925.

31. Garcia, *Seeking Refuge*, 94.

32. "American Baptist Churches v. Thornburgh (ABC) Settlement Agreement," U.S. Citizenship and Immigration Services, last updated October 28, 2008, https://www.uscis.gov/laws/legal-settlement-notices/american-baptist-churches-v-thornburgh-abc-settlement-agreement, accessed January 25, 2018.

33. Coutin, "From Refugees to Immigrants," 0901–0925.

34. Since the Salvadoran Civil War, Salvadorans have contended with temporary protected status (TPS), deferred enforced deportation (DED), the American Baptist Churches (ABC) settlement, the Illegal Immigration Reform and Immigrant Responsibility Act (IIRIRA), and the Nicaraguan Adjustment and Central American Relief Act (NACARA). See Mountz et al., "Lives in Limbo," 335–356.

35. Garcia, *Seeking Refuge*, 12.

36. Coutin, "From Refugees to Immigrants," 0901–0925.

37. David Smith, "Trump Renews Threat to Shut down Government over Border Wall," *Guardian*, July 30, 2018; Philip Elliott, "President Trump Is Demanding $25 Billion for a Border Wall amid Outcry over Family Separation," *Time*, June 19, 2018.

38. Mary Small, "A Toxic Relationship: Private Prisons, and US Immigration Detention," Detention Watch Network, December 2016, https://www.detentionwatchnetwork.org/sites/default/files/reports/A%20Toxic%20Relationship_DWN.pdf.

39. Levin, *Cold War University: Madison and the New Left in the Sixties*, Studies in American Thought and Culture (Madison: University of Wisconsin Press, 1973), loc. 1605–1608, Kindle.

40. William Stanley, "Self-Defense, Class Oppression, and Extortion: Alternative Views of State Violence," in *The Protection Racket State: Elite Politics, Military Extortion, and Civil War in El Salvador* (Philadelphia: Temple University Press, 1996), 14.

41. Ronald Reagan, interview by Walter Cronkite, CBS News, March 3, 1981, http://www.presidency.ucsb.edu/ws/?pid=43497, accessed December 6, 2016.

42. Ignacio Martín-Baró, *Sistema grupo y poder: Psicología social desde Centroamérica (II)* (San Salvador: UCA Editores, 2014), 164.

43. Montes and Juan Jose, *Salvadoran Migration*.

44. "Case of the Massacres of El Mozote and Nearby Places v. El Salvador," Inter-American Court of Human Rights, October 25, 2012, http://www.corteidh.or.cr/docs/casos/articulos/resumen_252_ing.pdf, accessed December 22, 2017.

45. Binford, *El Mozote Massacre*, loc. 1422–1424.

46. Rufina Amaya, Mark Danner, and Carlos Henríquez Consalvi, *Luciérnagas en El Mozote* (San Salvador: Ediciones Museo de la Palabra y la Imagen, 1998); Binford, *El Mozote Massacre*, loc. 1430–1433.

47. UN Security Council, *From Madness to Hope: The 12-Year War in El Salvador*, report of the Commission on the Truth for El Salvador, S/25500, March 15, 1993, 38.

48. Binford, *El Mozote Massacre*, loc. 3087–3088.

49. Philippe Bourgois, "The Power of Violence in War and Peace: Post–Cold War Lessons from El Salvador," *Ethnography* 2, no. 1 (2001): 5–34.

50. Levin, *Cold War University*, loc. 163–164.

CONCLUSION

1. Penny Coleman, *Flashback: Posttraumatic Stress Disorder, Suicide, and the Lessons of War* (Boston: Beacon Press, 2007), 170.

2. Maurice Halbwachs writes, "The mind reconstructs its memories under the pressure of society." See Halbwachs, *On Collective Memory* (Chicago: University of Chicago Press, 1992), 51.

3. Virginia Nazarea, *Heirloom Seeds and Their Keepers: Marginality and Memory in the Conservation of Biological Diversity* (Tucson: University of Arizona Press, 2005), 50.

4. Jeffrey Olick, "The Guilt of Nations?," *Ethics & International Affairs* 17, no. 2 (2003).

5. Marco Rubio, personal communication (letter), February 28, 2017.

6. See "The American Indian and Alaska Native Population: 2010," U.S. Census Bureau, January 2012, http://www.census.gov/prod/cen2010/briefs/c2010br-10.pdf, accessed September 22, 2017.

7. The "boarding-school era" refers to a nineteenth- to twentieth-century period of state-sponsored terror when indigenous children were forcibly removed from their home environments and immersed in federally funded, Christian, English-speaking school environments in order to assimilate them into Euro-American culture. In 1892, Captain Richard H. Pratt, the founder of the Carlisle Indian School, wrote, "All the Indian there is in the race should be dead. . . . Kill the Indian in him and save the man." See Karl A. Hoerig, "Remembering Our Indian School Days: The Boarding School Experience," *American Anthropologist* 104, no. 2 (2002): 642–646.

8. Vince Tucker, "Columbus Did Not Discover America, He Invented Indians," *Focus* 45 (Summer 1992): 3–5.

9. Scott Wallace, "You Must Go Home Again: Deported L.A. Gangbangers Take Over El Salvador," *Harper's Magazine* 301, no. 1803 (2000): 47–56, http://scottwallace.com/PDF2010/HarpersGangs.pdf.

10. "What You Need to Know about the Violent Animals of MS-13," The White House, May 21, 2018, https://www.whitehouse.gov/articles/need-know-violent-animals-ms-13/, accessed July 3, 2018.

11. For example, Cecilia Menjívar and Néstor Rodríguez write, "A Salvadoran death squad member who described his training at SOA explained how the U.S. instructor in one course emphasized 'psychological techniques' and demonstrated new and more effective ways of using electric shocks during interrogations. On the final day of the course, students practiced techniques on real prisoners. 'They were peasants,' the death squad member recalled, 'no one noteworthy' (quoted in Crelinsten, 1995, 50). After the practice exercise, the U.S. instructor evaluated the class on what they had done right or wrong." See Menjívar and Rodríguez, eds., *When States Kill: Latin America, the U.S., and Technologies of Terror* (Austin: University of Texas Press, 2005), loc. 388–392, Kindle.

12. Nina Lakhani, "El Salvador Issues Warrants for Guerrillas Who Killed US Soldiers during Civil War," *Guardian*, July 25, 2017, https://www.theguardian.com/world/2017/jul/25/el-salvador-guerrilla-fighters-us-soliders-helicopter-killings, accessed November 17, 2017.

13. Menjívar and Rodríguez, *When States Kill*, loc. 6665–6667.

14. Erna Paris, *The Sun Climbs Slow: The International Criminal Court and the Struggle for Justice* (New York: Seven Stories Press, 2009), 11, Kindle.

15. Irina Carlota Silber, *Everyday Revolutionaries: Gender, Violence, and Disillusionment in Postwar El Salvador* (New Brunswick, N.J.: Rutgers University Press, 2011), 200–201.

16. United Nations Evaluation Group, *Norms and Standards for Evaluation* (New York: UNEG, 2016).

17. Department of the Army (DOA), *Insurgencies and Countering Insurgencies*, FM 3-24/MCWP 3-33.5, May 2014, 11–12.

18. Martha Minow, *Between Vengeance and Forgiveness: Facing History after Genocide and Mass Violence* (Boston: Beacon Press, 1998), 144.

APPENDIX

1. K. Charmaz, *Constructing Grounded Theory: A Practical Guide through Qualitative Analysis* (Los Angeles: Sage, 2010), 133.

2. J. A. S. Corbin, *Basics of Qualitative Research*, 3rd ed. (Los Angeles: Sage, 2008).

3. Linda Tuhiwai Smith, *Decolonizing Methodologies: Research and Indigenous Peoples*, 2nd ed. (New York: Zed, 2012).

4. Eduardo Viveiros de Castro, *Cannibal Metaphysics*, ed. and trans. Peter Skafish (Minneapolis: Univocal, 2014).

5. Casper Bruun Jensen, "A Nonhumanist Disposition: On Performativity, Practical Ontology, and Intervention," *Configurations* 12 (2004): 229–261.

6. Corbin, *Basics of Qualitative Research*.

7. G. Deleuze and F. Guattari, *A Thousand Plateaus: Capitalism and Schizophrenia* (Minneapolis: University of Minnesota Press, 1987), 24.

8. Carlos Benjamín Lara Martínez, "*La hora de Sofía*: Memoria histórica del movimiento campesino de Chalatenango" (PhD diss., Universidad Nacional Autónoma de México, November 2016), 15.

9. Irina Carlota Silber, *Everyday Revolutionaries: Gender, Violence, and Disillusionment in Postwar El Salvador* (New Brunswick, N.J.: Rutgers University Press, 2011), 91.

10. Lindsay Pérez Huber, "Disrupting Apartheid of Knowledge: Testimonio as Methodology in Latina/o Critical Race Research in Education," *International Journal of Qualitative Studies in Education* 22, no. 6 (November–December 2009): 639–654.

11. Tuhiwai Smith, *Decolonizing Methodologies*.

12. Leigh Binford, *The El Mozote Massacre: Human Rights and Global Implications*, rev. and expanded ed. (Tucson: University of Arizona Press, 2016), loc. 492–495, Kindle.

13. Marcella Althaus-Reid, *Indecent Theology: Theological Perversions in Sex, Gender and Politics* (New York: Routledge, 2000), 134.

14. Russell Bisop, "Freeing Ourselves from Neocolonial Domination in Research: A Kaupapa Maori Approach to Creating Knowledge," in *The Landscape of Qualitative Research*, 3rd ed., ed. Norman K. Denzin and Yvonna Lincoln (Los Angeles: Sage, 2008), 173.

15. Atlas.ti (computer software), version 7.5.16, GmbH, Berlin.

16. K. Charmaz, *Grounded Theory: Objectivist, Constructivist Methods* (Thousand Oaks, Calif.: Sage, 2000); Charmaz, *Constructing Grounded Theory*.

17. Charmaz, *Constructing Grounded Theory*, 133.

18. Judith Halberstam, *The Queer Art of Failure* (Durham, N.C.: Duke University Press, 2011), loc. 250–251, Kindle.

19. Ann Laura Stoler with Karen Strassler, "Memory Work in Java: A Cautionary Tale," in *The Oral History Reader*, Routledge Readers in History, 3rd ed., ed. Robert Perks and Alistair Thomson (Boca Raton, Fla.: Taylor & Francis, 2016), 375, Kindle.

20. Christopher R. Browning, "Remembering Survival: Inside a Nazi Slave-Labor Camp," in *Oral History Reader*, ed. Perks and Thomson, 314.

21. Silber, *Everyday Revolutionaries*, 186–187.

22. Francis Good, "Voice, Ear and Text: Words, Meaning and Transcription," in *Oral History Reader*, ed. Perks and Thomson, 466.

INDEX

ABC lawsuit. *See American Baptist Churches v. Thornburgh*
Abrego, Leisy, 124
accountability, 104, 143–144, 154–155
acculturation, 78
affective management, 29–32
Agencia Nacional de Servicios Especiales de El Salvador. *See* National Agency of Special Services of El Salvador
agriculture, 3, 6, 57, 62–65, 149, 176n25; in U.S., 60–61
airlines, 20, 25–26
Althaus-Reid, Marcella, 86, 87, 160
American Baptist Churches v. Thornburgh, 144
amnesia: collective, 106; state, 9
ANESAL. *See* National Agency of Special Services of El Salvador
ANGEC. *See* National Association of Parcels and Culture Managers in El Salvador
ankle monitors, 47–49
anthropology, 63, 158, 169–170n26
arms transfers, 124, 135–136, 188n6
Asociación Nacional de Gestores de Encomiendas y Cultura. *See* National Association of Parcels and Culture Managers in El Salvador
assimilation, 78, 79
asylum, 123, 124; denial of, 144, 145

bodily hexis, 30
bodily logic, 112, 122
Boff, Clodovis, 84–85
Boff, Leonardo, 84–85
border wall. *See* U.S.–Mexico border: wall
Bourdieu, Pierre, 118, 121, 132, 140, 184n14, 186n35
Bourgois, Philippe, 146, 180n2, 185n16
Boym, Svetlana, 55, 56

Bush, George W., 43
bus industry, 113–116

CAFTA. *See* Dominican Republic–Central America Free Trade Agreement
Calderón, Felipe, 43
campesinxs, 2–4, 168n16; agency of, 85–86; and conflict navigation, 119; in detention facilities, 50–51; and everyday violence, 117–119, 121; and fashion, 79; and food, 57–61; and liberation theology, 85; and nostalgia, 55–56; seen as insurgents, 101
cannabis. *See* marijuana
caravans, 51
caretaking, 65–66
CARSI. *See* U.S. Central American Regional Security Initiative
cartels, 42–44, 46, 173n9
CBP. *See* U.S. Customs and Border Protection
Central American Minors program, 7, 75, 170n27
"chicken buses," 115–116
Ching, Erik, 3, 141, 188n16
CIA. *See* U.S. Central Intelligence Agency
client-centeredness, 30
clients, of couriers: complaints of, 30; and documentation, 31, 35; in El Salvador, 19; transnational base of, 13–14; in U.S., 28–29
Cold War, 102, 105–108, 137–139, 145, 183n46
communism, 101, 102, 108
compassion fatigue, 31
counterinsurgency, 101, 109–110, 139–140, 147, 154–155; effect on migration, 135, 140, 143–144, 150
couriers, 2, 13–20, 158; interaction with clients, 19, 28–32; as physical links, 25. *See also* women: as couriers

ABOUT THE AUTHOR

MIKE ANASTARIO is a sociologist and professor in the psychology department at the Central American University (UCA) in San Salvador, El Salvador. His research interests include social memory, violence, and agrarian worlds.

Available titles in the Latinidad:
Transnational Cultures in the United States series